MOORISH
SPAIN

RICHARD
FLETCHER

MOORISH
SPAIN

UNIVERSITY OF CALIFORNIA PRESS
Berkeley • Los Angeles

University of California Press
Berkeley and Los Angeles, California

First Paperback Printing 1993

First published in 1992 in the United States by
Henry Holt and Company, Inc.
and in Great Britain by
George Weidenfeld & Nicolson.

Library of Congress Cataloging-in-Publication Data
Fletcher, R.A. (Richard A.)
Moorish Spain / Richard Fletcher.
p.   cm.
Includes bibliographical references and index.
ISBN 0-520-08496-9 (pbk.)
1. Spain—Civilization—711–1516.   2. Muslims—Spain—History.
3. Spain—Civilization—Islamic influences.   I. Title.
DP99.F56   1993
946'.02—dc20   93–11117
                                                                          CIP

Printed in the United States of America

10   09   08   07   06   05   04
14   13   12   11   10   9   8   7

To
Houston and Lucinda Shaw Stewart
incomparable travelling companions
in
Al-Andalus and the Maghrib

ACKNOWLEDGEMENTS

Grateful acknowledgement is made to reprint the following: graph on p. 37 from Richard W. Bulliet, *Conversion to Islam in the Medieval Period* (Harvard University Press, 1979); extracts on pp. 67–8 and 93 from Colin Smith, *Christians and Moors in Spain*, vol. 1 (Aris and Phillips, 1988); Koran extract from A. J. Arberry, *The Koran Interpreted* (Oxford University Press, 1964). Poetry: on pp. 72, 87, 89, 90, 111 and 129 from A. R. Nykl, *Hispano-Arabic Poetry* (Slatkine Reprints, 1974); on pp. 91 and 96 from J. T. Monroe, *Hispano-Arabic Poetry* (Slatkine Reprints, 1974); on pp. 91 and 96 from J. T. Monroe, *Hispano-Arabic Poetry* (University of California Press, 1974); on pp. 96 and 97 from David Goldstein, *The Jewish Poets of Spain* (Penguin, 1971); on p. 109 from David Wasserstein, *The Rise and Fall of the Party Kings* (Princeton University Press, 1985); on p. 161 from L. P. Harvey, *Islamic Spain 1250–1500* (Chicago University Press, 1990); and on p. 163 from Roger Wright, *Spanish Ballads* (Aris and Phillips, 1987).

CONTENTS

ILLUSTRATIONS
AND MAPS

13 A casket of wood and ivory carved at Cuenca for a member of the princely dynasty at Toledo in 1049–50 now in the Museo Arqueológico Nacional, Madrid (MAS, Barcelona)

14 A silk textile of the eleventh century (Musée de Cluny, Paris)

15 The Almohad banner captured by Alfonso VIII of Castile at the battle of Las Navas in 1212 (Editions d'Art Albert Skira)

16 The Torre del Oro at Seville (Spanish National Tourist Office)

17 James I of Aragon conquers Valencia: fresco of *c.*1300 (MAS, Barcelona)

18, 19 Mudejar church architecture, in the Aragonese town of Teruel (Spanish National Tourist Office)

20 Mudejar military architecture at Coca (Spanish National Tourist Office)

21 An example of Mudejar ceramics (Museo Arqueológico Nacional, Madrid)

22 Averroes as represented in a western manuscript of the thirteenth century (Bibliothèque National, Paris)

23 Christian and Muslim playing chess together, from an illustrated manuscript of Alfonso X's treatise on the game (Escorial, Madrid)

24, 25 The Synagoga del Tránsito in Toledo (Spanish National Tourist Office)

26 Granada, the Alhambra: the Court of the Lions (Colin Grant)

27 Granada, the Alhambra: the Court of the Myrtles (Colin Grant)

28 The enforced baptism of the Moors of Granada in 1499: detail from the Capilla Real, Granada, High Altar by Philippe Biguerny (MAS, Barcelona)

Maps

PREFACE TO THE
PAPERBACK EDITION

This book is intended as an introduction to the history and culture of Islamic Spain between the Berber invasion of the early eighth century and the expulsion of the Moriscos by Philip III in the early seventeenth. It lays no claim to deep or original scholarship. The reader I have had in mind in writing it is the inquisitive traveller in Spain who might want to know something more than a guidebook can tell him about the people who built the mosque of Córdoba or the Alhambra at Granada.

The favourable reception of the hardback edition has given rise to the suggestion that the book might have potential for use in university courses which touch on the Spanish middle ages. In an attempt to make it more suitable for this purpose I have expanded the 'Notes on Further Reading', in particular to embrace some of the better works whose publication was associated with last year's quincentenary of the conquest of Granada in 1492.

Although the book is avowedly intended for the general reader and therefore lacks the scholarly apparatus of footnotes, formal bibliography and so forth, I may permit myself to claim that it is not merely a synthesis of modern secondary works. Extensive if unobtrusive use of original sources has been made, some of them not hitherto exploited in this context. To give two minor examples from chapter 7, 'Convivencia', I am not aware that the interest of the Sobrado slave-list or of the career of Gilbert Anglicus has previously been noted in print. The sources for these are, respectively, Pilar Loscertales de G. de Valdeavellano (ed.), *Tumbos del Monasterio de Sobrado de los Monjes* (Madrid, 1976), Vol. II, no. 108; and F. Udina Martorell (ed.), *El "Llibre Blanch" de Santas Creus* (Barcelona, 1947), nos. 50, 104, 114, 139, 148, 157.

I take this opportunity of drawing the reader's attention to an error of interpretation in chapter 3. Professor Richard W. Bulliet's graph of the rate of conversion (reproduced at p. 37) relates not to the whole of the indigenous population of Al-Andalus but only to that proportion of it who converted to Islam. In other words, his 100% is the total number of converts, not the whole population. We cannot yet guess what the numerical relationship between those converts and the entire population might have been. I am grateful to my friend Roger Collins, to whose work on early medieval Spain I owe much, for pointing this error out to me.

Some critics have taken exception to the tone of impatience which they have detected in chapter 9. That chapter was composed in the late summer of 1991. I have to confess that events and pronouncements in the Hispanic and American worlds in the course of 1992 have in no way led me to wish to modify my strictures on academic and media credulity. But the reader need not agree.

Finally, it is good to report that Hispano–Muslim studies continue to flourish as never before. In particular the recovery and interpretation of archaeological material proceeds apace. It is probably from this quarter that we may anticipate the most significant gains to our understanding of Moorish Spain over the coming years.

Richard Fletcher
Nunnington, York
May 1993

MOORISH
SPAIN

1

ROMANCE AND REALITY

In the year 711 a Berber army under Arab leadership crossed the Straits of Gibraltar from Morocco in continuation of a series of raids which had been going on for some time. The army was commanded by a general named Tariq who is said to have given his name to his landfall on the northern side of the Straits: *Jebel Tariq*, 'the Rock of Tariq', Gibraltar. In the following year a battle was fought between the invaders and the army of Spain under its king Roderic or Rodrigo and – astonishingly – Tariq's troops were victorious. King Roderic was slain and the invaders went on to take the capital city, Toledo. Within a very few years the entire peninsula lay at their feet. As in England in 1066, the fortune of a battle had decided the fate of a kingdom.

In Spain it had decided very much more than this. The early eighth-century conquest signalled the beginnings of an Islamic presence in the Iberian peninsula that would endure for the better part of a thousand years and whose impress upon peninsular culture is still discernible. What is more, Islamic Spain would come in time to offer the fruits of a higher civilisation to barbarian Europe beyond the Pyrenees. European acceptance of this legacy, hesitant at first and then full-hearted, decisively affected western culture, not just in Europe but also in those New Worlds discovered and settled by Europeans in the early modern period. So much may be said to have stemmed from Tariq's raid. That is why, in the last resort, Moorish Spain is worth trying to understand.

We are ourselves responsible for some of the obstacles that prevent understanding. Consider this passage, for example:

Beautiful and fierce, seductive and pagan, Andalusia is a world unto itself.

1

Probably no other region in Europe is so romantic, mysterious and atmospheric . . . with its incredible Moorish legacy, its vast mountains, parched plains, superb cities and magical villages.

The words are those of a British travel brochure designed to appeal to the discerning holidaymaker who sets his sights higher than the bars and fish and chip shops of, say, Torremolinos. Banal they may be, but they hold out a promise which echoes existing expectations – of romance, mystery and atmosphere. Such expectations are fairly recent. They gained currency during the Romantic movement of the nineteenth century. For the English-speaking world two authors in particular seem to have been largely responsible for this image of southern Spain: Washington Irving (1783–1859) and Richard Ford (1796–1858). Irving, a member of the United States legation in Madrid from 1826, travelled widely in the south and published his very popular *Tales of the Alhambra* in 1832. Ford, who lived for three years in Seville in the 1830s and also travelled indefatigably, published his *Handbook for Travellers in Spain* in 1845, a work which was long to remain the indispensable companion for English visitors. These two works, and others which bobbed along in their wake, did much to shape Anglo-American assumptions about the character of Spain, especially southern Spain, her people and their customs. These assumptions have left their mark in surprising places; for instance in the deservedly celebrated children's tale of Ferdinand the Bull. The brochure quoted above shows that they are still very much alive.

Any attempt to understand the history and culture of the Iberian peninsula must take account of that 'incredible Moorish legacy': but the enquirer should be prepared to find the reality less exotic than the stereotype. Less exotic, yes, but certainly unfamiliar to those habituated like Irving and Ford to the cultural traditions of the English-speaking peoples. Consider the most famous architectural monument of southern Spain, the great mosque of Córdoba, built in stages between the late eighth century and the late tenth. Here is a building which is constructed in accordance with an architectural aesthetic which is utterly different from that governing the design of the places of worship of the Christian west. In a church there is a line of tension which runs from west to east; the eye is led unerringly to the altar. There is no comparable focus in the great mosque. True, it has (like other mosques) a *mihrab* or prayer-niche in the south wall, to indicate the *qibla* or direction of Mecca and to provide a sounding-chamber from which the imam may recite the word of God. The *mihrab* receives special architectural and decorative emphasis but it does not exert a 'pull' in the way that the altar does in a Gothic cathedral. Muslim worship can take place wherever the worshipper is standing or kneeling, and involves no mediating priesthood. There is no 'holy of holies': the entire hall of prayer, with its 800-odd columns and its two-tier horseshoe arches, is a holy place. And this it emphatically is: even the most thick-skinned of visitors, the most assertively secular spirits have found themselves subdued and calmed by the tranquil, reposeful air of the place, for which we must be grateful to the cunning of successive architects.

But it is not uniformly calm. At its heart lies architectural evidence of strife. Herein lies a moral tale – yet another! – about the unwisdom of permitting corporate bodies who are the guardians of great buildings to be swayed by passing architectural fashion. After the Christian conquest of Córdoba in 1236 the mosque was turned into the city's cathedral. Early in the sixteenth century the bishop and chapter decided to improve their cathedral by installing what in Spain is called a *coro*, that is to say the walling-in, in stone, of the area of the choir: the effect is to create a building within a building. Many cathedrals were doing this in the fifteenth and sixteenth centuries. When the city fathers heard of these plans they protested to the king, showing in this, as Ford put it, 'a taste and judgement rare in corporate bodies'. The king of Spain then was the Hapsburg Holy Roman Emperor Charles V (Carlos I in Spain). Charles had been brought up in the Low Countries, he had not been king of Spain for very long and he had never visited Córdoba. The corporation's protest was to no avail. The bishop and chapter went ahead with their plans. A few years later Charles paid his first visit to the city, where the ecclesiastical dignitaries proudly showed off their improvements. Charles's comment must rank as one of the most crushing royal rebukes on matters architectural ever delivered: 'You have built here what you, or anyone else, might have built anywhere; to do so you have destroyed what was unique in the world.' Posterity has unhesitatingly endorsed the king's opinion: the harmony of the mosque is wrecked by the horrible architectural pustule inserted by the bishop and chapter in the sixteenth century. (There is one delicious irony here. In the very same year as that of his visit to Córdoba Charles commissioned the building of a colossal palace by a pupil of Michelangelo, to be inserted into the Moorish palace-complex of the Alhambra at Granada. But Charles's palace is both magnificent and beautiful. The *coro* of Córdoba is neither.)

We may condemn the *coro* as a disastrous error of taste, but bishops and chapters have to concern themselves with proclaiming Christianity. Their addition to the mosque made an unambiguous assertion of their religious allegiance which would have been commended in many quarters at the time. It is easy for us to condemn this too – a good deal easier than it was in the sixteenth century – but before we do so we should remember that the mosque itself had done precisely the same thing: it was built on the site of a former Christian church. The siting of the mosque was a gesture of Islamic triumphalism, an architectural manifesto.

Two things have emerged so far. The mosque of Córdoba has been the scene of religious conflict; and in its original, Islamic state it represents in form and function something different from our western experience. It is the architectural face of the Other. With the latter point in mind let us consider two much smaller works of art which were created in Spain at roughly the time when the mosque was taking on its final (Muslim) form in the latter part of the tenth century. One is a circular ivory casket about the size of a tea-caddy, now preserved in the Victoria and Albert Museum in London. The inscription in Arabic round the bottom of the lid tells us that it was made in the Islamic year of the Hijra 359, that is 969–70 AD, to the commission of a high-ranking official in the service of the caliph of Córdoba. It has suffered over the centuries: about a quarter of the lid has been broken off, and the carvings which decorate its entire surface have been worn smooth and indistinct by much handling. But enough remains to mark it as an exquisite work of art. The composition is satisfying, the detail of the carving displays skill of a very high order. Unusually, it includes three human figures: the representation of the human form was not encouraged among Islamic artists. In addition to these it features lively hunting scenes where hounds pursue their prey through luxuriant undergrowth, and static pairs of birds and beasts. The tone of the scenes is accessibility. There they are, naturalistic figures whom we can instantly understand, engaged in straightforward activities which need no explanation – sitting, chatting, pursuing, gazing. It's accomplished, elegant, pleasing. The piece radiates an easy, undemanding charm: altogether very livable-with.

With that contrast a work in a different medium: the fresco from the church of Sant Quirze de Pedret in the eastern Pyrenees, now preserved in the Diocesan Museum of Solsona. Here is something completely different in style and feeling, so much so that it might almost come from a different world. Who is the highly-stylised figure in the roundel whose features seem to express terror or anger or both? Why the bird? What is going on here? Whatever it is, it is powerful and primitive and disturbing. In fact, the human figure is praying. This would not be obvious to anyone who did not happen to know that the attitude of

Christian prayer was standing (or lying) with arms outstretched in the form of a cross, until the feudal age when it changed to the submissive posture of a vassal kneeling with hands clasped before his lord. The bird needs explanation too. One might just guess from its splayed tail-feathers that this represents a peacock: but why a peacock? The answer lies in St Augustine's *City of God*, Book XXXI, chapter 4, where he records his belief that the peacock's flesh had the God-given property of resisting putrefaction after death; whence the peacock became a common Christian symbol of immortality in late antique and early medieval art. The Pedret fresco does not yield up its meaning at a glance; it is not accessible in the way that the ivory casket is. Nor is it remotely elegant or charming. It seems rather to speak to us from a narrow, troubled world of pain and fear where only the hope of immortality provided consolation.

When we looked at the mosque of Córdoba it was the Islamic world which emerged as mysterious and other. In the ivory casket it seems to become accessible, at any rate in contrast with the Pedret fresco. But it is the latter which, so to say, belongs to us; in the sense that it is a product of a western European and Christian culture. Of course, it will rightly be objected that it is absurd to gauge the character of a civilisation on the strength of a single work of art. And it would be easy to assemble objects which could be brought to teach a diametrically opposite lesson. But what has been offered here is not just a conjuring trick. The two works of art are not, as it happens, unrepresentative of their respective civilisations. There is a startling potential for misunderstanding, for simply not finding any points of contact at all, in the encounter between two such dissimilar cultures. However, they did meet; and that meeting is one of the themes of this book.

*

The Iberian peninsula is the area of Mediterranean Europe where the most prolonged and intimate encounter between Christendom and Islam occurred before a Christian political power became eventually dominant. In Sicily, Islamic rule endured less than three centuries; in Greece, not much more. The most lasting traces of this encounter are to be found in the principal languages of the peninsula. The vocabulary of modern Spanish and Portuguese (and Gallego and Catalan – but not Basque) has been colonised by hundreds of words derived from Arabic. Take up a dictionary and observe the number of terms beginning with the letters *al-*; not all are derived from Arabic, but most of them are. Large numbers of them are words connected with agriculture, trading, crafts, and civil administration broadly defined: for example, *algodón*, from which we derive our word 'cotton'; *almazara* (oil-mill), *almendra* (almond), *álaga* (a type of wheat), *alhóndiga* (granary), *alcaicería* (silk exchange), *albañil* (mason), *almoneda* (auction), *alcabala* (excise). Neither need the sample be confined to words beginning with this prefix. The Arabic word *suq*, 'market', has provided Spanish with *zoco* and related terms; the square at the heart of the older part of Toledo is still known as the Zocodover. The *lechín* is a variety of olive tree, and from its fruit, the *aceituna*, is pressed *aceite*, olive oil, which will be stored in an earthenware jar, the *jarra*. Place-names derived from the Arabic are thickly strewn on today's maps of Spain and Portugal: Medinaceli, Alcalá, the river Guadalquivir, the Algarve, Játiva, Calatayud.

The visitor to Granada who goes straight from the plaster arabesques of the Alhambra to the astonishing eighteenth-century plasterwork of the sacristy of the Cartuja will know at once that the one has in some sense made the other possible, that the later work is in some large and important if indefinable manner the descendant of the earlier. Again and again in looking at Spanish arts and crafts we are brought up against this sense of a debt to the aesthetic traditions of the Islamic world, especially in the media of brick, plaster, wood, leather, pottery and textiles. The consequences – for the furnishing and decoration of the Spanish home, for instance – may not have been uniformly happy, but there can be no doubt about the nature and direction of the debt.

These are two obvious ways, the linguistic and the artistic, in which Iberian civilisation has benefited from its Moorish heritage. There are many others. Perhaps the most significant for the historian is an indirect one. The Islamic presence in Spain has furnished generations of Christian Spaniards with a potent national myth. Between the ninth and the thirteenth centuries Moorish dominion in the peninsula was slowly and fitfully rolled back towards its southern coastline until all that was left was the little state of Granada which endured until 1492. The beneficiaries were a number of Christian principalities which originated obscurely in the northern mountains and came in the course of their expansion southwards to take on the names and contours of the historic kingdoms of the medieval period – León, Castile, Aragon, Catalonia, Portugal. The impulses which propelled this expansion were predictably earthy ones: demographic pressure, land-hunger, the demands of a predatory nobility, advances in military technology, the appetites of transhumant sheep and cattle. However, the clerical propagandists of the royal and aristocratic elites which directed and profited from the expansion came to present it in a different and more respectable light. Thus there emerged the notion of the *Reconquista*, the

Reconquest: a sacred patriotic struggle to wrest power from alien hands and restore Christian dominion. The myth was irresistible. In the eighth century Spain saved Europe from the advancing hordes of Islam by sacrificing herself. In the ensuing medieval centuries she remade herself through the glorious epic of a crusading reconquest sustained by faith: the cross won back the fatherland from the crescent.

Like most national myths it has both an ennobling side and a more sinister reverse – in this instance a legacy of intolerance and xenophobia. Again like successful national myths, it proved readily adaptable to different circumstances. In the sixteenth and seventeenth centuries Counter-Reformation Spaniards were encouraged to see themselves as upholding Catholicism against the menace of heresy just as their ancestors had upheld Christianity against Islam. In the twentieth the Nationalist regime of General Franco could successfully play upon the myth in negotiations with the United States. Spain's experience in upholding European values fitted her to be in the front line of defence against Communism. The sickle replaced the crescent: the enemy's symbol retained the same menacing shape.

There was yet another way in which the encounter of Christian and Muslim in medieval Spain has powerfully affected later and distant human experience. Medieval Spaniards and Portuguese worked out by trial and error ways in which to administer large tracts of newly-conquered territory and to govern their inhabitants. Thus, when an overseas empire was acquired in the sixteenth century, models and precedents existed for the guidance of those whose task it was to rule it. In this as in so much else there was little that was new about the so-called 'early modern' period of the sixteenth and seventeenth centuries. Colonial Mexico and Peru and Brazil were medieval Andalusia writ large. Much that is central to the subsequent experience of Latin America follows from this.

In today's conditions the most awkward feature of Spain's national historical mythology is precisely what gave it potency in the past – its inbuilt hostility to Islam. Perceived as alien, how can Islam's positive contributions to peninsular culture be accommodated harmoniously in a vision of the national past? If Muslims and Muslim observances have been persecuted or frowned upon for centuries in Spain, if Africans in general have been regarded with fear and contempt, how can acknowledgement of indebtedness be gracefully made, hostility give way to amity? It is obvious that these questions have a special relevance today. The western world has become acutely and painfully conscious in recent years of the need to understand the culture of Islam. The peoples of Islam cannot, as too often in the past, be neglected, bullied or exploited. If there are difficulties in the way that the peninsular peoples have liked to interpret their past – and it is most important that their partners in a European Community should be aware both of the interpretation and of its difficulties – perhaps it is timely to hasten the dismantling of that mythology. The plain fact is that between 712 and 1492 Muslim and Christian communities lived side by side in the Iberian peninsula, clutched in a long, intimate embrace: sharing a land, learning from one another, trading, intermarrying, misunderstanding, squabbling, fighting – generally indulging in all the incidents that go to furnish the ups and downs of coexistence or relationship. National myths have to simplify if they are to be widely accessible and acceptable. But this scene was not a simple one: it was diverse and boisterous and crowded with life.

The most fortunate beneficiaries of this coexistence were neither Christian nor Muslim Spaniards but the uncouth barbarians beyond the Pyrenees. The creative role of Islamic Spain in the shaping of European intellectual culture is still not widely enough appreciated. Apart from anything else, it is a most remarkable story. The scientific and philosophical learning of Greek and Persian antiquity was inherited by the Arabs in the Middle East. Translated, codified, elaborated by Arabic scholars, the corpus was diffused throughout the culturally unified world of classical Islam in the ninth and tenth centuries until it reached the limits of the known world in the west. And there, in Spain, it was discovered by the scholars of the Christian west, translated into Latin mainly between 1150 and 1250, and channelled off to irrigate the dry pastures of European intellectual life. The rediscovery of Aristotle's works by this route decisively changed the European mind. Navigational devices such as the astrolabe made possible the voyages of discovery to east and west. Newton's work would have been inconceivable without the knowledge of mathematics transmitted through Spain. The advances in medical science of the seventeenth century were grounded upon Arabic observation and practice. Europe's lead in resourcefulness and creativity, the vital factor in the history of the world for the six centuries preceding our own, was founded in large part on intelligent grasping at opportunities offered by the civilisation of Islam; and that proffer came through Spain. Islamic Spain was not just an exotic bit of orientalia quaintly moored in the Iberian peninsula which has left behind some pretty flotsam for tourists to take photographs of. It played a significant part in the formation of the Old World's civilisation.

*

Thus far the Islamic presence in Spain has been considered from a western and Christian point of view. We should also attempt an assessment of its culture in the wider context of Islamic civilisation as a whole. During the Middle Ages al-Andalus – as Moorish Spain was always known in the Arabic-speaking world – was little regarded in the Middle Eastern heartlands of Islam. For the mandarins and intellectuals of sophisticated Damascus, Cairo or Baghdad, al-Andalus was a distant frontier outpost of Islam on the fringes of the known world, irredeemably dowdy and provincial. Yet from this dingy backwater there emerged some of the finest works of Islamic art and culture: for example, the great mosque of Córdoba, the Cuenca school of ivory-carving, the poetry of Ibn 'Ammar, the philosophy of Ibn Rushd (better known to the west as Averroes), the medical treatises of Ibn Zuhr, the Giralda of Seville and the Alhambra of Granada. Here too there are puzzles to be investigated.

This is to indicate some of the ways in which Moorish Spain might be thought to lay claim to our attention. But before we proceed further with the enquiry it will be as well to introduce the land which medieval Muslim and Christian shared, for the benefit of those who do not know it.

A preliminary difficulty – of which doubtless the reader must already have become aware – is to decide what to call it. This is not a new problem: take for example the opening sentences of the description of Spain by the eleventh-century geographer al-Bakri.

People say that in ancient times it was called Iberia, taking its name from the river Ebro. Later it was known as Bética, from the river Betis which runs past Córdoba. Later still it was called Hispania after a man named Hispan who had once ruled there. Some people say that its true name is Hesperia, which is derived from Hesperus, the evening star in the west. Nowadays we call it al-Andalus after the Andalusians who settled it.

Objections can be raised against nearly all the available options. 'Hispania' and 'Hesperia' sound precious and pedantic. 'Iberia' risks being confused with the region of that name in the Georgian Caucasus. 'Spain' as a term for the whole peninsular land mass between the Pyrenees and the Straits of Gibraltar is open to the objection that it will inevitably suggest the modern state of Spain and thereby exclude the area covered by modern Portugal. The political designations of the Middle Ages were applied to territories whose size and shape oscillated wildly. Castile did not exist in the year 800, by the year 1000 it was a modest county of the kingdom of León, by 1300 it was the largest state in Europe. Al-Andalus meant nearly the whole of the peninsula in the eighth century, but by the late thirteenth it meant the tiny principality of Granada. Religious labels are misleading. 'Islamic' Spain always contained sizeable communities of Christians and Jews, 'Christian' Spain, similarly, communities of Jews and Muslims. Ethnic designations are even more misleading. The language of common speech in al-Andalus, for Christians and Jews as well as for Muslims, was Arabic; but to speak as some have done of 'Arabic' Spain is to give the impression that the land had been colonised by the Arabs, whereas the number of Arabs who settled there was very small. 'Moorish' Spain does at least have the merit of reminding us that the bulk of the invaders and settlers were Moors, i.e. Berbers from northwest Africa. But we shall need to bear in mind that they overlay a population of mixed descent – Hispano-Romans, Basques, Sueves, Visigoths, Jews and others.

The reader who looks for consistency of verbal usage in this book is going to be disappointed. When I use the term 'al-Andalus' I understand by it that area of the Iberian peninsula under the control of Muslim authority, and the phrases 'Moorish', 'Muslim' and 'Islamic Spain' are to be regarded as synonymous with it. I shall try to avoid using 'Spain' to indicate the whole land mass but I do not expect to keep to this well-meant resolution. I offer my apologies in advance to those who inhabit the peninsula today who are politically independent of the Spanish monarchy (in Portugal) or who think that they ought to be (in the Basque country, Galicia and Catalonia).

The peninsular land mass is formidable: in its size, in its structure and in the demands it makes upon the peoples who live there. Spain and Portugal today, including the Balearic Islands, cover an area of 229,000 square miles. (For purposes of comparison, modern France stands at 204,000, England and Wales at 58,000, Texas at 262,000.) This area is very diverse: in its physical relief, in the climate that this produces, in the human economic activities which relief and climate together encourage or compel, in the social and institutional arrangements which have been devised over two thousand years of recorded history. The most distinctive physical features of the peninsula are its mountains. Spain and Portugal are more mountainous than any other European country, excepting only Switzerland and Norway. There are five systems whose ranges are consistently over 3000 feet high, sometimes very much more. In the north, of course, there are the Pyrenees. In the northwest the Cantabrian mountains and their related southwesterly extensions serve to shut away the northern and northwestern coastal territories of Asturias, Galicia and northern Portugal. To the south of the river Ebro, running from northwest to southeast through the modern provinces of Soria and Teruel, is a great sweep of mountainous territory. This is joined about half-way along it, at right angles, by another band of mountains running from northeast to southwest, of which the highest peaks are to be found in the Sierra de Guadarrama to the north of Madrid. Finally, in the southeast, there is the Sierra Nevada near Granada and its related ranges such as the Sierra de Segura a little to the north. (The Spanish word *sierra* literally means 'saw', and was applied to these ranges because of their jagged peaks.) River systems divide these ranges from one another. All the major rivers save one drain towards the Atlantic coast. The exception is the Ebro, running from its headwaters in northern Castile on a south-easterly course past Tudela and Zaragoza to join the Mediterranean at Tortosa. (There are some lesser rivers which drain into the Mediterranean, such as the Llobregat at Barcelona and the Turia at Valencia, but only the Ebro is navigable for the sea-going craft of the ancient and medieval world for some considerable distance upstream.) The major rivers which drain to the west are, working from north to south, the Duero (Portuguese Douro), the Tagus, the Guadiana and the Guadalquivir. Each is fed by a number of tributaries. The Duero system divides the Cantabrian mountains from the Guadarrama ranges. The Tagus flows along the south side of the latter. Between it and the Guadiana lie the ranges of the Montes de Toledo and the Sierra de Guadalupe, of lesser height than the mountains mentioned so far. The same may be said of the Sierra Morena which lies between the systems of the Guadiana and Guadalquivir.

The land which lies between these mountain ranges is itself for the most part of fairly high altitude: the tableland or *meseta*, rarely falling below 1200 feet, level, sometimes rolling, uneventful country. Truly low-lying land is only to be found in the coastal strip which runs round the periphery of the entire peninsula. In some parts this strip is narrow, as for example on the south coast between the Sierra Nevada and the Mediterranean. In other regions it is broader, as in southern Portugal. Sometimes it reaches far inland up the river valleys, as is the case with the Tagus and the Guadalquivir.

There are, broadly speaking, three climatic and therefore economic zones. The northern and western coastal territories have an Atlantic climate comparable to that of Ireland, western Britain and Brittany. It is temperate and it is damp; an area of mixed farming where livestock was always more important than tillage and where fishing played a significant part in the local economy. On the *meseta* there are violent contrasts of temperature: it is very hot in the summer, but the winters are long and bitterly cold. The soil is light and easily worked; apart from patchy scrub there is no woodland to speak of. This is the land where corn is king in the north, olives and vines further south. The *meseta* is roamed by vast herds of sheep, goats and cattle, seasonably transhumant from north to south in autumn and from south to north in spring. Along the eastern and southern coasts frosts are rare, rainfall is low, summers are exceedingly hot. The land is very fertile if properly irrigated. This is the area of intensive cultivation, of market gardening, of several vegetable crops each year, of exotic products such as sugar-cane, oranges, aubergines, rice — all of them, incidentally, words derived from Arabic.

We must take account, therefore, of marked contrasts between regions; of a tension between centre and periphery; of a south and east which have always been better favoured and richer than the north and west (until, that is, the opening-up of an Atlantic economy). Observe how the major cities from the Roman period or even earlier have tended to be on the southern or eastern coasts or in the fertile river valleys: Barcelona, Tarragona, Tortosa, Zaragoza, Valencia, Cartagena, Murcia, Granada, Málaga, Córdoba, Seville, Cadiz, Mérida, Badajoz. Exceptions prove the rule. Rulers have sometimes deliberately sited administrative capitals precisely in the centre of the peninsula and simply for that reason: so the Visigothic kings did with Toledo, so Philip II did with Madrid. It was pilgrimage which put Santiago on the map. It was overseas imperial responsibilities which did the same for Lisbon and Corunna. Bilbao was a product of the Industrial Revolution.

The mountainous nature of the terrain made for difficulty of internal communication in the Iberian peninsula, before the coming of the railway and the internal combustion engine. The road system of Roman Hispania, maintained by the Visigothic kings who succeeded to Roman authority in the fifth century, enabled troops to be moved with speed from place to place. The Berber armies of the early eighth century could turn these same roads to good account. But bulk goods — oil, wine, wool, hides, corn — moved very slowly, at the pace of oxen, mules and donkeys: and very expensively — in the late antique Mediterranean world overland freight was about ten times as expensive as transport by water. Commercial considerations therefore reinforced the tendency for the periphery of the peninsula to look outwards rather than inwards: external communication was comparatively easy. Catalonia's cultural contacts have traditionally been closer with southern France and the Ligurian coast of Italy than with Castile. It is not by accident that the surviving prehistoric monuments of Portugal and Galicia find their closest counterparts in Brittany and the western parts of the British Isles. What needs special emphasis in any account of Moorish

Spain is the ease of contact between southern Spain and northwest Africa: the Straits at their narrowest are only twelve miles wide. In his poem 'Spain' – of 1937, later disavowed – W. H. Auden called the land 'that arid square, that fragment nipped off from hot Africa'. How right he was. The relief, climate and ecology of southern Spain find their closest parallel in Morocco. Shackled to Castile by the chance of history, Andalusia has a natural partner in Barbary, the land of the Berbers, to which indeed she was once linked until the land-bridge burst and the waters of the Atlantic gushed in to make the Mediterranean. Again and again in the course of this book the significance of contact and conflict across the Straits of Gibraltar during the Middle Ages will become apparent.

In the perspective of Iberian history as a whole the most important consequence of geography has been the great difficulty that a single political authority has always had in enforcing its will over the entire peninsula. Peninsular unity has never been natural. It has been an artificial condition achieved only with effort, fragile to maintain. Any strains imposed upon this unnatural condition normally result in the surfacing of fissile tendencies: the peninsula breaks down into its regional components. Of this tendency, too, we shall meet examples.

2

THE SECRET OF
THE TOWER

A king of Spain in ancient time built a tower in which he deposited a
secret. He sealed the tower with a mighty padlock, and laid upon his
successors the obligation each by turns to add an extra padlock so
as to preserve ever more inviolable whatever was concealed within.
Twenty-six kings came and went, respecting his wishes. Then there
succeeded a rash and headstrong young king named Roderic. Resolved
to penetrate the tower's secret, and against the advice of all his
counsellors, he had the twenty-seven padlocks opened. Then he
entered the chamber within. On its walls were painted Arab horsemen,
scimitars at their belts, spears brandished in their right hands. In the
middle of the room stood a table made of gold and silver set with
precious stones, upon it carved the words: 'This is the table of King
Solomon, son of David, upon whom be peace.' There was an urn on the
table, which was found to contain a scroll of parchment. When this was
unrolled, the following words were revealed: 'Whenever this chamber
is violated, and the spell contained in this urn is broken, the people
painted on these walls will invade Spain, overthrow its kings, and
subdue the entire land.'

This is a version of one of several legends, recorded in both Christian
and Islamic sources, which came to cluster round the memory of the
last days of the Christian Visigothic kingdom of Spain on the eve of the
invasion from northwest Africa which destroyed it. It is easy to
understand why such a myth was needed and how it could grow.
Christian Spaniards who had been conquered wanted a scapegoat: the
legend made Rodrigo into one by dwelling on his disregard of
traditional royal obligation. The conquerors needed the legend too:

they could take comfort from the thought that their invasion of Spain had been sanctioned by prophecy and destiny.

Not all the elements in the story are legendary. Toledo was indeed the capital city of Spain under the Visigothic kings of the sixth and seventh centuries, and they did indeed adorn it with splendid public buildings. Roderic was – as we have already seen – the last of this line of monarchs, and he was defeated and killed in attempting to defend his kingdom against Moorish invaders from northwest Africa early in the eighth century.

So far, so good. No one disputes these bare bones of the story of the invasion. It is when we try to clothe them with a little more flesh that our difficulties begin. It is not that we are short of information about the Moorish conquest. On the contrary, we possess a great deal. The trouble is that the surviving narratives were composed several centuries after the events which they describe, as a few examples will show. The earliest known historian of Moorish Spain whose work has come down to us was Ahmad ar-Razi who was writing in about 950, and his chronicle survives only in a fourteenth-century translation into Portuguese. The anonymous work entitled *Ajbar Machmua* ('Collection of traditions') is a compilation of the eleventh century. Ibn Idhari, who composed an important history of Islamic Spain, was working in Morocco around the year 1300. The most elaborate and comprehensive such history was the work of al-Maqqari, another Moroccan, who died as late as 1632. These were conscientious chroniclers, but they composed their works in a social and intellectual environment which was utterly different from that of the years of the conquest. Furthermore, they conceived of their task as primarily one of collecting and recording current traditions: they did not attempt to sift the grains of scientific historical truth from the spoil-heaps of legend.

The historical sources from the Christian side display the same sorts of shortcoming in their accounts of the Moorish conquest. The later they are, the fuller of detail they are, the more concerned their authors to peddle reassuring national myth to the readers of their own day. No more than their Islamic counterparts were they 'scientific' historians as we understand the term today. This could be said, for example, of archbishop Rodrigo of Toledo whose Latin history of Spain, the *De Rebus Hispaniae*, was composed in about 1240; or of king Alfonso X of Castile (d. 1284), known as Alfonso *el Sabio*, the Learned, who sponsored the production of vernacular historical chronicles in the second half of the thirteenth century.

Strictly or near-contemporary sources of evidence for the Moorish conquest are three: a short narrative from the Christian side, a single but crucial administrative document from the Islamic side, and a small amount of archaeological evidence. The narrative is an anonymous work in Latin prose known as the *Chronicle of 754*. It takes its name from the date of the latest events mentioned in it, and it is assumed that it took on its final shape in or shortly after that year. The author may have been a cleric of Toledo. A powerful case has recently been made for supposing that the *Chronicle of 754* furnishes a more reliable account of events in Spain during the first half of the eighth century than any other surviving narrative sources. What it has to tell us of the circumstances of the conquest is as follows.

A series of raids and incursions from Arab-held north Africa were launched against Spain in the earliest years of the eighth century. These went on 'for some time' and involved the laying waste of 'several provinces'. Then in the year 711 Musa ibn Nusayr, the governor of north Africa, sent an army under the command of Tariq to invade Spain. Another army, commanded by Musa himself, followed shortly afterwards. Roderic had become king of Spain in the same year 711, but in the face of opposition. Fighting between Roderic and his rivals occurred. In the following year, 712, a battle was fought between Roderic and Tariq which proved to be decisive. The place of the encounter ('at the Transductine promontories') cannot now be identified with certainty; it may have been between Algeciras and Jérez. Roderic was defeated and killed. Musa proceeded to Toledo where he executed a number of prominent people and devastated the country round about. He went on northeastwards to the valley of the river Ebro where he took the principal city of the region, Zaragoza. There was much devastation and loss of life. The archbishop of Toledo, primate of the Spanish church, abandoned his flock and fled. Before the end of 712 Musa left Spain, recalled by the Umayyad caliph to Damascus. He took with him a number of lordly Visigothic captives and huge quantities of booty in the form of bullion and jewellery. Before he left he entrusted the administration of the conquered provinces to his son 'Abd al-Aziz, who spent the three years of his governorship (712–15) extending and consolidating his father's conquests until they embraced the whole of the Iberian peninsula.

This narrative, more plausible in itself than the later accounts with which it is at variance, can to some degree be corroborated from contemporary evidence originating elsewhere. For example, the chronicler's information concerning the flight of the archbishop of Toledo is confirmed by the appearance of his name among the attenders of a church council in Rome a few years later. Archaeological evidence within Spain also brings some general confirmation of the anonymous writer's story. Some settlement sites have been excavated which show signs of violent destruction at a period which can be dated by the evidence of coins to about 711–13, and more may well be revealed by future excavation. We cannot of course *prove* that such destruction occurred in the course of the invasion, but it looks likely. The most sensational discovery of material remains dating from this period occurred in 1857 at Guarrazar, near Toledo: the votive crowns presented by a succession of seventh-century Spanish kings to a (presumed) religious community, buried for safekeeping at a time of turmoil, never recovered by their guardians, accidentally turned up eleven centuries later, and now among the most precious treasures of the National Archaeological Museum in Madrid. Were they deposited in 712 as rumours of a battle in the south, of the defeat of the king, of the northward advance of an alien army, drifted through to Toledo? Were the priests who deposited them slaughtered in Musa's devastation? We cannot tell: but looking upon these jewel-encrusted golden crowns we can sense something of the booty which Musa took back with him to Damascus.

The administrative document survives only in much later copies but is agreed by all scholars to be reliable. It is the text of a treaty made between 'Abd al-Aziz and a certain Theodemir, and it is dated according to Muslim usage to the 4th day of the month of Rajab in the 94th year after the Hijra; that is, in the Romano-Christian calendar, 5 April 713. Theodemir was the lord of seven named towns in the southeast of Spain, Alicante on the coast and places in its hinterland such as Lorca and Orihuela. In return for their submission Theodemir and his people were promised their personal safety and the free practice of the Christian faith in their churches. Theodemir himself was confirmed in his lordship. In return he and his people were not to give aid to deserters from or enemies of the conquerors, and they were required to pay an annual poll tax partly in money (one silver dinar) and partly in kind (specific measures of wheat, barley, must – unfermented grape-juice – vinegar, honey and oil).

There are some grounds for supposing that comparable treaties were made with other local authorities in Spain, for example with the city of Pamplona. Only those places which offered armed resistance to the conquerors were subjected to the full rigour of Islamic custom, summary execution of all adult males, enslavement of women and children: this grim fate seems to have befallen the inhabitants of Córdoba, Zaragoza and possibly Mérida. In these dealings the conquerors followed well-established precedents which the Arab leaders had used in their subjugation of Syria, Egypt and Persia. Under Islamic law both Christians and Jews, as 'Peoples of the Book', were permitted the exercise of their religion. Settlement on terms made possible the continued mobility of the Arab armies (since they were not tied down in garrison duties) and thus allowed the rapid subjugation of large areas of territory. Such settlements also involved the minimum of dislocation at the local level. Theodemir continued in his position as a local magnate, and his people tilled their fields and tended their olives and paid their taxes as they had done before: only the management was different.

The *Chronicle of 754* makes it clear that by about 720 all the lands under the control of the Visigothic kings had been pacified by the invaders. It should be borne in mind that these lands comprised not just the Iberian peninsula but also the Visigothic province of Septimania, that is to say the area of Mediterranean France stretching from the Pyrenees to Provence which was then administered from Narbonne.

Who were these conquerors, who had so quickly and so completely overturned the strongest western European monarchy of their day? It is customary to refer to these stirring events as the 'Arab' or the 'Islamic' invasion and conquest of Spain. But only in a very limited sense was it either Arab or Islamic: it was mainly Berber. The Berbers were, as they still are, the indigenous inhabitants of northwest Africa, the Maghrib. The word 'Berber' was not of their own coinage and has no ethnic connotations. It derives from the Latin term *barbari*, meaning 'barbarians' or 'outsiders'. The Romans applied the term indiscriminately to all the peoples who ringed their empire; for some reason – we do not know why – the application of the term to this particular group of barbarians seems to have stuck. The Berber peoples were divided among a number of tribal confederacies and these were further subdivided into clans and families. Their economy was mainly a pastoral one, varied by inter-tribal raiding for cattle, slaves and women. Although they traded, they knew neither money nor towns. They had no written culture and their religious beliefs seem not to have advanced beyond a simple animism. They had no form of political organisation beyond the elders of each clan and their only 'political' activity was the prosecution of the feuds which arose from raiding. They were a group of peoples altogether at a much less advanced stage of civilisation than their neighbours of the Mediterranean basin.

The conquest of the Maghrib was one of the longest and bloodiest episodes in the extraordinary expansion of the Arab peoples which followed the preaching of Muhammad. Within about a century of his death in 632 the empire of Islam extended from Kabul to Agadir, from the Aral Sea to the Gulf of Aden. The north African conquests of Islam were made initially at the expense of what was left of the Roman Empire, governed then, of course, not from Rome (which had long been within the Lombard kingdom of Italy) but from Constantinople: a vulnerable political structure internally weakened by the ravages of bubonic plague and the economic dislocation which it brought in its train, and beset from without by old enemies such as the Persians and new ones such as the Slavs. The Roman provinces of north Africa fell swiftly to the Arabs. They conquered Egypt in the years 640–42, Cyrenaica and Tripolitania (i.e., roughly, the northern parts of modern Libya) in 643–47, and the province of Africa proper (which the Arabs called Ifriqiya, i.e. today's Tunisia) by 670 when the new city of Kairouan, to the south of Tunis, was founded. But then the pace of conquest slackened. The Berbers put up a fierce resistance to the Arab armies. They were nominally subjected by the early years of the eighth century, but continued to mount sporadic rebellions against Arab rule until the 740s and 750s. One way of taming the Berbers, and of simultaneously profiting from their fighting skills, was to encourage or compel their enlistment into Arab-led armies for the prosecution of military campaigns elsewhere. The prospects of adventure and plunder, possibly even of land, would appeal to the Berber warrior-tribesmen. Regular military discipline would break down clan loyalties and values; regular religious discipline would turn them into good Muslims. This thinking probably influenced the Arab leadership to undertake the raids on southern Spain which occupied the years before 711.

It is not clear, from the meagre sources that have survived, why raiding should have turned into conquest. Partly, perhaps, it may have arisen from the inner dynamics of the early Islamic polity. The caliphs of the Umayyad dynasty who presided from Damascus over the vast, sprawling Islamic empire which had erupted with such speed in the seventh century depended for their survival upon the allegiance of an Arab aristocracy imbued with a warrior ethic. (In this respect they were not unlike the rulers of other early medieval successor-states to the Roman empire, such as the Merovingian and Carolingian kings of the Franks in Gaul and Germany.) Prudent rulers respected the habits and needs of their predatory nobilities. Expand or go under: this could have been the motto of any early medieval ruler, whether Christian or Islamic.

Factors which today we might call environmental may have played a part. As we saw in the last chapter, the ecologies of Morocco and of southern Spain are remarkably akin. The difference between them is one of degree: Spain is a little more gentle, tame and lush than her harsher, fiercer, more arid partner across the Straits. It was natural for the Berbers to cast covetous eyes upon these tempting pastures. Comparable factors may have helped to decide the limits of the conquest. After a few years the conquerors abandoned the Asturias, that dank region tucked between the foggy Cantabrian mountains and the Bay of Biscay, where the olive does not grow and where the sodden forests are roamed by herds of – to the Muslim hateful – swine. Just so in other areas did big mountain masses administer a check to early Arab expansion, for instance the Taurus range in northern Syria, or the Caucasus between the Black and Caspian Seas. The Pyrenees are fairly easy to pass at their eastern, Mediterranean end. Hence the existence of Visigothic Septimania, and hence its conquest by the invading armies from Africa. But here too the intrusive presence was short, lasting little more than a generation. This brevity, however, owed as much to political forces as to environmental ones, as we shall see in due course.

If we wish fully to understand the conquest and its context we must give some attention to Spain's preceding historical experience. The Moorish conquest, as we have already stressed, was remarkably quick: a decisive battle, followed by a few mopping-up operations. The invaders did in four years what it had taken the legions of Rome two centuries to encompass. Two observations suggest themselves: they pull in different directions but are not irreconcilable one with the other. First, the ease of conquest was due partly to the legacy of Rome. Four centuries of Roman rule had seen a degree of ordered uniformity imposed upon the Iberian peninsula for the first time in history. The language of the empire, Latin, became the language of law, government and polite society. Recruitment of Spaniards into the Roman army locked Spain firmly into the imperial embrace; returning veterans diffused Roman habits and ideals into the remotest parts of the peninsula. The same might be said of commerce. Spain's primary products – her corn, oil and wine, her minerals, her horses – were greatly in demand in the Mediterranean world. The uniform coinage of the empire and the reasonable safety of travel encouraged commercial enterprise. Landowners both big and small, entrepreneurs, traders, could all profit. The palatial villas of the aristocracy that have been excavated in the valleys of the Guadalquivir, the Guadiana and the Ebro are a testimony to, among other things, market-orientated agricultural production. Old towns prospered under the *Pax Romana* and new ones were founded. Their names can still remind us of their imperial origins – Caesar Augusta (Zaragoza), Legio (the city of the legions, León) – and in some their public buildings, as for example the theatre at Mérida or the aqueduct that still strides across Segovia, continue to attest to their civic pride, their spirit of emulation and their fervent desire to be as Roman as they possibly could. Rapid communication between them was ensured by the network of Roman roads and bridges. Some of the latter still stand, as for instance the bridges over the Duero and the Guadalquivir at Salamanca and Córdoba respectively. One feat of engineering, the bridge over the Tagus near the present frontier between Spain and Portugal, built in the time of the emperor Trajan (98–117) who was himself a native of Spain, so impressed the invaders that they called it simply *'the* Bridge', al-Qantara, now Alcántara: though heavily restored it still stands as one of the proudest feats of Roman engineering, flanked by the temple which shelters the tomb of its designer.

To this grid or pattern of Roman culture must be added one final element in the process of Romanisation – the Christian church. St Paul referred in one of his epistles (Romans 15) to a desire to preach the gospel in Spain, but it is doubtful whether Christianity reached Spain in the apostolic age of the church. (The legend that St James the Great preached in Spain and was buried at Santiago de Compostela in the extreme northwest is a myth got up several centuries later.) However, the new faith certainly reached Spain early on in the Christian centuries, perhaps from north Africa rather than from Italy or southern Gaul. By the time that Christianity became the official religion of the Roman empire in the fourth century a network of Christian communities and their bishops existed in the principal cities and towns, even though it is likely that much of the rural hinterland remained to be converted.

When the western Roman empire crumbled in the fifth century its place was taken by a number of kingdoms under the control of Germanic rulers and their aristocracies – the Ostrogoths (and later on the Lombards) in Italy, the Burgundians in southeastern Gaul, the Franks in northern Gaul. It is most important to grasp that some of these successor-states were themselves highly Romanised. The Visigothic kingdom of Spain forms a particularly telling example.

The Gothic peoples had lived for centuries in proximity to the Roman empire in the lands to the north of the imperial frontier along the river Danube. Already during this period they had begun to adopt some of the trappings of Roman culture from their more civilised neighbours. Pressed from the east by the rise of a new confederacy of nomadic peoples in central Asia, the Huns, the Goths were permitted to enter the Roman empire as refugees in the year 376. There ensued a period of migration within the bounds of the empire and of sporadic hostilities with the authorities, in which the best-known incident was the sack of

Rome by the Gothic king Alaric in 410. Shortly afterwards, in 418, the branch of the Gothic peoples known as the Visigoths, or western Goths, were settled under treaty with the imperial government in southern Gaul where they set up a kingdom ruled from Toulouse. By the time of their invasion and conquest of Spain in the reign of king Euric (466–84) they had become effectively integrated into the culture of the Roman world in which they had now lived for a century.

Romanitas – 'Roman-ness' – was what the Germanic elites who took over the empire strove towards. They had everything to learn, and they showed themselves remarkably versatile and adaptable in adjusting to the new world in which they found themselves. Visigothic Spain was Roman Spain under changed management. The Visigothic rulers issued codes of law in Latin, modelled on Roman law. They issued coinage whose design echoed imperial exemplars. They maintained Roman administrative practices and repaired Roman public buildings. One of them, king Leovigild (569–86), even indulged in the imperial practice of founding cities – Reccopolis, named after his son Reccared (now Zorita, east of Madrid), and Victoria (now Vitoria) which commemorated his victory over the Basque tribes to the north of his kingdom. They showed themselves devoutly, even aggressively, Christian.

One explanation, then, for the speed of the Moorish conquest lies here. Roman order, inherited and maintained by the Visigothic kings, made for a united Spanish state. The decisive blow once dealt in battle, the kingdom would collapse into the hands of the invaders. Just so had other well-governed polities folded in the face of Islam, whether provinces of an empire such as Egypt or indeed an empire itself such as Persia.

The other observation, as has been said, pulls against this one. It is possible to exaggerate the degree of order and unity in both Roman and Visigothic Spain. (This is partly because most of our surviving sources are what might be called 'centralist'. A lawcode such as the Visigothic one naturally tends to focus attention upon the king as lawgiver. We know practically nothing about how the law was actually administered in the provinces.) The Roman empire and its Germanic successor-states depended for their functioning upon the active administrative role of local elites or bosses – landed magnates with a stake in the provincial urban capital, patrons of clients and retainers, buffers between their dependents and the tax-man, givers of employment, organisers of charity when times were hard, providers of public entertainments such as races or bullfights, wielders of influence with the local judge or bishop (who might well, indeed, be related to them). For the local community such people as these probably loomed larger and mattered more than the remote figure of the king. A would-be conqueror could proceed on his way striking a series of deals with the local bosses. If we may generalise from the case of Theodemir, this was perhaps exactly what 'Abd al-Aziz was doing in the years 712–15.

One further element in Spanish society at the time of the conquest must be mentioned: the Jewish communities. Jews had been settled in Spain from at latest the first century of the Christian era. It may be that St Paul had been attracted by the idea of a mission to Spain through awareness of the Jewish congregations there. They seem for the most part to have been concentrated in the cities of the east and south, and in the Balearic Islands. Unfortunately, very little is known of them from their own records, which amount to not much more than a handful of inscriptions. Our principal source of information about them is furnished by successive royal enactments against them preserved in the Visigothic lawcode. These edicts make ugly reading, especially to a twentieth-century mind and to historians who cannot but be aware of later outbursts of anti-Semitism in medieval and modern Spain. Two things need to be borne in mind in considering this legislation. First, the sixth and seventh centuries saw steady persecution of the Jews in the east Roman or Byzantine empire. In this respect the Visigothic kings were once more aping *Romanitas*; and so were their contemporaries in other successor-states such as the Lombard and Frankish kings of Italy and Gaul. There was therefore a context for anti-Jewish persecution in the early medieval Mediterranean world. Second, there is some reason to suppose that the persecutions were rather less effective in practice than the kings and bishops who initiated them had intended.

When all is said and done, however, the Jewish communities of Spain about the year 700 must have been disaffected towards their Visigothic masters. Their engagement in external trade and their relations with Jewish congregations elsewhere must have made them aware of the fortunes of their co-religionists in other parts of the Mediterranean world. It may be significant that king Egica (687–702) enacted a law prohibiting Spanish Jews from engaging in foreign trade. They cannot have been ignorant of the fact that Jews in Syria and Egypt were distinctly better treated under Islamic rule – in accordance with Koranic precept – than they had been under Roman. Precisely what part the Jewish community leaders played in forwarding the Moorish conquest cannot be known. They may well have played a role in negotiating local treaties of the sort referred to above. In general, it is difficult to envisage them as not having been at the very least benevolently disposed towards the invaders.

During the forty-odd years that followed the initial conquest Spain was ruled by governors, based in Córdoba, who were in theory appointed by the Umayyad caliphs in Damascus but in practice seem to have been answerable to the Arab governors of Ifriqiya based in Kairouan. This is a very obscure period, but with the help of the all-important *Chronicle of 754* eked out by a few other scraps of evidence we can dimly make out the shape of events. Four important developments may be discerned. In the first place, the conquerors' hold was consolidated by the distribution of land on which to settle the rank and file of the armies. Not all the aristocratic landholding families of Visigothic or Hispano-Roman descent were dispossessed by any means. Theodemir is a case in point of one who survived, and as we have seen there may have been plenty of others like him. On the other hand, the landed estates – presumably both ample and widespread – of the Visigothic monarchy must have come into the hands of the Arab governors; so too, probably, the estates of those who resisted the invaders such as the warriors of king Roderic's army and the notabilities of the cities that resisted such as Córdoba and Zaragoza. These lands would have been available for distribution, which we are told was done 'by lot' during the governorship of As–Samh between 718 and 721. However the lottery may have been conducted, it looks as though the results were rigged: for the Arab minority among the conquerors got the most fertile lands, while the Berber majority were palmed off with the less favoured lands in the centre and north of the peninsula or in the more mountainous regions of the east and south. This inequality of distribution was to have serious consequences.

Immigration, secondly, provided the manpower for settlement. It is a critical question whether it also provided the womanpower. The most authoritative estimate puts the number of Arab and Berber *warriors* who settled in Spain in the wake of the conquest at between 150,000 and 200,000. If they were accompanied, or later joined, by their wives, children, clients and slaves we should have to multiply that figure by perhaps four or five or six to arrive at an idea of the total number of immigrants to eighth-century Spain. If on the other hand these were unattached warriors who acquired women and slaves for themselves in Spain, then the ethnic significance of the invasions will have been less marked. Common sense would suggest that both processes – single and group migration – occurred. If the immigrants approached one million persons in the course of the eighth century this would represent a substantial shift in the ethnicity of the peninsular population. How substantial is a question that cannot confidently be answered, since our information about the demography of late antique and early medieval

Spain is almost non-existent. Guesstimates by plausible guessers put the population of the Iberian peninsula at around the four-million mark in the late Roman period. It is unlikely to have grown by the year 700, seeing that in Europe as a whole the early medieval period seems to have been a time of demographic stasis or even recession.

The population of the conquered was reduced partly by violence and partly by emigration to safer regions. One such emigrant we have already met, the archbishop of Toledo who fled to Rome. Others were involuntary, like the lordly Visigoths whom Musa carried captive to Damascus in 712. (Some of the latter may have entered the caliph's service there. When the Anglo-Saxon traveller Willibald and his companions were arrested during a visit to the Holy Land a few years later (about 724), they were released through the good offices of 'a certain man from Spain' and his brother 'who was the chamberlain of the king of the Saracens'; an odd encounter.) Others emigrated to parts of the peninsula where they would be safe.

The third significant development of these years was the withdrawal of the conquerors from the Asturian region. This was connected – though whether as cause or as consequence our sources are too meagre to tell us – with the successful rebellion there of a Christian nobleman called Pelagius or Pelayo. Later Spanish historians of a nationalistic bent would imbue these events with a significance that they did not have at the time. Pelagius did not 'initiate the Reconquest of Spain from the Moors'. He founded a tiny Christian principality which could serve as a haven for refugees from the Islamic south. One day, far in the future, it would grow into the medieval kingdom of León-Castile. But nobody could possibly have foreseen that in the eighth century.

Finally, Arab-Berber forays beyond the Pyrenees brought confrontation with the Frankish kingdoms in Gaul. Obedient to the imperative of expansion in search of booty and captives, Islamic armies raided deep into Gaul. Toulouse was besieged in 720; Autun, in Burgundy, was sacked in 725. Their celebrated defeat at the hands of Charles Martel near Poitiers – traditionally dated 732, but 733 looks more likely – was a less decisive battle than has sometimes been claimed: Islamic armies were devastating Provence throughout the late 730s. The context in which the battle of Poitiers *does* have significance is a Frankish rather than a Spanish one. It marked a stage in the process by which a new northern Frankish dynasty, the Carolingians – usurpers, yet anointed kings from 751 – established effective rule over Aquitaine, where only a shadowy overlordship had existed before. Direct confrontation on Spanish soil between Christian Frank and Arab-Berber Muslim would occur in the next generation during the reign of Charles Martel's grandson and namesake — Charlemagne.

In 739 the Berbers of the Maghrib rebelled against their Arab masters and in the following year the revolt spread to Spain. It is not difficult to understand the Berbers' grievances. They had lost their independence after years of struggle. Although by this date their acceptance of the Islamic faith was probably complete, this had not made them the equals of their conquerors. Throughout their empire the Arab elite regarded non-Arab Muslims as second-class citizens; and they were particularly scornful of the Berbers. To these general issues should be added the special grievances of the Berbers of the Iberian peninsula which sprang from the unequal distribution of land. It is small wonder that these resentments should have exploded in 740.

The Berber revolt initiated a period of chaos in the public affairs of al-Andalus. The rebellion itself caused widespread damage and economic dislocation. Furthermore, there were rivalries between the Arab forces (whether from north Africa or from the Middle East) which were sent to suppress it. Spain entered upon a period of endemic civil war. Meanwhile, at the other end of the Mediterranean, the authority of the Umayyad caliphs at Damascus was crumbling. In consequence, their attempts to exert control over their far-flung western provinces were steadily less effective.

Peninsular affairs at this juncture cannot be properly understood without some reference to these stirring, indeed seismic, events in the history of Middle Eastern Islam. From 661 onwards supreme authority within the Islamic community had lain with the Umayyad dynasty of caliphs governing from Damascus. The Umayyads were an Arab family ruling in Arab interests. They generated in the Middle East exactly the same sort of resentments that festered among the Berbers of the Maghrib and the Iberian peninsula. The difference was that those excluded from influence and status in the east were not simple Berber clansmen but Persian, Iraqi, Syrian and Egyptian bureaucrats, soldiers, businessmen, professional people: a formidable opposition, if it could be organised and articulated. And this is precisely what happened. A rival dynasty, known as the Abbasids because they were descended from the Prophet's uncle 'Abbas, skilfully exploited the opposition and in 750 succeeded in ousting the Umayyads and taking the caliphate for themselves. The Abbasids were to keep the office in their family for the next five centuries.

The replacement of the Umayyads by the Abbasids, it has been said, 'was more than a mere change of dynasty. It was a revolution in the history of Islam.' It had a special significance for the history of al-

Andalus. In the first place, the Abbasids shifted the whole centre of gravity in the Islamic world further eastwards, from the shores of the Mediterranean to Persia. The shift was symbolised by the foundation of a new capital city at Baghdad in 762. One of the effects was to make the western outposts of Islam even more remote from the Islamic heartlands. Secondly, the Abbasid revolution precipitated a coup in the political affairs of al-Andalus by a member of the dispossessed Umayyad family which had the effect of rendering the peninsula politically independent of the caliphate in Baghdad.

The first Abbasid caliph took steps to eliminate all the members of the Umayyad family on whom he could lay hands, earning thereby the nickname of al-Saffah, 'the shedder of blood'. One of those who escaped him was a young man named 'Abd al-Rahman who contrived to make his way to the Maghrib. He crossed to Spain in 756 and managed to establish himself in Córdoba. With hindsight the coup of 756 and the establishment of the Umayyad dynasty which was to rule al-Andalus until 1031 came to appear as a decisive turning-point. But matters could not have been perceived in this way by contemporaries. 'Abd al-Rahman and his followers were just another element in the hugely complicated and messy faction-fighting which had been the norm in the peninsula since the outbreak of the Berber revolt in 740. Whether 'Abd al-Rahman would survive, or go under like other factional leaders before him, remained to be seen.

As matters turned out, 'Abd al-Rahman survived for thirty-two years after his initial coup d'état, and in the course of this period he gradually enlarged and stabilised his authority. Thus, for example, he took control of Toledo and its region in the years 761–64, but had to defend himself against rival contenders there as late as the year 785. Seville and the southwest were not securely under his control until the mid-770s. Not until about 780 was he – and then precariously – master of the Ebro valley and the northeast. The imposition of Umayyad rule upon al-Andalus was gradual, and its maintenance demanded constant watchfulness. The centralised state of the peninsular Umayyads was indeed in the fullness of time to be an imposing political system: but the authority of the early amirs – the title which they applied to themselves, and which we may now use of them – was fragile and vulnerable.

One consequence of this was that their Christian neighbours to the north could exploit the amirs' weakness. Alfonso I, the son-in-law of Pelagius who ruled the little Asturian principality from 739 to 757, and his son Fruela I (757–68), laid waste the region between the Cantabrian mountains and the valley of the river Duero and compelled many of its inhabitants to migrate northwards into the Asturias and Galicia. Thus they at once significantly enlarged their resources of manpower and created a depopulated – or very sparsely populated – buffer zone of territory, a no-man's-land between themselves and the Muslim south. An important point about the political geography of the Iberian peninsula in the early Middle Ages should be noticed here. As we have seen, Toledo was the capital city of the Visigothic kings. Under the Umayyad amirate it was replaced by Córdoba. Just as the Abbasids shifted the centre of gravity of eastern Islam from Damascus to Baghdad, so the Islamic presence in Spain shifted *its* centre from Toledo to Córdoba, from the central *meseta* to fertile Andalusia. Simultaneously, the emergence of small nuclei of resistance in the north, of which the Asturian principality was the first, altered the focus of Christian culture in a similar fashion but a different direction. It is convenient to think of the Iberian peninsula from the eighth century onwards for several hundred years as being broadly divided into three roughly horizontal bands, whose individual proportions continually fluctuated: a Muslim zone in the south, a Christian zone in the north, and between them the *tierras despobladas*, the unsettled lands of the frontier zone.

Another Christian neighbour who dabbled in peninsular affairs – and got his fingers badly burnt – was Charlemagne. The background to his intervention was in part the expansion of Carolingian power into Aquitaine, already alluded to, which had been going on since the time of Charles Martel. Under his son Pippin (the father of Charlemagne) the Carolingian advance continued into the Muslim province of Septimania. In 759 the inhabitants of Narbonne massacred their Arab-Berber garrison and handed the town over to Pippin. Carolingian dominion had reached the Mediterranean and the Pyrenees. The question was, when and where would the Frankish steamroller stop? It could be only a matter of time before Frankish armies made an appearance on the southern side of the Pyrenees.

From the Spanish side, the background to Charlemagne's intervention was 'Abd al-Rahman's attempt in the 770s to make the authority he claimed in the northeast a reality by subduing the local bosses who had dug themselves in during the chaotic years of the mid-century. Naturally, they looked elsewhere for protectors. It was an appeal from the governor of the city of Zaragoza that brought Charlemagne to Spain in 778. The expedition disastrously misfired. The governor changed his mind and refused to admit the Franks into Zaragoza. They had no alternative but to withdraw. As they were returning through the western Pyrenees the rearguard of the Frankish army was set upon by the Basques and destroyed in the pass of Roncesvalles. The only person to profit from the operation was the amir of Córdoba, who captured Zaragoza in the following year and thereby consolidated his authority in the valley of the Ebro.

The defeat at Roncesvalles and the death there of Charlemagne's vassal Roland were later to inspire the grandest and most sombre of the Old French epics, the *Chanson de Roland*. But though it looms large in literature, in sober history Roncesvalles was a fairly insignificant affair. Later Frankish initiatives were to be more important. Here the key figure was Charlemagne's son Louis, for whom a sub-kingdom of Aquitaine was created in 781. Louis took advantage of divisions in al-Andalus over the succession to the amirate at the end of the century to mount expeditions which proved more successful than his father's. These culminated in the conquest of Barcelona in 801. Following this, a Frankish 'march', or frontier province, was set up in Catalonia. Louis seems to have attempted to set up a similar march at the western end of the Pyrenees based on Pamplona, which had submitted to him in 806, but here he was less successful. The history of this region is almost impenetrably obscure during this period, but it would seem that in the ninth century an independent Basque principality of Pamplona slowly emerged, which would later come to be known as the kingdom of Navarre.

*

Isidore of Seville, the great scholar-bishop of the Visigothic period, composed a celebrated passage in praise of his country about ninety years before the Moorish conquest:

Oh loveliest of all lands thou art, mother Spain, holy, everlastingly happy!

The author of the *Chronicle of 754*, not surprisingly, took a rather different view of his world:

Who could number these disasters? Human nature could not relate the ruin of Spain, nor the quantity and degree of her sufferings, not even if every bodily member were to be turned into the tongue.

The eighth century was probably the bleakest in the entire recorded history of the Iberian peninsula. We have to say 'probably' because it is also the most obscure to us. The surviving sources are so meagre, in consequence so difficult to interpret, that we can do very little more than trace the indistinct outlines of convulsive public events. We have no means at all of measuring the cost in terms of human suffering. The exodus of refugees from the peninsula shows that some, at least, wanted to get out and had the means to do so. Certain among them achieved prominence in the Frankish kingdom. Here are two examples.

A mysterious character called Pirmin is the earlier of the two. Historians have for long debated his origins – Irish? Frankish? Visigothic? – but it is now generally agreed that he was a native of Visigothic Septimania. He turns up in the eastern part of the Frankish kingdom where he founded the monastery of Reichenau, on an island in Lake Constance, in 724. He went on to found others, for example Murbach in Alsace in 728, and his surviving writings show that he envisaged them as mission-stations for the evangelisation of the peoples to the east of the Rhine. He busied himself in this work until his death in 753. Another refugee, and this time certainly of Visigothic extraction – he may have come from the Ebro valley – was Theodulf, who joined Charlemagne's court in the 780s and rose to be bishop of Orléans. He was an accomplished Latin poet, a Biblical scholar and a theologian: an important figure in the revival of learning which took place under the patronage of Charlemagne. Theodulf was himself a connoisseur and a patron. The chapel he built at Germigny-des-Prés, beside the Loire upstream from Orléans, still stands (though much restored).

Pirmin and Theodulf were well-connected and moved in the highest political and ecclesiastical circles. That, after all, is why we hear about them in our sources, which are themselves works composed by and for this small elite. There were certainly plenty of others who flocked towards the Frankish kingdom, of humbler station, of whom we can just catch the faintest glimpses. In Catalonia, for example, a number of charters recording grants of land to be resettled and colonised in this marchland refer to the settlers as *Hispani*, 'Spaniards', a term which in this context designates refugees, Christian immigrants from the Muslim south.

The period of maximum turbulence and dislocation in the peninsula as a whole seems to have been the half-century or so after the outbreak of the Berber revolt in 740. Breakdown of public order, disruption of administrative structures and legal routines, faction-fighting and vendettas, the forcible transfer of communities from one place to another, random slave-raiding and cattle-rustling – all the things to which Theodulf referred in one of his poems, perhaps with an inward shudder, as 'overwhelming disasters' – all these must have had the gravest social and economic consequences, at which we can only guess. In some areas these would last for centuries. In the *tierras despobladas* olive groves and vineyards would go untended, grass and scrub would encroach on road and threshing floor, squatters in the abandoned towns would look round in alarm for their children at the thud of collapsing masonry. Cities like Salamanca would not rise from their rubble again until the twelfth century.

In the areas more or less under the control of the amirs of Córdoba, the main question posed for the bewildered indigenous populations was this: how should they adjust to their new masters, who spoke a strange language, professed an alien faith and observed a different law? The manner – the variety of manners – in which this question was to be answered in the ninth century would go far to shape the character of an emergent Hispano-Muslim civilisation.

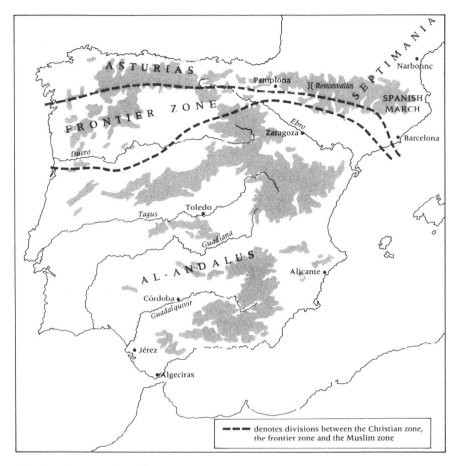

The Iberian Peninsula c. 800

3

THE CURVE
OF CONVERSION

The ninth century is a little less obscure to us than the eighth, but it must be said that the illumination is fitful. However, we must take the sources as we find them and do with them what we can. They have nothing to say directly about the most important process of all that was going forward, the conversion of the indigenous population of al-Andalus to Islam and the development thereby of an Islamic society in the Iberian peninsula. It is clear from the much fuller sources that have come down to us from the tenth and eleventh centuries that by then a large proportion of the population was Muslim. Can we discover anything about the occasions and momentum of conversion?

It would be incorrect to think of the Arab-Berber conquerors as filled with missionary zeal. In the first place, the Berbers were themselves only partly 'Islamicised' at the time of the invasion. Secondly, Islamic law guarantees toleration for Christians and for Jews as 'Peoples of the Book', peoples to whom God has granted a partial revelation, reserving the fullness of it for his prophet Muhammad. It may be a grudging toleration but it is toleration nonetheless, and we have plenty of evidence that it was normally observed in al-Andalus. Only pagan idolaters might be subjected to forcible conversion, and there were none of these left – in theory at least – in the Visigothic kingdom at the moment of its collapse. Third, there was a consideration of fiscal interest: non-Muslim subjects of a Muslim regime bore the heaviest weight of taxation. Under early Islamic custom, Muslims were exempt from taxation apart from the obligatory almsgiving which was one of the five so-called 'Pillars of Islam' (alongside the profession of faith, prayer, fasting and the pilgrimage to Mecca). But non-Muslim subject

35

peoples paid poll taxes and land taxes which provided the state with its revenues. In the last chapter we saw 'Abd al-Aziz negotiating with Theodemir in 713 for the payment of precisely these taxes. For the Muslim authorities, therefore, there would have been a certain disincentive for encouraging conversion. The more conversions that occurred, the less the government could hope to raise in tax.

In these circumstances, conversion to Islam would come about not by means of missionary pressure but through the nudging of other social forces of a kind which tend to be inconspicuous to the historian. Let us suppose, by way of example, that a prominent person in a family or a street or a village goes over to Islam – perhaps following marriage into a Muslim family – then friends, kinsfolk, neighbours may follow. In towns especially, the adoption of Islam could have opened the doors to all sorts of opportunities for employment, as clerks, for instance, in an expanding bureaucratic government. There are parallels here to the impulses which much later on, in European colonial empires, led thousands of budding government servants to adopt Christianity. Once the Islamic (or any other) 'establishment' is perceived as 'here to stay', people will drift into it. The process is self-reinforcing, for the consequent diminution and demoralisation of the non-ruling communities will stimulate further defections.

It was forces such as these, we may suggest, that brought about conversion to Islam in al-Andalus just as they did in other parts of the Islamic world such as Ifriqiya or Egypt. Only one serious attempt has been made to investigate the rate at which conversion took place. The method devised, by the American historian Richard W. Bulliet, hinges upon the analysis of patterns of name-giving recorded in medieval Islamic biographical dictionaries. Such dictionaries were a common genre of historical writing in the medieval (and later) Islamic world, and they furnish a prodigious amount of biographical and genealogical information. For an Andalusian example we might cite the *History of the Judges of Córdoba* composed by the scholar al-Khushani, a native of Kairouan who settled in Córdoba in the middle years of the tenth century. It was usual in these works for the compiler to provide the genealogy of each individual who was included in the dictionary. Bulliet was struck by the fact that as an ancestry was traced backwards from generation to generation a moment would come when a series of 'mainstream' Islamic names – such as 'Ali, Ahmad, Muhammad, Umar, etc. – gave way to non-Islamic ones, such as (in our context) Tudmir, Rudruq, Lubb, that is to say the Visigothic names Theodemir, Roderic and Lope; and *that* changeover, at *that* generation, represented (he argued) the moment of a shift from a non-Islamic to the Islamic faith in that family. Bulliet went on to argue that if one pooled all the genealogical information of this sort and then pegged it to a rough chronology by allowing a number of years to each generation, a graph representing the rate of conversion in any given area of the early Islamic world would emerge. The methodological objections are, of course, only too obvious. How long is a generation? What if some of the genealogies are false? But, argued Bulliet, these objections should not matter if the statistical sample is large. For certain parts of the Islamic world, such as Egypt, Syria and Persia, the sample was very large indeed. For al-Andalus it was small. Yet the graph yielded by this modest amount of Andalusi evidence corresponded to those furnished by information from better-documented Islamic societies. This is what it looks like.

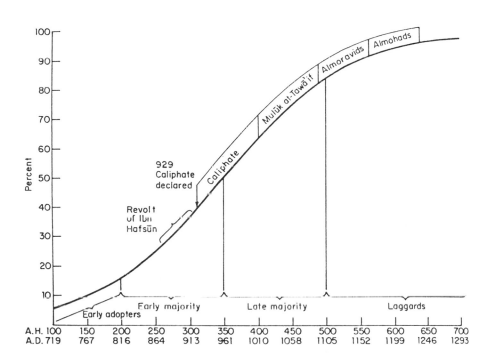

Let us take these findings as a working hypothesis. By about 800 only some 8% of the indigenous population of al-Andalus had become Muslims. This had risen to about 12.5% by the middle of the ninth century. Thereafter the figure increased by leaps and bounds. It had doubled, to 25%, by about 900 and by 950 this figure had doubled again. By about the year 1000 the proportion stood at something like 75%, after which the curve flattened out. There was therefore, on Bulliet's showing, a sudden surge into the Islamic fold from about the middle years of the ninth century. Can this trend be corroborated from any other sources?

One possible such source is an architectural one. The first mosque in Córdoba was built on a central site in the city near the Roman bridge over the river Guadalquivir. It was rebuilt by 'Abd al-Rahman I towards the end of his reign in the years 784–86. The building was enlarged by 'Abd al-Rahman II between 833 and 848; further extended by al-Hakem II between 961 and 966; and finally enlarged once more by the vizir al-Mansur between 987 and 990 into the structure which still stands today. While there may be several reasons for a ruler to extend and embellish a noble religious edifice – piety and self-glorification among them – the most obvious is surely the most convincing. Successive extensions to the mosque were necessary to accommodate a steadily growing number of Muslim worshippers. The chronology of the architectural additions, in the century and a half from the 830s to the 980s, suggestively matches Bulliet's curve of conversion.

A series of bizarre and tragic events which took place in Córdoba in the middle years of the ninth century may point in the same direction. A number of Christians publicly denounced Islam and suffered the full penalty which Islamic law exacts for this offence – death. The first of these self-sought 'martyrdoms' was experienced by a man named Isaac on 3 June 851. His story was written up shortly afterwards by the Christian priest Eulogius – who was himself to be executed in 859 – in the work *Memoriale Sanctorum*. It is an instructive tale.

Isaac was a member of a prominent and wealthy Christian family of Córdoba. He received a good education and was an accomplished speaker of Arabic. When he grew up he entered the service of the government and rose to the rank of what Eulogius calls *exceptor reipublicae*, by which he probably meant *katib*, or secretary; a high posting for a non-Muslim. But he experienced a religious vocation, resigned his post, and became a monk at the monastery of Tábanos, a little way outside Córdoba to the north. This was in 848. Three years later Isaac made his way back to Córdoba, presented himself before the *qadi* – the officer appointed to administer Islamic law and maintain standards of religious observance in the city – and announced that he wished to be instructed in the Islamic faith. The *qadi* expounded the faith to him. Isaac then cursed and abused Muhammad and called on the *qadi* to become a Christian. The *qadi*, completely flabbergasted, struck Isaac in the face, who then burst out, 'How dare you strike a face which resembles the image of God?' The *qadi*, calmed by his advisers, then said, 'Perhaps you are drunk, or in the grip of some frenzy, so that your utterances are out of control.' This Isaac vigorously denied: on the contrary, he was 'on fire with a zeal for righteousness' and ready to die for his beliefs. And this, after a brief period of imprisonment during which the matter was referred to the amir, he duly did.

It is of great interest to find the son of a Córdoban Christian family being brought up fluent in Arabic and then entering the civil service. Eulogius tells us these things casually, just to fill in the background to the encounter with the *qadi*: evidently they deserved no special comment. The same may be said of the ostensible pretext for Isaac's interview with the *qadi* on his return to Córdoba: the implication is that the *qadi* was accustomed to instructing prospective converts to Islam. In other parts of the writings of Eulogius and of his friend Paul Alvarus (who wrote an account of Eulogius' death) anxieties are voiced which seem to tally with this. They and presumably others among the Christian community were worried about the decline of Christian observance and the attractions of Arab-Islamic culture. This mood accords well with a period when the rate of conversion to Islam seems to have been gaining momentum.

Isaac had seemingly wound himself up into a state of elation by the time of his confrontation with the *qadi*. This may have something to tell us of the spiritual atmosphere of the monastery of Tábanos. (It may also have something to tell us of the literary influence upon Eulogius of the passion-stories of those earlier Christian martyrs who fell victim to Roman persecution.) The community there furnished several of the martyrs who met their deaths between 851 and 859. It seems to have been a place where consciousness of an Islamic threat to Christianity was stoked up to maximum heat.

How real was this threat? One of the most interesting features of the writings of Eulogius and Paul Alvarus is the light they shed on social relationships and religious affiliations in ninth-century Córdoba. These relationships and affiliations seem to have been fairly easy and fluid. The number of mixed marriages between Muslim and Christian is striking. Several cases are reported of Christian converts to Islam who subsequently apostasised and returned to Christianity; of converts from Islam to Christianity; of differing confessional allegiances within a single family. Eulogius tells us of these cases simply because they led to disaster. We must make a large allowance for those that did not.

The zealots who sought martyrdom were regarded with wariness by their co-religionists. The movement was condemned by bishop Reccafred of Seville. It was this condemnation, indeed, which prompted Eulogius and Paul Alvarus to compose their works. These were not simply commemorations of the martyrs but also apologetic works designed to justify the martyrs' actions and defend the executions as 'true' martyrdoms. This polemical edge to their writings is one factor which makes it so difficult to handle them as historical evidence. Another is their very isolation. The works cast a shaft of welcome light upon Córdoba in the middle years of the ninth century. But Córdoba was obviously a special and unusual place – the capital city of al-Andalus, the seat of amiral power and government. What was happening to the Christian communities in, say, Zaragoza or Valencia or Seville or Lisbon? We do not know.

Another Christian response to the steady advance of Islam among the population of al-Andalus was emigration. Now the cases of Pirmin, Theodulf and the *Hispani* of Catalonia, mentioned in the last chapter, serve to remind us that this was no new phenomenon. The fact remains that we do hear more about emigration from al-Andalus to the Christian principalities of the north in the course of the ninth century. Consider, for example, the case of the monastery of Samos, near Lugo, in Galicia. A monastic community had existed there in the Visigothic period, attested by a surviving inscription, but had subsequently withered away. Ramiro I, king of the Asturias from 842 to 850, desirous of restoring monastic life there, entrusted the task to an abbot named Argericus; and the document recording this transaction makes clear that Argericus was an immigrant from al-Andalus. A little later, in 857, presumably after the death of Argericus, Ramiro's successor king Ordoño I put the monastery in the charge of two monks, Vicentius and Audofredus, who had recently arrived from Córdoba. It is interesting to find that they left Córdoba at the very period of the martyr movement. One wonders whether their decision to leave was prompted by it.

It was doubtless such people as Vicentius and Audofredus who brought news of the martyrdoms to the Asturias and fostered the growth of a cult of the martyrs there. In 883 king Alfonso III acquired the relics of Eulogius from the amir Muhammad I and the focus of the cult was transferred from Córdoba to Oviedo. There was a great deal else that the immigrants to the Christian principalities brought with them. They brought, for example, distinctive artistic traditions of the school often labelled 'Mozarabic'. ('Mozarab' and 'Mozarabic' are derived from the Arabic term *musta'rib*, meaning 'Arabised'. The term is usually employed to denote the culture of those Christian communities who continued to live under Islamic rule in al-Andalus.) The monastery church of San Miguel de Escalada near León, built shortly after 900, is a good example of Mozarabic architecture. Like Samos, it was colonised by monks from Córdoba. Among them was one named Magius who was the artist who painted the illustrations in one of the earliest surviving Mozarabic manuscripts, a copy of the *Commentary on the Apocalypse* by the eighth-century monk Beatus of Liébana, now preserved in the Pierpont Morgan Library in New York. Its highly stylised forms and its vivid colours are characteristic of Mozarabic illumination.

The quickening of the momentum of conversion to Islam was one of the silent processes of the ninth century. Another was an upswing in the economic life of al-Andalus. Here too we have to argue back from the conditions of the better-documented tenth century. The economy of al-Andalus was strong and buoyant in the tenth century. Because economic growth was everywhere an exceedingly slow affair in the early Middle Ages, it follows that this buoyancy must have been preceded by a period of gestation in the ninth. Here again al-Andalus fits into a wider pattern of change. Historians and archaeologists are agreed that in the period between – very roughly – 550 and 750 the Mediterranean world as a whole experienced a long economic recession. The turn of the tide came from about the middle years of the eighth century; there were signs of growth during the ninth; and the ensuing three centuries were a time of sustained expansion.

In the overwhelmingly agrarian economy of early medieval Europe this economic upswing must have been based in the last resort upon rural prosperity. Unfortunately, it is about the countryside of al-Andalus that we are least informed. It is a reasonable guess that, after the turbulent eighth century, the relative peace and order of the ninth enabled a hard-working peasantry more confidently and successfully to exploit a land which at least in the south and east of the Iberian peninsula is naturally fertile. Agricultural prosperity supported towns and the traders who lived in them. The ninth century seems to have been a time when far-flung trading networks were established. It was said that the amir 'Abd al-Rahman II bought a famous necklace that had belonged to one of the wives of the Abbasid caliph Harun al-Rashid (786–809). True or not, the story may be taken as a symbol of the peaceful contacts – not simply commercial ones, as we shall see – which were opening up between al-Andalus and eastern Islam during this period. (The necklace had an exotic subsequent history. After the collapse of the Umayyad system in the eleventh century it passed into the hands of the rulers of Toledo. The last of these, al-Qadir, ended his life as ruler of Valencia. Through him the necklace came into the possession of the Christian conqueror of Valencia, Rodrigo Díaz, better known as El Cid. Much later on it was among the treasures of the famous constable of Castile Don Alvaro de Luna which were forfeit to the crown on his execution in 1453. The necklace is last heard of in the possession of queen Isabel, the consort of Fernando, the conqueror of Granada in 1492.)

More prosaic, but strictly contemporary, information is provided by the geographer Ibn Khurradadhbih whose work, dedicated to an Abbasid ruler, was completed in about 885. He tells us that slaves and furs were traded 'on the western sea' – by which he meant the western parts of the Mediterranean – and shipped eastward from there. The slaves, he says, were Slav, Greek, Frank and Lombard. It is likely that slave-traders from Sicily, which was in Muslim hands from about 830, were in a position to ship Greek and Lombard (i.e. Italian) slaves to the east. But Frankish and Slavonic slaves most probably came by way of al-Andalus. Slaves could be acquired there by means of raiding. Among the 'martyrs' of 851 there was a young man named Sanctius (Sancho), a native of Albi in southern France, who had been captured as a boy, possibly during a raid into southern Gaul recorded in 841, and then brought up to serve as a slave-soldier in the amir of Córdoba's army. They could also be acquired by purchase. By the middle of the tenth century merchants of Verdun, we are told, made a speciality of transporting slaves from the Slavonic regions of eastern Europe down to Spain for sale there: the traffic could have been in existence at a much earlier date. Other specialists were the Vikings. Andalusi sources, like Frankish or Irish or English chroniclers, confine their attentions to the destructive role of the Vikings as pillagers. In 844 they attacked Seville, in 859 it was the turn of Algeciras. They took captives, of course, as part of their plunder. In 858, for example, they managed to capture the royal women of the little state of Nakkur, near Melilla, whose ransom was paid by Muhammad I of Córdoba. In 861 they captured king García of Pamplona. But we need to remember that they also *brought* captives with them, for sale as slaves: trading and raiding went hand in hand. Irish and Anglo-Saxon slaves, as well as Frankish and Slavonic ones, probably reached al-Andalus in Viking ships in the course of the ninth century. As for the furs to which Ibn Khurradadhbih refers, doubtless they were supplied by the Vikings too – just as they supplied Middle Eastern Islam with the exotic furs that trappers brought back from the Arctic north or the great forests of Russia.

The drafting of slaves, howsoever acquired, into the Andalusi armies was a highly significant development. In this as in much else the amirs of Córdoba were following in the footsteps of the Abbasid caliphs in the east, who were recruiting slaves (often, ethnically, Turks) on a large scale from the early ninth century onwards. ('Slave' is perhaps a misleading term, since by no means all such soldiers were unfree: 'mercenary', or simply 'professional', might be more appropriate.) A standing professional army – further evidence of the government's wealth – freed the amirs of Córdoba from dependence on the caprice of vendetta-ridden Berber clansmen. We are told by an eleventh-century source that the amir al-Hakem I (796–822) was the first ruler of al-Andalus to establish a professional army. In his day it was essentially a palace guard of 2000 cavalry, quartered in the city next to the amir's residence. But it grew: by the middle of the tenth century there was a standing army of about 60,000. The soldiers who served in it were popularly known as 'the silent ones' because they had no, or very little, knowledge of Arabic – which serves to confirm their generally foreign origin.

Change in the military organisation of the Umayyad state was only one of several ways in which the amirs of Córdoba copied the governmental system of the Abbasid caliphs of Baghdad. Indeed, the leading modern historian of al-Andalus, the French scholar Evariste Lévi-Provençal, even went so far as to describe the state as 'an exact, if smaller copy' of the Abbasid system from the early ninth century onwards. Lessons may also have been learnt, directly or indirectly, from another highly sophisticated political system, that of the east Roman or Byzantine empire. Embassies were exchanged between Constantinople and Córdoba in 840. The manufacture of precious silk textiles was a monopoly of the amirs, just as it was of the Byzantine emperors; and the former, like the latter, distributed them annually to deserving dignitaries.

We first hear of a chancery on the Abbasid model during the reign of the amir 'Abd al-Rahman II (822–52). It was situated in a building next to the palace and employed a staff of secretaries – among them the 'martyr' Isaac – for the rapid multiplication of documents. It is evident that writing already played a significant part in the business of government. During the same reign we hear of the adoption of elements of the court etiquette developed by the Abbasids after Persian models, designed to make the ruler more remote, imposing and difficult of access. 'Abd al-Rahman was himself a man of intellectual cultivation: he collected books (often imported from the eastern Islamic lands) and was reputed a skilful poet. He established an exile from the east, the celebrated singer and musician Ziryab, at Córdoba in the early part of his reign. Ziryab established a kind of *conservatoire* at Córdoba where young musicians and singers could study. Through him the musical traditions of the east were brought to al-Andalus, and also his own additions to them. He is said to have been the first to add a fifth string to the four-stringed lute. (The word 'lute' and its fellows in the languages of western Europe are derived from Arabic.) But Ziryab brought more than music. At Córdoba he established himself as a kind of Andalusi Beau Brummell. From him fashionable Córdoban society learnt how to cook and serve a dinner after the smartest fashion of Baghdad. He introduced new hairstyles, encouraged the use of toothpaste and laid down what clothes were to be worn at what seasons of the year. Until his death in 857 he was an important influence in the transmission of eastern Islamic culture to the outpost of western Islam in al-Andalus.

By this date Córdoba was, if not always a tranquil, at least a loyal and a well-governed city. It had not always been so. In 805 there had been a conspiracy in Córdoba against the amir al-Hakem I. He suppressed it mercilessly: seventy-two persons were crucified. In 818 there were serious urban riots against the government in the suburb of the city on the south side of the river Guadalquivir. After these had been put down, again with great brutality, al-Hakem had the suburb removed. Its inhabitants were sent into exile, their houses were demolished and the entire area was turned over to arable cultivation. After this Córdoba gave no more trouble. Other areas, however, did.

To read Lévi-Provençal's great work is to gain an impression of the Umayyad amirs as almost constantly engaged in 'suppressing provincial revolts'. This is one way of looking at things but it may not fully accord with the realities of the ninth century. It is as well to remember that geography encouraged the political fragmentation of the peninsula; that Roman and Visigothic centralism had depended upon the active and benevolent role of local magnates; and that the imposition of Umayyad rule after the chaotic years of the mid-eighth century had been slow. Furthermore, the organisation of the frontier areas of al-Andalus by the Umayyads was such as to encourage the continuing dominance of local magnate elites.

We have seen that the Carolingian rulers of the Franks established marches on the fringes of their empire whose governing classes had the primary task of defence. So too did the Umayyads. The marches were called *tugur*, a term which literally means 'front teeth'. As they emerge into the light of history in the ninth century there were three of them: an Upper or Eastern March in the valley of the river Ebro; a Middle March, usually governed from the strategically nodal point of Medinaceli; and a Lower or Western March embracing Extremadura and the central parts of modern Portugal. Each was governed by a military officer, a *ka'id* or general, rather than a civil governor as was the practice in the provincial divisions of the south. The marcher generals were a long way from the seat of government in Córdoba, they necessarily had command of troops and they governed areas which were poorer, less densely populated and less urbanised than the south. In these circumstances a *ka'id* could be to all intents and purposes an independent ruler of his marcher principality. Both he and it would be fairly rough and ready; the lutes, toothpaste and smart parties of Ziryab and his circle might as well have been on a different planet.

An example of such a family of local dynasts is the Banu Qasi. They claimed descent from a Visigothic count named Cassius – hence the family name – who was said to have come to terms with the conquerors after 712 (like Theodemir in the southeast). We do not possess enough reliable historical evidence with which to test this claim: it sounds implausible. It is certain, however, that the family did descend from a line that was neither Arab nor Berber. They are therefore an example of a *muwallad*, or 'convert' (literally 'adopted') family. The earliest traceable member of the family was a certain Musa ibn Fortun who made himself briefly master of Zaragoza after the death of 'Abd al-Rahman I in 788. Fortun is an Arabisation of the Latin name Fortunius; Musa is an Arab name which carried special resonance in al-Andalus as the name of the leader of the expedition which overthrew the Visigothic kingdom. Musa ibn Fortun would appear to have been the first convert to Islam within his family; and thus a persuasive illustration of Bulliet's thesis.

Musa's son, also called Musa, was *ka'id* of Tudela by 842. In that year he cooperated in a military campaign against the Asturian kingdom conducted by a general sent up from Córdoba for the purpose, but quarrelled with him afterwards and declared himself at enmity with the amir. Although Musa was defeated by the amir in person in 843, he seems to have been regarded as so indispensable – or maybe was just so immovable – that he was reinstated in the government of Tudela in 844. He showed himself a loyal vassal in that same year, assisting 'Abd al-Rahman to beat off a Viking attack. Three years later, however, in 847, he again rebelled. He was to remain an effectively independent ruler over the cities and territories of Zaragoza, Tudela and Huesca until his death in 862.

In part Musa's strength derived from his connection with the family of the rulers of Pamplona. He married the daughter of king García (he who was captured by the Vikings in 861). Between the rivalries of the amirs of Córdoba, the kings of Pamplona and the kings of the Asturias, Musa was an adroit survivor. He also troubled the Frankish realm: in 856 he sacked Barcelona and captured two Frankish counts. He was evidently seen as worth placating by diplomatic means, for when he was defeated by king Ordoño I of the Asturias at Albelda in 860 'presents' from the Frankish ruler Charles the Bald were found in his ransacked camp.

After Musa's death the amir Muhammad I was able to recover his power over the Upper March in the Ebro valley, but not for long. In the winter of 871–72 Musa's sons Mutarrif and Isma'il rose in revolt again. Mutarrif fell into the hands of the amir in 872 and was crucified in Córdoba. Isma'il, however, and after him his nephew and then great-nephew, were able to maintain their independence until 907. They had to fight hard to do so, against almost annual expeditions from Córdoba against them. But what is really significant is that it was not military might that brought them down in the end, but intrigue and patronage. The amirs encouraged dissension in the enormously ramified clan of the Banu Qasi, and raised up a rival family, the Tujibids, to supplant them. Ironically, but perhaps not surprisingly, the Tujibids in their turn would one day become independent of rule from Córdoba.

Comparable events occurred in the Middle and Lower Marches in the course of the ninth century. One example will suffice. At Mérida, capital of the Lower or Western March, a certain 'Abd al-Rahman ibn Marwan rose in rebellion in 868. His has all the appearance of another well-entrenched local family like the Banu Qasi. The rebel's father Marwan had been appointed governor of Mérida early in the reign of the amir 'Abd al-Rahman II. It is certainly another case of a *muwallad* or convert family. Marwan had been nicknamed al-Djilliki, 'the Galician', because he descended from a *muwallad* family which originated in northern Portugal or southern Galicia. The rising was crushed and as a precautionary measure the fortifications of Mérida were destroyed. Ibn Marwan was taken to Córdoba where he served, in more-or-less honourable captivity, in the amir's army for the next seven years. In 875 he had a quarrel with a high-ranking official of Arab descent – a point which may be of significance – who insulted and struck him. Ibn Marwan left Córdoba and returned to the west where he held out with a few companions in a castle near Mérida until forced to surrender. Incredibly, he was not compelled to return to Córdoba but was permitted to settle at Badajoz (then a new, modest and unfortified settlement) under promises of good conduct. Predictably, in 877 he declared renewed dissidence by undertaking the fortification of Badajoz and by appealing for aid to the Christian king of the Asturias, Alfonso III. In 878 Ibn Marwan defeated the army sent from Córdoba against him and captured its general, whom he sent captive to his ally Alfonso III. Apprehensive of a larger army despatched against him, Ibn

Marwan fled shortly afterwards to the Asturian court, where he remained until 884. In that year he returned to Extremadura and managed to re-establish himself at Badajoz. Surviving precariously at first, he was able to profit from the disturbed circumstances of the amirate in the later ninth century – the death of Muhammad I in 886, the very short reign of his successor al-Mundhir (886–88), the troubled early years of the next amir, 'Abd Allah – to dig himself in more securely, professing a nominal obedience to Córdoba but in practice ruling independently. Ibn Marwan died in about 890. Successively his son, grandson and great-grandson ruled his Extremaduran principality from Badajoz. It was not until 930 that Córdoban control was reimposed.

These are two examples – there are others – of the troubled history of the marches in the ninth century. They show how easy it was for the frontier areas to drift away from the precarious authority of the amirs. There were other disturbances which occurred very much nearer the centre of power. The most serious of these was the rebellion – so-called – of 'Umar ibn Hafsun.

Ibn Hafsun was a member of a landed family near Ronda. Like the Banu Qasi and the Banu Marwan this was a *muwallad* family: Ibn Hafsun claimed descent from a Visigothic count named Alfonso. The family had gone over from Christianity to Islam in the early years of the ninth century. 'Umar Ibn Hafsun, evidently a somewhat wild young man, quarrelled with one of his neighbours and killed him. This was in 879. Disowned by his father he fled to Morocco, but returned to Spain in the following year and established himself at Bobastro, a few miles to the east of Ronda: this was an almost impregnable site overlooking the upper waters of the river Guadalhorce where it runs through the narrow Chorro gorge, in some of the wildest mountain scenery in the Iberian peninsula. (It is a region much favoured by the makers of 'paella westerns'.) He took to a life of brigandage, quickly began to attract followers, and went from strength to strength. After defeating a series of expeditions sent against him he was eventually forced to surrender in 883, and – like Ibn Marwan in 868 – was taken to Córdoba where he was drafted into the army. He served on one of the campaigns against the Banu Qasi. However, and again like Ibn Marwan, 'Umar ibn Hafsun was not integrated into Córdoban society: he was mocked as a neo-Muslim by officials of Arab descent. So he deserted, and returned to Bobastro, where once more he flourished as a brigand leader. It is said by one source – a late one – that he won the affections of the peasantry of the area by interposing himself between them and the representatives of authority to protect them from excessive taxation and forced labour. In 888 a force sent from Córdoba against Archidona, one of the towns by then within Ibn Hafsun's power, crucified the commander of the garrison, another *muwallad*, between a dog and a pig: but atrocities did not weaken the spirit of Ibn Hafsun and his men. His zone of influence became more and more extensive. At its most ample his principality stretched from Cartagena to the Straits, and inland to Ecija, Baena and Jaén. Just as the Banu Qasi looked to the kings of Pamplona or Ibn Marwan to Alfonso III, so too Ibn Hafsun turned for aid to the Aghlabid rulers of Kairouan, also to Alfonso III. Although his position was weakened after about 900, he managed to survive until 917. Only afterwards, when his sons fell out and quarrelled amongst themselves, was the government in Córdoba able to re-establish its authority. Bobastro was repossessed in 927.

'Umar ibn Hafsun's career may be interpreted in various ways, some more plausible than others. Was he simply a fugitive from justice, a skilful and opportunistic brigand, inspired perhaps by the example of Ibn Marwan or Musa ibn Musa, operating in a region where banditry has been endemic from the earliest times until almost within living memory? Did he lead a movement of protest on behalf of the oppressed peasantry in a land without justice? Was he, as a *muwallad*, frustrated, cut off from the lucrative patronage of the establishment in Córdoba, an alienated provincial scorned by sleek metropolitan courtiers? Was he just a particularly vivid illustration of the limitations of central power over a segmentary society dominated by feud, in a region of peculiarly intractable terrain? Was he a sort of 'hinge' figure in a world of fluid allegiances?

The last of these unanswerable questions relates to Ibn Hafsun's religious affiliations. When Bobastro was finally subdued by the amir 'Abd al-Rahman III in 927 a church was found in the fortress, and when the ten-year-old remains of Ibn Hafsun's body were exhumed – to be taken to Córdoba for public crucifixion – it was found that he had been buried after the Christian fashion. It is hard to know how seriously to take these reports. The later they were composed, the more detailed and circumstantial they become: it is a chronicler writing in about 1300 who furnishes the exact date of Ibn Hafsun's conversion to Christianity, 899! The reports appear to derive from a news sheet issued by the government at the time – a frequent vehicle of Umayyad propaganda – which referred to Ibn Hafsun as an 'infidel'; but another version of this text makes clear that his 'infidelity' lay in his dealings with the Shi'ite regime of the Aghlabid rulers of Kairouan. It may be, as has been suggested, that the stories of Ibn Hafsun's Christianity were 'no more than rumours put out to discredit a dead but dangerous man in the eyes of his followers'.

The 'rebellions' of the Banu Qasi, of Ibn Marwan and of 'Umar ibn Hafsun tend to be grouped together by historians as '*muwallad* revolts'. It is true that among the features which these movements had in common was a leadership which was not of Arab or Berber descent. It is further suggested that *muwallads* or converts were being excluded from power and influence in ninth-century al-Andalus and that the *muwallad* rebellions were movements of protest by men who, though Islamic by faith, were regarded as outsiders on grounds of ethnicity. On this showing al-Andalus in the ninth century was experiencing the same sort of tensions as Middle Eastern Islam in the eighth, and starting to resolve them in a similar manner. The Abbasid revolution sprang from the resentment of converts against the Arab elite. Its outcome was a community at once more open and more integrated, an Islamic society whose members were defined by religion and culture rather than ethnicity. In the same way, it has been argued, in al-Andalus the ninth century saw 'the creation of a society that was culturally and institutionally Islamic, rather than tribal in nature'.

It is difficult, with any conviction, to cast Musa ibn Musa in the role of resentful outsider. There, surely, was a man who had all that he could desire; so at any rate seem to have thought those contemporaries who nicknamed him 'the third king of Spain' (alongside the amir of Córdoba and the Christian king of the Asturias). Neither can one easily see 'Umar ibn Hafsun as the sort who might have been bought off with a lucrative posting in the civil service; not exactly a man for a desk job, one might judge. Outsiders like the Christian Isaac could rise to positions of administrative responsibility, even eminence, in the ninth century, and would continue to do so in the tenth.

Nevertheless, contemplating the turbulent ninth century, one is left with a sense that the processes which have been glanced at in this chapter – conversion, 'martyrdoms', emigration, economic expansion, *muwallad* rebellions, contact with the east, institutional borrowings – were all somehow interconnected and may have something to tell us about the emergence of an Islamic society in the Iberian peninsula. This was a gradual development. If Bulliet's calculations are approximately correct, only one in eight of the indigenous population had adopted Islam by 850, only one in four by 900. One may suspect that conversion occurred a good deal more slowly in the countryside than in the towns, just as had conversion from paganism to Christianity in the late antique period. Confessionally speaking, Muslims did not outnumber Christians and Jews until the second half of the tenth century.

The most justly celebrated monument to the piety of the amirs is the great mosque of Córdoba. This is a building which 'makes a statement' of the most emphatically Islamic kind. It is principally, of course, a confessional statement. This is where the rituals of Muslim worship were performed; this is where, from the steps of his *minbar* or pulpit – like the tenth-century Andalusi one which survives in Fez – the imam could contemplate with satisfaction the swelling number of believers gathered for Friday prayers. But there was more to it than this. The mosque was different, shriekingly different, from the Roman architecture of Córdoba. It intruded upon and took possession of the open, public space of an antique Mediterranean city. And it was a vehicle for the instruction of the people, its walls not scrubbed clean as they are today for the tourist, but plastered with information and exhortation and instruction from the palace and the chancery next door in handsome Kufic script.

In the name of God, the Merciful, the Compassionate. Glory to God, who has ordained the triumph of those who obey him and the humiliation of those who resist him . . . By the great favour and gift that God has granted us, giving us victory and triumph in all that we undertake, exalting our friend and humiliating our enemy, ennobling our days and allowing us to trample infidel ground under foot, delivering to us his fortresses and mansions so that we may go to and fro within them as we please, now in the abundance of his giving has rendered to us that stronghold of criminals, Bobastro . . .

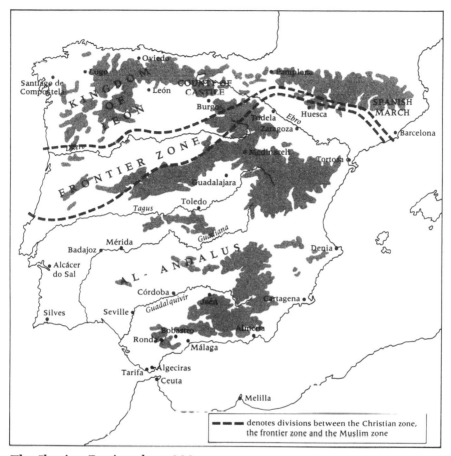

The Iberian Peninsula c. 900

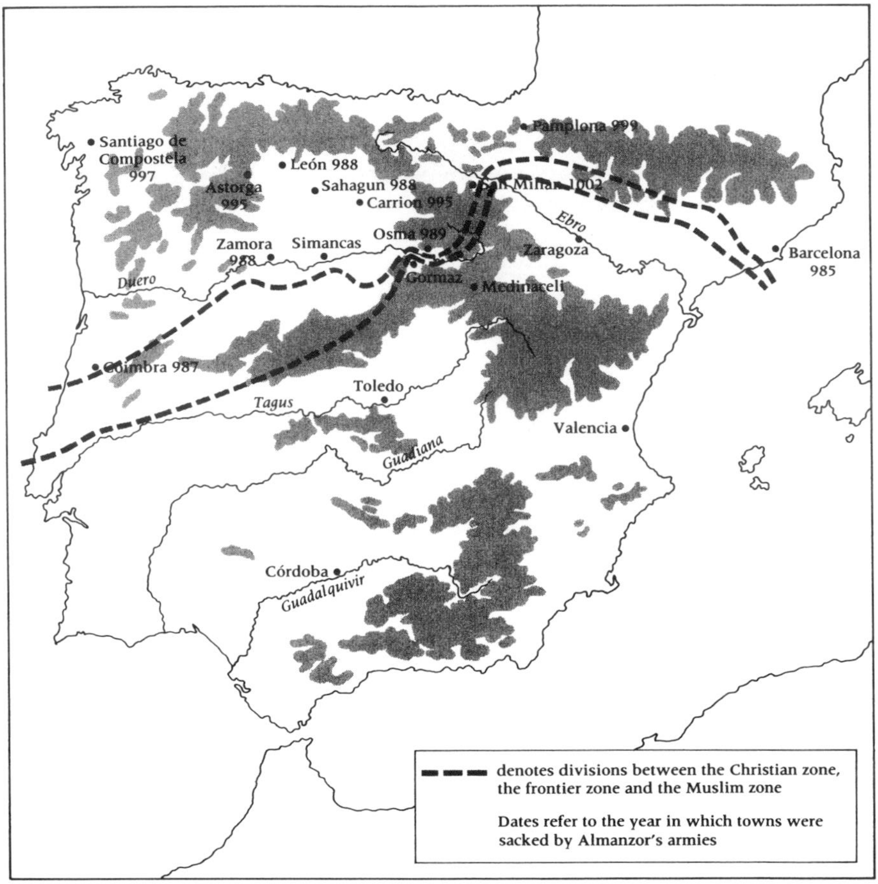
Santiago de Compostela 997
Astorga 995
León 988
Sahagun 988
Carrion 995
Pamplona 999
San Millan 1002
Ebro
Zamora 988
Simancas
Osma 989
Gormaz
Medinaceli
Zaragoza
Barcelona 985
Duero
Coimbra 987
Toledo
Tagus
Guadiana
Valencia
Córdoba
Guadalquivir
denotes divisions between the Christian zone, the frontier zone and the Muslim zone
Dates refer to the year in which towns were sacked by Almanzor's armies

The Campaigns of Almanzor

4

THE CALIPHATE
OF CÓRDOBA

With the tenth century we seem to move into a new atmosphere. In 912 the amir 'Abd Allah died in his palace in Córdoba and was succeeded by his grandson 'Abd al-Rahman III, during whose very long reign of nearly fifty years (912–61) the Spanish-Islamic state reached the peak of its power and renown. This position of eminence was maintained by three succeeding rulers: 'Abd al-Rahman's son al-Hakem II (961–76), and then the vizir al-Mansur, usually westernised as Almanzor, and his son 'Abd al-Malik, who governed successively in the name of the puppet ruler Hisham II (976–1009). This golden age was followed by a sharp crisis in the early part of the eleventh century, after which time the state based at Córdoba was never again to enjoy the status of a superpower which it had briefly enjoyed in the tenth.

'Abd al-Rahman III's father Muhammad was born of the union between the amir 'Abd Allah and the Christian princess Onneca or Iñiga, the daughter of a king of Navarre who had been sent to Córdoba as a hostage in the 860s. 'Abd al-Rahman himself was the child of a union between his father Muhammad and a slave-concubine, a Christian captive possibly from the same Pyrenean region, named Muzna (perhaps originally Maria?). In his immediate ancestry, therefore, the new ruler was three-quarters Spanish, or perhaps more accurately Hispano-Basque, and only one-quarter Arab. He had blue eyes, a light skin and reddish hair. We are told that he used to dye his hair black to make himself look more like an Arab. This was only one of several ways in which 'Abd al-Rahman was skilled at the business of what today we would call projecting an image of himself.

Titles emphasised his loftiness. 'Abd al-Rahman III chose as his *laqab* or honorific name *al-Nasir li-dini 'llah*, 'he who fights victoriously for the faith of Allah'. His most imposing titles were those of *khalifa*, 'caliph', and *amir al-mu'minin*, 'prince of the believers', publicly adopted – and it is significant that we know the precise date – at the Friday prayers on 16 January 929. Elaborate – and for visiting envoys mystifying – protocol governed the daily routine of the caliphal palace. Processions and ceremonies marked the regular occasions, annual during the first half of the reign, when the caliph personally took the field at the head of his troops: the solemn trooping of the standards from the great mosque of Córdoba, the caliph's inspection of his army on the *Fahs al-suradik*, the 'Field of the Royal Encampment' to the north of the city. Newsletters and panegyric poets celebrated the ruler's military exploits and his piety. He seems to have been the first of his line to have employed an official historian to record his deeds.

The work of this historiographer, Ahmad ibn Muhammad ar-Razi (d. 955), has not survived in its original form. However, copious extracts from it have been preserved, along with much else of great interest, in the writings of the eleventh-century Córdoban historian Ibn Hayyan. It follows that we are better informed about the reign of 'Abd al-Rahman III than we are about the reigns of any earlier amir of al-Andalus. While it is gratifying to have such full information, the fact that for the most part it emanates directly or indirectly from the government must induce caution in the historian of today who tries to use it. It is rarely possible to check the assertions of 'Abd al-Rahman's propagandists against independent evidence. We must be prepared to take what they have to say with a pinch of salt – sometimes a generous one.

What they have most to tell us about is warfare. The rulers of Córdoba had to undertake military initiatives on two fronts in the tenth century: within the Iberian peninsula, against the Christian states of the north; and outside it, against the principalities of north Africa across the Straits of Gibraltar to the south. The former involved them in warfare by land, the latter necessarily in warfare by sea. Because our evidence has survived unevenly we know a good deal more about the peninsular operations than we do about the maritime, African ones. It is possible, however, that in the context of Andalusi foreign policy as a whole Africa was more weighty than Europe.

There had been an important change in the political and religious complexion of north Africa in the early years of the tenth century, which in turn can be understood only against the larger background of the development of Middle Eastern Islam. We need to go back for a moment to the middle years of the seventh century. Less than a generation after the death of the Prophet, between 656 and 661, there had occurred a split in the Islamic community between the Sunnis and the Shi'ites. It was a schism which has endured to the present day. In essence what was at stake was the location of authority within the Islamic community, but there rapidly appeared divergences of doctrine and religious practice between the two sides: a rival form of Islam had emerged. In the eighth and ninth centuries Shi'ite propagandists recruited widely in the Islamic world – and secretly, which makes their progress hard to follow. It seems reasonably clear that one of these propagandists decided to 'target' the Maghrib in the closing years of the ninth century. His teaching was successful, and there resulted from it the emergence of a small Shi'ite state whose leader in 910 proclaimed himself *al-Mahdi*, 'the guided one'. His dynasty came to be called the Fatimids because they claimed descent from the Prophet through his daughter Fatima (a claim which the Sunnis disputed). In 912 the Fatimids founded a new capital, al-Mahdiya, between Sousse and Sfax on the coastline of modern Tunisia. From this base they were well-placed to expand east and west along the littoral of north Africa between the desert and the sea, and to prey upon the islands and shipping of the Mediterranean.

It was probably in response to Fatimid pretensions that 'Abd al-Rahman III adopted his new titles in 929. These titles were of the utmost solemnity. *Khalifa* means 'successor' (to the Prophet). In theory, there can be only one caliph in the Islamic world. 'Abd al-Rahman's assumption of the title, it has been suggested, was intended to mark a break with the Abbasid (Sunni) caliph in Baghdad. But al-Andalus had enjoyed a *de facto* independence from Middle Eastern Islam for nearly two centuries: there would have been no sense, in the year 929, in breaking with distant Baghdad. It is more likely that the new titles were intended to assert claims upon the religious loyalties of those who might be 'poached' by the Fatimids. The peoples in question were the Berber inhabitants of the western Maghrib.

The Fatimids posed an economic threat as well to the Umayyad rulers of al-Andalus. The Mediterranean trading networks established in the ninth century were vulnerable to Fatimid seapower. On land, their westward expansionary tendencies could threaten the trans-Saharan caravan routes which were in existence by the same period. From Sijilmasa in southern Morocco to the Niger valley near Timbuktu there stretched a route of some 1400 miles, negotiable by camel-train, along which flowed commodities that vitally contributed to the power of the caliph of Córdoba: gold and slaves.

'Abd al-Rahman III's north African policy took the classic form of a combination of subsidies and ships. He cultivated good relations with the Berber chieftains of the area, to prevent their drifting into a Fatimid orbit or troubling him in other ways – for example by the sheltering of dissidents such as Ibn Hafsun. He also took measures designed to ensure an Umayyad presence on the waters of the western Mediterranean. To this end he commissioned coastal fortresses, watchtowers and other installations: the fortifications of Tarifa are dated by an inscription to 960, and the dockyards of Tortosa, similarly, to 944. Tortosa, at the mouth of the river Ebro, was probably chosen as a naval arsenal because of the proximity of extensive pine forests; the twelfth-century geographer Idrisi furnishes the interesting information that Tortosan pine was immune from attack by insect predators. There were other important naval bases at Denia, Almería, Málaga, Algeciras, Seville, Silves and Alcácer do Sal near Lisbon. (The Atlantic bases were perhaps primarily concerned with defence against enemies from northern waters, such as the Vikings who were active along the Atlantic coast between 966 and 971.) 'Abd al-Rahman III also established bridgeheads on the south side of the Straits by capturing Melilla in 927 and Ceuta in 931. From these bases fleets could patrol the coastline of al-Andalus and launch raids on Fatimid territory. From the African outposts a watchful eye could be kept on the internal affairs of the Maghrib through a network of spies. The father of the historian Ahmad ar-Razi was a merchant of the Maghrib who purveyed political intelligence as well as slaves to the court of Córdoba.

In the event, Fatimid power shifted eastwards rather than westwards. In 969 their armies overran Egypt and shortly afterwards the seat of Fatimid government was transferred to the new city they founded there, Cairo. Thereafter the Fatimid rulers were primarily concerned with the power-politics of the Middle East – where they were the dominant Islamic power until the arrival on the scene of the Seljuk Turks a century later – rather than with the more westerly parts of north Africa. Nonetheless, the prudent rulers of Córdoba remained alert to potential danger from the Maghrib. Their eleventh-century successors showed less wisdom in this as in other matters – with disastrous consequences for themselves.

An overland expedition within the Iberian peninsula against the Christian states of the north was generally termed a *sa'ifa*, from which the Spanish word *aceifa*, meaning 'campaign', is derived. As we have seen in an earlier chapter, these Christian principalities had originated in the eighth century. By adroitly exploiting the weakness of their Muslim neighbours, they had come by the early years of the tenth to occupy slightly more extensive territories and in doing so had pushed the *tierras despobladas*, the unsettled frontier zone, further to the south. At the eastern end of the Pyrenees was a cluster of little principalities which contemporaries called the *Marca Hispanica*, the 'Spanish March' organised by the kings of the Franks, especially Charlemagne's son Louis the Pious (d. 840). The most important of these was the county of Barcelona, which by the year 900 stretched a few miles down the Mediterranean coast southward from the city of Barcelona itself. These Catalan principalities still owed a nominal loyalty to the Carolingian kings of France but were in practice independent. Further to the west, in the Basque country, the little kingdom of Pamplona (or Navarre) had been joined by a neighbour, the county – later to be the kingdom – of Aragon. By the early years of the tenth century the rulers of Navarre were beginning to cast covetous eyes on the rich lands of the Rioja region just to their south. The most westerly of the Christian kingdoms, in the Asturias, had grown prodigiously in the course of the ninth century and by the time of 'Abd al-Rahman's accession reached as far south, in places, as the valley of the river Duero: its kings had just transferred the main seat of their power from Oviedo in the Asturias south over the Cantabrian mountains to the city of León on the northern half of the central *meseta*. Thenceforward they would be known as kings of León. The kingdom had spawned an eastern subdivision, the county of Castile in the upper valley of the Ebro, by the mid-ninth century. During the course of the tenth the counts of Castile would gradually emancipate themselves from the control of their overlords the kings of León. These then were the principal targets of the Córdoban armies of the tenth century: León, Castile, Navarre, Aragon and Barcelona.

To get an idea of what this warfare was like it might be useful to look at one of these campaigns in some detail. This one culminated in a battle – in itself fairly unusual – at Valdejunquera, a little to the southwest of Pamplona, on 26 July 920, in which the Christian forces were badly defeated. This disastrous outcome stimulated Christian chroniclers into taking up their pens, so that this is one of the relatively rare occasions when we can compare Christian and Muslim accounts of the same event. 'On account of our sins many of our people fell there,' observed one writer; 'a great slaughter of the Christians,' noted a monk of the Pyrenean monastery of San Juan de la Peña. The town of Burgos, seat of the counts of Castile from its foundation in 884, was laid waste. Another chronicler recorded that two bishops were captured in the fighting: the ten-year-old nephew, Pelayo, of one of them was shortly afterwards sent to Córdoba as a replacement hostage to secure his uncle's release; five years later he met a martyr's death there.

Thus far the laconic accounts from the Christian side. Ar-Razi's narrative, preserved by Ibn Hayyan, is a great deal fuller.

In this year 308 [= 23 May 920–11 May 921] there took place al-Nasir's expedition against enemy territory which is known as the Muez campaign. He led it in person from his capital right into the heart of the enemy lands, a warrior in a holy cause. This was the first expedition against the infidels under his personal command. After lengthy appropriate preliminaries [i.e. the ceremonial muster at Córdoba] the army set out on 13 Muharram [4 June 920] and made camp at Guadalajara on 24 Muharram [15 June]. On that day al-Nasir appointed Sa'id ibn al-Mundir as governor of Guadalajara. From there he penetrated deeply into enemy territory, laying it waste, destroying the fortresses of Osma and San Esteban, and many monasteries and churches.

The barbarian rulers Ordoño of Galicia [i.e. León] and Sancho of Pamplona, assisted by their infidel vassals and neighbours, came forth to do battle with the Muslim army. A violent conflict ensued between them in which the Muslims, well-led and strong in morale, routed the infidels. God turned the unity of those two barbarians into disunity and their many into few. The defeat took place on 6 Rabi' I [25 July]. Those who fled took refuge in the castle of Muez where they were closely besieged until they were almost dead from thirst. The fortress was taken by assault four days later and its inmates surrendered. The combatants among them were put to the sword in the presence of al-Nasir, more than 500 of their counts and knights. Al-Nasir returned by way of Alava, where he destroyed the town of [illegible: Burgos?] and others nearby, and made his way back to Córdoba in triumph. The campaign had lasted three months.

Ar-Razi's narrative may be supplemented by an even fuller account from the pen of another near-contemporary writer, Arib ibn Sa'id, and by a panegyric poem on the exploits of 'Abd al-Rahman III by the court poet Ibn 'Abd Rabbihi. The latter tells us that Osma was left behind 'like a blackened piece of charcoal'. Ibn Sa'id furnishes some interesting additional details on the Muslim army's itinerary and tactics, as well as a few gruesome sidelights on the campaign: there were, for example, too many heads of the Christian dead for the mule- train to carry back to Córdoba where they were to be set up on stakes round the city walls.

The background to this campaign was the incipient expansion of the principality of Pamplona/Navarre from its mountain nucleus in the Pyrenean valleys southwards towards the fertile lands of the upper Ebro which we now call the Rioja. From the perspective of distant Córdoba, a good 350 miles away, this meant trouble on the frontiers – but trouble of a minor kind, not to be compared, for example, to the threat from Fatimid north Africa. Why could not the amir of Córdoba leave the management of it to his marcher lords such as the Tujibids of

Zaragoza? One answer to this question is implicit within it: the amir could not risk allowing his marcher barons to become overmighty subjects through successful frontier warfare. 'Abd al-Rahman III's forebears had expended precious resources in trying to tame the Banu Qasi of the Upper March, as we saw in the last chapter. No amir in his right mind would want to go down that road again. From this angle, the Valdejunquera campaign – and others like it – was as much about the amir making his presence felt among his nominal subjects as it was about administering a check to his relative the king of Navarre. Details furnished by our sources about changes of officials are significant here. The new governor of Guadalajara, Sa'id ibn al-Mundir, was one of the amir's most reliable servants from early in the reign until his death in 938. Thus the campaign provided opportunities for the exercise of patronage: appointing trusted men to govern restive areas.

The campaign also provided booty. We hear in Ibn Sa'id's account of the plundering of Osma, San Esteban, Clunia and Calahorra; of the treasures and the 1300 horses seized at Muez; and of the foodstuffs found at Vigucra. The Muslim army could live off the land and its soldiers could be duly rewarded in accordance with Islamic law from the booty taken. Above all, the amir's coffers could be replenished. In this context the most surprising feature of the Muslim narratives is their report of the slaughter of large numbers of captives. (Could it be that the figures are greatly exaggerated? 500 is a suspiciously round number, and it shows a tendency to grow in the retelling, to 1000 for example in a later source.) In the normal course of things the higher-ranking prisoners would have been ransomed and the lesser ones sold into slavery; and we know of course that on this occasion some of them *were* held for ransom, like the two bishops mentioned in one of the Christian accounts of the campaign. Captives were usually killed out of hand only if they had treacherously broken one of the agreed conventions of war, for instance by previous ill-treatment of *their* prisoners or failure to observe truces or safe-conducts. It is possible, though we are not told this, that some such misdemeanours might have been held to have occurred during or before the Valdejunquera campaign.

Such ransoms and sales of captives were extremely lucrative. We do not know what price could be demanded for a bishop in the early tenth century but we may be sure that it was no small sum. Regular campaigning was thus an important source of revenue for the government in Córdoba. In this respect the preoccupations of the rulers of al-Andalus matched those of other European rulers of their day. Kings such as Henry the Fowler of Germany (919–36) or his son Otto I

(936–73) beat up their Slavonic neighbours with the same regularity and the same predatory intent as marked the amir of Córdoba's dealings with his Christian neighbours in northern Spain.

Naturally, for the Umayyads as for the Ottonians, matters did not always go as well as they evidently did in the year 920. Nineteen years later a Leonese army under king Ramiro II inflicted a shattering defeat on 'Abd al-Rahman III at Simancas, near Valladolid. The caliph, as he was by then, nearly lost his life: his tent was captured by the Christian forces, and with it his standard, his armour and his own copy of the Koran. Never again did he take the field in person against the Christians.

Generally speaking, however, the Muslims held the military advantage over the Christians throughout the tenth century. After the death of Ramiro II in 950 the succession to the throne of León was disputed between rival claimants who sought help from the rulers of Navarre and Castile in prosecuting their claims. Córdoban diplomacy easily exploited this tangled web. During the last years of 'Abd al-Rahman's reign and in the early part of his son al-Hakem's, the Leonese rulers were in effect the clients of the caliphs. Later still, during the years when the vizir Almanzor had taken over the government during the minority of the caliph Hisham II, Córdoban military ascendancy became even more assertive. Almanzor was in power between 981 and 1002, during which period he is credited by our sources with undertaking no less than fifty-seven victorious campaigns against the Christian north. The most celebrated of these occurred in 997, when Almanzor's armies penetrated to the extreme northwest to sack the city of Santiago de Compostela and carry off the bells from the church of its patron St James to Córdoba. There they remained until the Christian conqueror of Córdoba, king Fernando III of Castile, sent them back to Compostela in 1236.

Such a record of Andalusi military success in the tenth century must have owed as much to good organisation as to good generalship or good fortune. Recruitment to the army drew on three sources. Each *kura* or province of al-Andalus was required to furnish a certain number of soldiers for the amiral (or caliphal) army. Owing to the loss of all the administrative archives of Córdoba from this period we have hardly any precise knowledge about how the system worked in practice. A fragmentary document from the year 863, preserved like so much else in the work of the eleventh-century historian Ibn Hayyan, throws a little light on the matter. From it we learn, for example, that the province of Elvira (present-day Granada) was required to provide 2900 cavalrymen for a campaign against the Christian Asturian kingdom, the province of Algeciras only 290. (The discrepancy is possibly to be explained by the circumstance that the bulk of local Algeciran forces were committed to coastal defensive duties.) This source of recruitment could evidently furnish fairly large contingents in total, and we should remember that as the territorial extent of Córdoba's effective authority increased in the tenth century so too did the amount of military service on which the government could call. As against this, our sources unite in condemning these local levies as inefficient and unreliable.

In the second and far more important place, the army was recruited from mercenaries. As we saw in the last chapter, this development is said to have begun in the reign of al-Hakem I in the early part of the ninth century. The palace guard then instituted grew steadily. It drew partly upon volunteers from Christian northern Spain or the Berber Maghrib, attracted to it by the prospects of good pay just as Scandinavians were attracted at the same period into the Varangian guard of the Byzantine emperors in Constantinople. However, this section of the armed forces seems to have been made up predominantly from captives taken in war – and the 'martyr' Sancho of Albi whom we met in the last chapter is a case in point – or slaves acquired by purchase from native, Maghribi, French or Viking dealers. The Berber and Black African soldiers were known in Andalusi slang as 'Tangerines' because so many were imported through Tangier. These, the crack troops of the armed forces, could be reinforced from a third source of recruitment. This was formed by the service of volunteers who wished to undertake a spell of *jihad* or 'holy war' against the enemies of Islam – rather as, two or three centuries later, western knights would put in a bit of time crusading in the Middle East. In the Islamic world of the tenth century Spain was known colloquially as the *Dar Djihad*, 'the land of *jihad*'. These volunteers must have formed only a small proportion of the armed forces, but perhaps they made up in zeal what they lacked in numbers.

Arms factories near Córdoba could produce 1000 bows and 20,000 arrows every month, 1300 shields and 3000 tents every year. Stud farms for breeding horses were to be found in the basin of the river Guadalquivir, on the lush pastures of the Camargue-like marshland known as Las Marismas bounded by Seville, Huelva and Cadiz. It is a curious fact that wheeled traffic was not generally used in the Islamic world at this period. In its absence transport was furnished by camels and mules. Camels were imported from Africa and herded between campaigns on the semi-desert between Murcia and Lorca. Mules were brought over from the Balearic Islands: Ibn Hawkal, an Arabic traveller and geographical writer who visited al-Andalus in 948, reckoned that

Majorcan mules were the best in the world. The distances covered in a short space of time in land campaigning such as the Valdejunquera expedition of 920 testify to the efficiency of military transport. On occasion as appropriate, troops for use on land might be moved by sea, as for example in 997 when Almanzor sent some of his forces to Galicia by sea – presumably from one of the Atlantic naval bases such as Silves – for the raid on Santiago de Compostela.

Fortifications dotted the land frontier just as they did the coasts of al-Andalus. They are traceable today in place-names, often in the physical survival of constructions. Some were modest affairs, art providing the most rudimentary assistance to nature in the fortification of a hilltop. Others were very impressive indeed. The best of the lot is the enormous castle of Gormaz in the modern province of Soria, rebuilt on the orders of the caliph al-Hakem II in 965 as an inscription above one of its gates witnesses. For intelligence of design and quality of construction, as well as for sheer size, Gormaz had no rival in the western Europe of its day and could hold up its head in the company of the best of Byzantine or eastern Islamic military architecture.

Military procurement in tenth-century al-Andalus must have stimulated a whole range of trades and crafts and skills. The economic pull of Córdoba was felt in places as far apart as Nigeria and Norway. Only a very rich government could have afforded such lavish diplomatic and military policies. We are told by a usually reliable contemporary authority that public revenues amounted to about 6½ million dinars – the gold coin minted at the state mint at Córdoba – per annum towards the end of 'Abd al-Rahman III's reign. But since we lack plentiful information about prices and purchasing power it is hard to know what to do with a figure like this.

Ibn Hawkal, the geographer who was so impressed by the mules of Majorca, is one of the two principal contemporary witnesses to the health and buoyancy of the Andalusi economy in the middle years of the tenth century. The other is a Mozarabic Christian cleric named Recemund, who ended his days as bishop of the Christian community of Elvira. Recemund had had a successful career as a civil servant under 'Abd al-Rahman III: in 955–56 he had been employed on a diplomatic mission to the German king Otto I. He matters in this context because in about 960 he commissioned a work known to scholars as the *Calendar of Córdoba* which contains much information about the practice of agriculture in al-Andalus.

Between them Ibn Hawkal and Recemund of Elvira enable us to chart the Spanish course of what has been called a 'green revolution' in the early medieval Islamic world. One of its most important features was the introduction of new crops to the Iberian peninsula. By the middle of the tenth century there had been acclimatised there, among others, the following: rice, hard wheat, sorghum, sugar-cane, cotton, oranges, lemons, limes, bananas, pomegranates, watermelons, spinach, artichoke and aubergine. One of our sources even allows us a glimpse, precious because unique, of the hazards involved in the process.

The doñegal variety of fig was introduced by al-Ghazal when he went from Córdoba to Constantinople as an envoy [possibly the embassy of 840 referred to in the last chapter]. He saw that fig there and admired it. It was forbidden to take anything from Constantinople. He took the green figs [apparently a seedling is meant] and concealed it among his books that he had wrapped up. When he took his leave he was searched but no sign was found of it. When he arrived in Córdoba he removed the plant from the wrappings, planted it and tended it. When it bore fruit he took it and presented it to the lord of Córdoba [presumably 'Abd al-Rahman II]. He told him about his ruse in procuring it and his lord thanked him.

Doñegal and other varieties of fig were cultivated as a cash crop in al-Andalus. By the early eleventh century Málaga figs – so-called from their point of export – were being sent as far afield as Baghdad.

A second important feature of the 'green revolution' was the wider diffusion of irrigation in the peninsula. Simple irrigation systems had certainly existed there in the Roman period, if not before. The contribution of the Arabo-Berbers was to introduce more complex systems, including new technology, and to diffuse the practice of irrigation more widely. The most famous system in Spain was that of the hinterland of Valencia on the eastern coast. Here the distribution of water for the *huerta*, the belt of irrigated land round the city, was and still is supervised by a Water Court sitting regularly in the city: the system of distribution and control bears striking resemblances to that of Damascus and it has been suggested that the Valencian system was introduced from Syria, possibly in the ninth century. The new technology consisted of the means to raise water artificially from its source in river, well or cistern prior to distribution, in other words the waterwheel fitted with buckets, powered either by the flow of water itself or by human or animal traction. Waterwheels were inexpensive to build and maintain. They undoubtedly became very widespread: the thirteenth-century poet al-Shaqundi claimed to have counted five thousand in the valley of the river Guadalquivir.

The combination of new crops and widespread irrigation brought incalculable economic and social benefits. Rice is cheap and nutritious. Hard (i.e. pasta) wheat will grow in a drier climate than soft (i.e. bread) wheat and because of the low water content of its grain will store for a long time without decay. The net effect of the cultivation of these and comparable crops was a population less exposed to famine. More eating of fruit and vegetables meant healthier people. Irrigation extended the growing season of each year and eased the farmer's dependence on the caprice of the weather. The result was greater productivity, stability of supply and prices, higher income for the grower, further encouragement to innovate and diversify. Taxation was light, as Ibn Hawkal noted, and there was a fluid market in land and labour. Generally peaceful political conditions prevailed in al-Andalus throughout the tenth century. The overall effect must have been a healthier and more prosperous population, thus providing the right conditions for demographic growth: encouragement of earlier marriage and larger families, possibly some increase in longevity.

Historians are agreed that there occurred an upward drift of the population of al-Andalus during this period, though one that it is impossible to quantify on the basis of the sources that have survived. One of its manifestations was the flourishing of city life: demographic growth provided the surplus rural population which might migrate to the towns, higher agricultural productivity the commodities to sustain the specialised economic and other activities of urban life. Many industries flourished in al-Andalus in the tenth century – mining, metalwork, ceramics, glass, woodwork and leatherwork, silk and woollen textiles, paper-making, book production, ivory-carving, to name but a few. As well as serving home markets, these sustained a considerable export trade. Some raw materials were exported: agricultural products like the Málaga figs; rare minerals like mercury from the cinnabar mines at Almadén, between Córdoba and Toledo, which was exported all over the Islamic world. Among manufactured products, textiles seem to have held pride of place: Ibn Hawkal singled out velvets and felts among woollen textiles, linen (which was exported to Egypt), and a whole range of silks. 'Their dyers work miracles,' he observed, and here we have yet another stimulus to trade, for some of the dyestuffs came from very far afield indeed: there survives by chance a letter from about the year 1000 written by a Jewish merchant based in Cairo part of whose business lay in trading brazilwood, the source of a much-sought-after red dye, from India to Spain.

Among the cities of al-Andalus, Córdoba stood out as by far the biggest. Disasters were to befall the city early in the eleventh century – of which more later – and it was to be reduced to a shadow of its former self. This has had the unfortunate effect, for the historian, of generating an element of unrealistic romance in all subsequent descriptions of the city as it was in its heyday under the caliphs. Once more, it is probably best to rely on the sober description of a contemporary. This is what Ibn Hawkal has to tell us.

The biggest city in Spain is Córdoba, which has no equal in the Maghrib, and hardly in Egypt, Syria or Mesopotamia, for the size of its population, its extent, the space occupied by its markets, the cleanliness of its streets, the architecture of its mosques, the number of its baths and caravanserais. Natives of Córdoba who have travelled to Mesopotamia say that it is about the same size as one of the divisions of Baghdad.

A little later he tells us 'perhaps Córdoba is not quite half the size of Baghdad but it cannot be far off it.' Attempts to estimate the size of Córdoba's population at this period are largely guesswork. Something in the region of 100,000 is a widely favoured figure. This would make the Córdoba of 'Abd al-Rahman III and al-Hakem II roughly equivalent in size to Constantinople, the other great city of the Mediterranean world, and several times bigger than even the largest towns of western Europe in the tenth century.

The urban nucleus was the Roman city of Corduba, whose walls of stone pierced by seven gateways were much admired by Ibn Hawkal. It should be remembered that he would probably have been more familiar with simpler walling of adobe or tamped earth on his north African and Middle Eastern travels. He recommended walking round the walls – 'You can do it in an hour' – for the views over the city and its suburbs. This walled city, bounded by the river Guadalquivir to the south, was largely given over to officialdom. Here were grouped the principal mosque, the palace of the caliphs, the chancery, mint, barracks, prison, and the residences of some leading officials. On all sides to the north of the river the walled nucleus was surrounded by suburbs – residential areas, markets, industrial zones, gardens, bathhouses, cemeteries – which imperceptibly turned into a countryside of market gardens and the *munyas* or country houses of the rich on the southern slopes of the Sierra de Córdoba.

The river was spanned by a handsome Roman bridge, which still stands today. The southern bank, cleared of settlement after the rebellion of 818, remained sparsely inhabited even at the period of Córdoba's maximum extent in the late tenth century. There was a large cemetery there, a leper colony, and a few more scattered *munyas*. Among the latter the most celebrated was the *Munyat Nasr*, attractively situated on the banks of the Guadalquivir. Originally built by one of the counsellors of the amir 'Abd al-Rahman II in the second quarter of the ninth century, it later became the home of the famous musician and courtier Ziryab. By the tenth century it was in the hands of the caliph, and often used for housing visiting notables such as the envoys from Constantinople in 949.

It was in 936 that 'Abd al-Rahman III began to build himself a new palace on a site outside Córdoba. From the first it was conceived as more than simply a palace-residence in the countryside of the *munya* type. It was to be a new centre of government of a grandeur fitting to the ruler's new dignity of caliph. No doubt 'Abd al-Rahman had in mind the ambitious building projects of earlier rulers whom he wished to ape; especially perhaps the colossal palace-complex of Samarra, north of Baghdad, built by the Abbasid caliphs about a century earlier. The site chosen was on sloping ground above the Guadalquivir valley some three miles to the west of Córdoba. It came to be called Madinat az-Zahra. Excavations carried out in the first half of this century have revealed much of the structure and decoration of the caliphal palace proper, and one can see why contemporaries were impressed by it. An enormous army of workmen toiled at the site; 10,000 it was said, which is just credible because there was a vast amount of levelling to be done. Roman remains in al-Andalus were pillaged for masonry that could be re-used. Marble was imported from north Africa. A Christian bishop – Recemund of Elvira, no less – was sent to the Byzantine empire to collect works of art, and he probably brought back craftsmen too, for the distinctive Byzantine style of the period has been identified in the decoration of the palace. Perhaps it was through the offices of Recemund that the emperor Constantine Porphyrogenitus sent, we are told, one hundred and forty columns.

The throne rooms were of the utmost magnificence, none more so than the so-called 'Hall of the Caliphs'. Its roof and walls were constructed out of sheets of variously tinted marble so fine as to be translucent. In the centre of the room stood a large shallow bowl containing mercury: it stood on a base which could be rocked, and it was so placed as to receive sunlight from a number of surrounding apertures. When the caliph wished to impress or alarm anyone who had been granted an audience he would sign to a slave to rock the bowl and the sunbeams reflected from the surface of the mercury would flash and whizz round the room like lightning. We are told that at the time of 'Abd al-Rahman's death in 961 there were 3750 slaves in the palace. There was a menagerie, an aviary and fishponds so extensive that the daily allowance of bread for their fish is said to have been 12,000 loaves. (Well, it's what our source tells us. Perhaps the loaves were extremely small.)

But there was much more to Madinat az-Zahra than just the caliph's palace and its gardens. The whole administrative service had been transferred there from Córdoba by the time Ibn Hawkal made his visit to al-Andalus in 948. People had been attracted there to provide what would today be called service industries by government subsidies for building houses. There were mosques, baths, markets, workshops, stables, gardens, merchants' quarters as well as residential areas. Ribbon development sprouted along the road between Córdoba and the new palace-city.

The impression it made upon a visitor from the very different world of northern Europe can be gauged from the contemporary account of a German mission to the court of Córdoba towards the end of the reign of 'Abd al-Rahman III. In 953 Otto I of Germany had sent John, abbot of the monastery of Gorze in Lorraine, to Córdoba. The occasion of the embassy was the desire of the German king to enlist the help of Andalusi naval power in suppressing piracy in the western Mediterranean. Abbot John ran into severe difficulties upon his arrival because the letters he carried with him were couched in terms hostile to Islam. A diplomatic impasse was reached because it was clearly impossible in the circumstances for the caliph to receive the German envoys, yet they could not go home without completing their mission. Matters had to be handled by intermediaries. A senior member of the Jewish community, Hasday ibn Shaprut, and a Christian bishop, another John, presumably the Mozarabic bishop of Córdoba, were charged with making arrangements. It was eventually decided to send a suitable ambassador back to Otto I to seek what our source calls 'more diplomatic letters'. The man chosen was that invaluable servant of the state, bishop Recemund. All this took time. It was not until 956 that Recemund returned from the German court with the appropriate letters. During the nearly three years since their arrival in Córdoba John of Gorze and his companions had been kept in a state of semi-captivity, seemingly fairly bewildered about what was going on. (We do not know where the envoys were housed, though it was evidently outside the city: one suspects that they were not considered important enough for the *Munyat Nasr* treatment.) It is at this point that our source, a life of John of Gorze composed shortly after his death in 974, may take up the tale.

When all these matters had been explained to him, John, released from almost three years of cloistered seclusion, was ordered to appear in the royal presence. When he was told by the messengers to make himself presentable to royalty by cutting his hair, washing his body, and putting on clean clothes, he refused, lest they should tell the caliph that he had changed in his essential being beneath a mere change of clothes. The caliph then sent John ten pounds in coin, so that he might purchase clothing to put on and be decent in the royal eyes, for it was not right for people to be presented in slovenly dress. John could not at first decide whether to accept the money, but eventually he reasoned that it would be better spent for the relief of the poor, and sent thanks for the caliph's generosity and for the solicitude he had deigned to show him. The monk added in his reply: 'I do not despise royal gifts, but it is not permitted for a monk to wear anything other than his usual habit, nor indeed could I put on any garment of a colour other than black.' When this was reported to the caliph, he remarked: 'In this reply I perceive his unyielding firmness of mind. Even if he comes dressed in a sack, I will most gladly receive him.'

On the day which had been agreed for John's presentation at court, all the elaborate preparations for displaying royal splendour were made. Ranks of people crowded the whole way from the lodging to the centre of the city, and from there to the palace. Here stood infantrymen with spears held erect, beside them others brandishing javelins and staging demonstrations of aiming them at each other; after them, others mounted on mules with their light armour; then horsemen urging their steeds on with spurs and shouts, to make them rear up. In this startling way the Moors hoped to put fear into our people by their various martial displays, so strange to our eyes. John and his companions were led to the palace along a very dusty road, which the very dryness of the seasons alone served to stir up (for it was the summer solstice). High officials came forward to meet them, and all the pavement of the outer area of the palace was carpeted with most costly rugs and coverings.

When John arrived at the dais where the caliph was seated alone – almost like a godhead accessible to none or to very few – he saw everything draped with rare coverings, and floor-tiles stretching evenly to the walls. The caliph himself reclined upon a most richly ornate couch. They do not use thrones or chairs as other peoples do, but recline on divans or couches when conversing or eating, their legs crossed one over the other. As John came into his presence, the caliph stretched out a hand to be kissed. The hand-kissing not being customarily granted to any of his own people or to foreigners, and never to persons of low and middling mark, the caliph none the less gave John his hand to kiss.

What an encounter it must have been! We are told a little about their subsequent discussions, though not about the results, if any, of the mission as a whole. One should very much like to know what presents a German king thought it suitable to send to a caliph of Córdoba. Let us hope that they were not perishable. We possess by chance a list of presents offered to the caliph by one of his most exalted subjects a few years earlier. Ahmad ibn Shuayd belonged to one of the richest and most powerful families of al-Andalus: in 929 he had been appointed to the rank of vizir, that is one of the small group of caliphal counsellors which numbered only about ten or a dozen men at any one time; ten years later he was, uniquely, promoted to the rank of 'double vizir'. It was on this occasion, in 939, that he presented his ruler with 500,000 gold dinars, 400 pounds of gold bullion, 200 bags of silver ingots worth 45,000 dinars, precious wood for making caskets, 30 lengths of silk, 5 rich 'heavy' tunics, 10 furs (of which 7 were Khorasan white fox), 6 outfits of Iraqi silk, 100 marten furs, 6 tents, 4000 pounds of spun silk and 1000 pounds of raw silk for the royal (monopoly) manufacture of *tiraz*, 100 prayer rugs, 15 silken hangings, 100 horses (15 of them Arab and 5 of them complete with harness and decorated saddles), 60 slaves (40 male and 20 female) and – a very timely present – large quantities of dressed stone and wood for the caliph's building works. I have slightly abbreviated this list, omitting some of the more commonplace presents. We should bear in mind that this was no routine gift. It was what a very rich man paid to buy one of the highest offices in the land. Untypical, therefore, but still a breathtaking revelation of the wealth available in al-Andalus at this period.

Otto I's embassy conducted by John of Gorze was not the only one to come from Germany. His son Otto II communicated with Córdoba in 974. Envoys from Constantinople were in Córdoba in 949 and 972. In 942 the caliph received an ambassador from Sardinia accompanied by a deputation of businessmen from the southern Italian city of Amalfi – at that date an important trading centre – who doubtless wished like John of Gorze to discuss commerce and security in the Mediterranean. As we have seen, there was plentiful coming and going between Córdoba on the one hand and, on the other, the Christian states of northern Spain and the Berber chieftains of the Maghrib.

These diplomatic exchanges were not confined to the discussion of affairs of state in a ceremonial setting. They could also be the occasion for intellectual exchanges which may have had far-reaching effects. The Byzantine embassy of 949 brought among its presents to the court of Córdoba a magnificent copy of the works of the first-century botanist Dioscorides. This author was the most famous pharmacologist of antiquity: Dioscorides was the first scientist to attempt a systematic study of the medicinal properties of plants. When his works arrived in al-Andalus there were no scholars there – at any rate, none known to the court – who could read Greek. An appeal was sent back to Constantinople, in answer to which a Greek monk named Nicholas was despatched to Córdoba in 951. Somehow a Sicilian Arab – the Arabs had conquered Sicily in the 830s – with a knowledge of Greek was also procured. Nicholas and the Sicilian expounded the text of Dioscorides to a group of Andalusi scholars which included Hasday ibn Shaprut.

We have already met Ibn Shaprut as the friendly intermediary between John of Gorze and the palace. However, there was much more to him than that. He was the caliph's personal physician, and a man renowned far and wide for his medical skill. He treated king Sancho the Fat of León for obesity in 964. Dunash ibn Tamim, the Jewish doctor to the Fatimid ruler of Egypt, dedicated a scientific treatise to him. Ibn Shaprut was a figure of eminence in the international Jewish community at large. He was the patron of Jewish-Andalusi poets such as Dunash Ha-Levi, the benefactor of the Talmudic academies of Mesopotamia, the author of a letter to the ruler of the 'Thirteenth Tribe', the Jewish Khazars of south Russia. He occupied an important position in al-Andalus as a trusted adviser as well as doctor to the caliph. For his services he seems to have been rewarded with some lucrative sinecure arising from the tolls and customs paid by merchants. Hasday ibn Shaprut is a remarkable testimony to the cosmopolitan character of the court of al-Andalus under 'Abd al-Rahman III, and to the heights to which Jews could rise in service to it.

But we must return to the medical scholars of Córdoba. The work of Dioscorides had already been translated into Arabic in the Middle East, but it would seem that this translation had not made its way to Spain by 951. The excitement aroused by this text points to some sort of intellectual ferment at Córdoba in circles close to – we might say under the patronage of – the caliph himself. Recemund of Elvira was another member of this network and his *Calendar*, with its abundant botanical and agronomical information, arises from shared intellectual concerns. Another member of the circle was Ibn Juljul who a little later, in the reign of al-Hakem II, was the author of a commentary on Dioscorides.

This cultivation of the arts of peace owed much to caliphal patronage. In medieval Islam, as in Christendom, it was part of a ruler's duty, and a great part of his glory, to be a patron of artists and wise men. Before the tenth century the rulers of al-Andalus had had little time, resources or inclination for filling this role. From the middle years of the tenth century their commitment to it was full-hearted. One example may be found in the decoration and furnishings of Madinat az-Zahra, another in the international (and interdenominational) team of scholars who pored over Dioscorides. The ruler who took his duties as a patron of learning most seriously was al-Hakem II.

'Abd al-Rahman III had ensured that his son received a first-rate education, and from an early age the boy showed intellectual potential. Al-Hakem's energies as scholar and patron went principally into building up at Córdoba one of the greatest libraries of the Muslim world. The eleventh-century scholar Ibn Hazm tells us that its catalogue alone ran to forty-four volumes of fifty folios apiece. Other writers assure us that the entire library comprised no less than 400,000 books. Incredible though we may choose to find these figures, we have reliable evidence that books were acquired for the caliph from as far afield as Persia and that he maintained a team of copyists in Córdoba for their rapid multiplication. (These copyists included, most interestingly and unusually, a woman, a poetess named Lubna.) Because royalty is a trendsetter, it is not surprising to find that we hear of other private libraries assembled in Córdoba at this period by the pious, the scholarly and the rich.

The city acquired in the tenth century a reputation for learning which spread very widely. The French scholar Gerbert of Aurillac – later to be pope as Sylvester II (999–1003) – came to Spain to study as a young man, in the 960s. As far as we know, he did all his studying in the monastic houses of Catalonia, but a French chronicler of only a generation later reported that he had gone as far as Córdoba 'for the sake of wisdom'. This account is unlikely to be true; its interest lies in showing that Córdoba's reputation as a centre of exotic learning quickly spread far and wide.

In this context of princely patronage the activities of the scientists who worked on Dioscorides are less surprising than they might have seemed at first sight. Another branch of science which profited similarly was astronomy. Here the leading name was that of Maslama, known as Maslama al-Madjriti, Maslama of Madrid: the first native of that city – then a very small and insignificant place – to have achieved renown. Maslama, born about 950 or so, was early attracted to Córdoba where he seems to have been associated with the intellectual circles under the patronage of the caliph. His most celebrated achievement was to adapt the astronomical tables of the great Middle Eastern astronomer al-Khwarizmi to the meridian of Córdoba on the basis of observations made in the year 979. He wrote several other works which in different ways cast light on the culture of al-Andalus in the tenth century. He translated Ptolemy's *Planisphere* into Arabic, another example of the reception of Greek science in tenth-century Spain. He wrote a textbook of commercial arithmetic, presumably to meet a demand among the business community of al-Andalus. He composed a treatise on the astrolabe, a simple guide to the construction and use of this critically important item of scientific technology, perhaps intended primarily for his pupils. These were many. He was a famous teacher, and several of his disciples achieved renown in mathematical and astronomical studies during the eleventh century. It seems likely that Maslama was in addition a master of astrology. We should bear in mind that this was then, and for many centuries to come, widely regarded as an exact science, a close relation of astronomy. Maslama may have been the official astrologer to the caliphal court. One historian says that he predicted the political disruption that occurred shortly after his death in 1007.

Only a few moved in the exalted circles of al-Hakem's learned court; and of course to fewer still in any age are granted the talents of a Maslama. The nature of our sources is such that the less prominent are less visible. It is all the more important to try to get a glimpse of them. Consider for example the Banu Zuhr family who formed a veritable dynasty of physicians. The first of them to practise medicine was Muhammad ibn Marwan ibn Zuhr (947–1032) of Seville. His son 'Abd al-Malik travelled and studied in the east, returned to Spain and practised medicine at Denia on the Mediterranean coast. His son Zuhr returned to Seville where he was the chief physician to its ruling family in the latter part of the eleventh century. His son 'Abd al-Malik was the court doctor to the first of the Almohad caliphs of al-Andalus in the mid-twelfth century and the author of several medical treatises. His son Muhammad, the great-great-grandson of the earlier Muhammad, who died in about 1200, was renowned as a doctor but still more so as a poet. The verse epitaph which he composed for himself became justly famous:

> You stopping here, please contemplate:
> Look at the place to which I now have been brought.
> The grave's earth covers my face, as if
> I never had trodden it before.
> I used to save men from the fear of death,
> Now I've become the hostage of death myself!

The successive generations of Banu Zuhr doctors lived, as we shall see, through turbulent times. But they owed their original grounding to the years of peace and plenty under the caliphs of the tenth century. There were doubtless many such skilled, prosperous, solid professional families who flourished like the Banu Zuhr, and our mental picture of the cities of al-Andalus would be incomplete without them.

*

It would be misleading to leave the reader with the impression that all was social harmony in al-Andalus in the tenth century. True, it was a more harmonious society than it had been in the ninth, vastly more so than it had been in the eighth. Some old tensions remained, and some new ones were created. We can explore these tensions by looking at what happened after the death of the caliph al-Hakem II in 976.

These were the years of Almanzor. His name has already been

mentioned more than once; now it is time to look more closely at his career. His full name was Abu 'Amir Muhammad ibn Abi 'Amir al-Ma'afari: al-Mansur, which means 'the Victorious', was a *laqab* or honorific title which he adopted in 981. He will be referred to here by the westernisation of the latter name, Almanzor. He was born in 938 into an old-established family of Arab descent settled near Algeciras. Some of its members had enjoyed a reputation as jurists or had achieved modest distinction in government service. Almanzor received a good education at Córdoba. Among his teachers was a celebrated rhetorician from Baghdad who had been invited to Spain by al-Hakem – yet another example of that ruler's patronage of learning. Thereafter Almanzor entered the administrative service with successive junior bureaucratic posts in Córdoba. These brought him to the notice of important people as a coming man of talent and ambition.

His great opportunity came in 967 when he was entrusted with the administration of the property settled by the caliph upon his favourite wife Subh – another concubine of Christian and Navarrese origin, carried off a captive to Córdoba. From that moment Almanzor's future was assured. As Subh's protégé and, it was whispered, her lover, he rose rapidly to become one of the leading civil servants of al-Andalus. When the caliph al-Hakem II died in 976 his son by Subh, Hisham II, was aged only eleven. The regency which governed in his name was a triumvirate formed of al-Mushafi, the first minister of the late caliph; the leading military man of al-Andalus, the general Ghalib; and Almanzor.

These three men embodied some of the tensions at the heart of al-Andalus. Ghalib was older than Almanzor. He was a freedman of the caliph 'Abd al-Rahman III who had come to prominence as long before as 946 when he had been entrusted with refurbishing the defences of Medinaceli, the headquarters of the Middle March, an area particularly vulnerable to attack from León and Castile in the reign of the warlike Leonese king Ramiro II. A contemporary source claims that Ghalib was actually a native of Medinaceli. He had won fame as a general by his campaigns both on the northern frontier and in the Maghrib. Emphatically a man of the camp rather than the court, he and Almanzor may be said to have symbolised the tensions between the provinces and the centre, or the military and the civil, which existed in al-Andalus. Nevertheless, the two men worked together in a complementary way for a few years. Almanzor got his first taste of military campaigning in Ghalib's company, and even married the old general's daughter.

They were drawn together by a common hostility to al-Mushafi.

Here was another elder statesman, who had been governor of Majorca as early as 947. His family was a modest one from the Valencia region, and of Berber descent. He owed his position entirely to al-Hakem II, who had promoted him to the highest offices of state. The death of the caliph left him vulnerable. Although he must have been a consummate politician he was widely disliked in the Córdoba establishment as an upstart and especially as a Berber. Although, as we have already seen, persons of Christian or Jewish background could rise to responsible positions in the bureaucracy, the directing elite in the most senior posts tended to be made up of men of Arab descent – or at any rate who claimed it. It seems to have been rare for Berbers to have had careers in the civil service. They were still regarded in the tenth century as second-class citizens, just as they had been two hundred years earlier. Here then was a different sort of tension, an ethnic one, which might divide ruling circles in al-Andalus. Almanzor certainly played on this in his rivalry with al-Mushafi. Not for nothing did he make much of his own Arab descent. He even claimed that a direct ancestor had been among the companions of Tariq in the invasion of Spain in 711 and that the family estates near Algeciras were a reward for his military prowess.

The intrigues which followed al-Hakem's death need not be followed in detail. It is enough to say that Almanzor managed to rid himself of al-Mushafi in 978: the former minister was disgraced, imprisoned and later murdered. Relations with Ghalib remained harmonious for longer, but in 981 it came to civil war and the elderly general was defeated: he met his death in the course of the battle, not by the sword but accidentally, by a fall from his horse. During these five years from 976 to 981 there had been three other significant political developments. First, the young caliph Hisham was encouraged to enter upon an adulthood entirely given over to the gratification of the senses. His time fully occupied with girls, he made no attempt to play any active political role. Second, Almanzor had acquired a reputation as a soldier – and popularity with the army – by undertaking a campaign against the kingdom of León in 977. Third, he had constructed a new palace-complex of his own to the east of Córdoba, which came to be known as al-Madina al-Zahira, 'the glittering city'. It was obviously intended to rival the caliphal complex of Madinat az-Zahra to the west of the city. To his new creation Almanzor transferred all the offices of government in 981.

By 981, therefore, Almanzor was established as a 'mayor of the palace' in al-Andalus. He remained the effective ruler of the state until his death in 1002. These were the years that were given over to his campaigns against the Christians, already alluded to. The expedition to

Santiago de Compostela in 997 was only the most daring and notorious of a series of hammer-blows which the Andalusi armies under Almanzor's leadership delivered to the Christian principalities. In 985 Barcelona was sacked, as well as the celebrated nearby monastery of San Cugat del Vallés. The Leonese outpost of Coimbra, in what is now Portugal, was plundered in 987. The same treatment was meted out to León and Zamora in 988, and to the monasteries of Sahagún and Eslonza. It was the turn of Osma in 989. In 995 no less a prize than García Fernández, the count of Castile, was captured: he died of his wounds in Córdoba. In the same year Carrión and Astorga were destroyed. In 999 Pamplona was attacked. In 1002 the Rioja was laid waste and the monastery of San Millán de la Cogolla was burnt.

It was on his way back from the Rioja campaign that Almanzor died, at Medinaceli. 'Our provider of slaves is no more,' the Córdobans are said to have lamented. But his power did not die with him. He was succeeded as the unofficial ruler of al-Andalus by his son 'Abd al-Malik, who continued his father's aggressive policies. Catalonia was raided in 1003, Castile in 1004, León in 1005 and Aragon in 1006. Had 'Abd al-Malik not died young in 1008 there is no reason to suppose that the policy would have been discontinued.

A Christian chronicler, noting Almanzor's death, wrote that he was 'seized by the Devil and buried in Hell'. He was a 'scourge' of the Christians and his removal from the scene was an act of 'divine mercy'. Almanzor himself had been ostentatiously pious, partly, we may be sure, to keep the good opinion of the *faqihs*, the religious leaders of Córdoba. He took a copy of the Koran written in his own hand on all his campaigns; he was ruthless in his punishment of departures from Islamic orthodoxy; he presented his wars against the Christians as a *jihad*. It was natural for Christian writers to present Almanzor as a Satanic scourge: there can be no doubt that his campaigns were terribly destructive of life and wealth. But there was nothing about him of the religious fanatic. The clinching point here is his employment of large numbers of Christian mercenaries in his armies. Without Christian noblemen to act as guides his army would never have found the way to Compostela in 997 (and handsomely they were rewarded for it too, with handouts of the precious *tiraz* silks).

The more one looks at Almanzor's wars the more they fit into the mould of the earlier campaigns discussed in this chapter such as 'Abd al-Rahman's Valdejunquera expedition of 920. Their aim was to extract tribute, plunder, livestock, slaves, treasure: not to strike a blow for Islam against Christendom. If he attacked churches and monasteries, as he certainly did, it was because they were rich in treasure, animals, dependents: not because they were Christian. (There is a fair amount of evidence to suggest that in Spain as in other parts of western Christendom at this date churches were used as places of secure deposit for bullion and valuables by the local nobility. Sacking a monastery was therefore something like raiding a bank. There is no reason to suppose that the religious convictions or observances of the staff of the bank were of any interest to the raiders.)

What was new about Almanzor's campaigns was their frequency and their intensity. What impulses drove him to undertake them, season after season, fifty-seven times in all? Possibly the strongest impulse was financial. The caliph al-Hakem II was said to have left an enormous reserve of cash in the treasury at his death in 976: forty million dinars, perhaps about six years' revenue. But Almanzor's rise to power and his maintenance of himself there was an expensive business. He built lavishly: al-Madina al-Zahira, a very considerable addition to the great mosque of Córdoba. He sought popularity by cutting taxes such as the hated levy on olive oil. His followers had to be rewarded and his enemies bought off by presents, sinecures, backhanders. He vastly increased the size of the army.

The last point is especially significant because of the manner in which it was done. The mushroom growth of the armed forces under Almanzor partly arose from the military requirements of al-Andalus, but circumstances in Africa seem to have been a more important factor. The eastward shift of Fatimid power to Egypt eased direct pressure upon Córdoba's influence in the Maghrib but left her rulers with the difficult task of exercising some control over the always turbulent Berber tribes. The expedient devised in the reign of al-Hakem II was to draft whole tribal units into the Andalusi army. This course of action was intensified under Almanzor's rule. Thousands upon thousands of Berbers were ferried across the Straits to al-Andalus where, still in their tribal units under their own tribal commanders, they became in effect the private armies of Almanzor and his son. This was a development fraught with peril. The Berber units were entering a land where ethnic rivalry between Arab and Berber was keen, and where Berbers were widely despised, distrusted and disliked. The units were not broken up but remained intact, their cohesion maintained by the bonds of language and tribal loyalty, reinforced by the hostility of the civil population. The Berbers were an alien element and the primary loyalty of their commanders was to Almanzor and his son, not to the institution of the caliphate of Córdoba.

The institution of the caliphate may have been fatally damaged by Almanzor himself. It had rested, in any case, upon a somewhat soggy intellectual foundation. The theory of authority in Islam dictates that there can be only one rightful caliph, one 'successor' to the Prophet. For the ruler of a breakaway state in the most westerly corner of the Islamic world to declare himself caliph, as 'Abd al-Rahman III had done in 929, was preposterous. Still, the caliphate of Córdoba had represented authority successfully in al-Andalus for the next half-century. What Almanzor had done was to show that constituted authority could be pushed aside. The caliph Hisham II outlived both Almanzor and 'Abd al-Malik, but in his 'reign' of thirty-three years he exercised not a shred of political power. What might happen if Almanzor's example were to prove infectious?

We leave al-Andalus in the early years of the eleventh century at a time of incipient governmental crisis – financial, military, and in the narrow sense of the word political. We may guess that it is easier for us to perceive this than it was for all but a few well-placed and acute contemporaries – or astrologers like Maslama. For nearly a century al-Andalus had been the richest, the best-governed, the most powerful, the most renowned state in the western world. The tenth century was the pinnacle of Córdoba's glory.

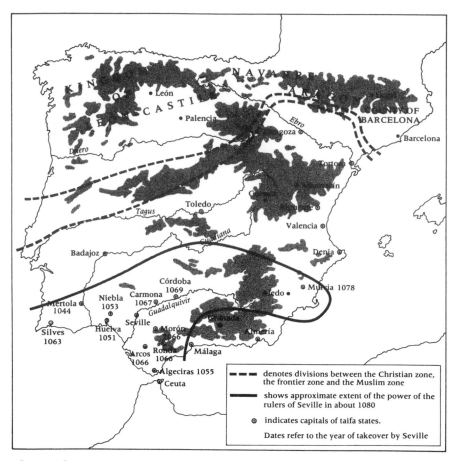

The Taifa States

5

THE PARTY KINGS

In the Islamic world the Arabic word *fitnah* is used to denote strife, and in particular sedition or rebellion against a duly constituted ruler. Prolonged or widespread *fitnah* has traditionally been interpreted as one of the signs of the imminence of the Day of Judgement, foretold in some of the most sombre passages of the Koran.

When the sun shall be darkened,
when the stars shall be thrown down,
when the mountains shall be set moving,
when the pregnant camels shall be neglected,
when the savage beasts shall be mustered,
when the seas shall be set boiling,
when the souls shall be coupled,
when the buried infant shall be asked for what sin she was slain,
when the scrolls shall be unrolled,
when Heaven shall be stripped off,
when Hell shall be set blazing,
when Paradise shall be brought nigh,
then shall a soul know what it has produced.

In this perspective, what occurred in al-Andalus between 1008 and 1031 must have suggested to contemporaries that that dreadful day was fast approaching.

After the death of 'Abd al-Malik the Umayyad dynasty attempted a comeback. A great-grandson of 'Abd al-Rahman III deposed the feeble

Hisham II, proclaimed himself caliph in his place as Muhammad II, captured Almanzor's palace-complex of al-Madina al-Zahira and razed it to the ground. These events occupied the winter months of 1008–09. The Berber generals chose another descendant of 'Abd al-Rahman III, Sulayman, as a rival caliph. Sulayman appealed for military aid to the count of Castile, Sancho García, who responded positively. The two men, Christian and Muslim, joined forces, marched on Córdoba and defeated Muhammad II in November 1009. Sulayman was proclaimed caliph. Muhammad fled to Toledo and in his turn appealed for aid to another quarter of the Christian north. In response to his appeal the two most prominent figures in Catalonia, the count of Barcelona and the count of Urgel, led their armies to the south and defeated Sulayman and his Berbers in May 1010: the year 1010 came to be known as 'the year of the Catalans' among Andalusi chroniclers. Muhammad took possession of Córdoba but was assassinated there in July. Hisham II was restored to the office of caliph by his followers. Sulayman marched on the capital and gained possession of the palace of Madinat az-Zahra where he established a base for his Berber troops. From there he blockaded the city for the next two and a half years.

During this period the Berbers rampaged uncontrollably over the southeastern parts of Spain, living off the land and extorting protection money from the cities, doing untold damage by their depredations. Meanwhile, the situation of the Córdobans became very wretched. The city was crowded with refugees from the surrounding countryside. A wet spring in 1011 brought serious flooding of the Guadalquivir. An outbreak of plague occurred. The government was so hard up that it was driven to the expedient of selling off some of al-Hakem II's splendid library. In May 1013 Córdoba surrendered. Sulayman's Berber followers, who had already wrecked the palace at Madinat az-Zahra, sacked and plundered the city. What remained of the caliphal library was dispersed. Enormous numbers of the citizens were massacred. The great scholar-to-be, Ibn Hazm, then aged about nineteen, witnessed the slaughter and later named over sixty distinguished scholars who met their deaths. One of them, the biographer Ibn al-Faradi, lay unburied where he had been cut down for three days. The caliph Hisham II disappears from view, presumed murdered.

Sulayman presided as caliph for three years but it cannot be said that he ruled. His Berber followers treated Córdoba as a city under enemy occupation and instituted a reign of terror, killing and looting as they pleased. Their generals prevailed upon the caliph to allot them fiefs for their support. Helplessly he handed out provincial governorships — often, one suspects, doing no more than recognising a de facto state of

1. The interior of the great mosque at Córdoba.

2. Ivory casket made in Córdoba in AH 359/AD 969–70.

3. Fresco of a figure praying, from the Pyrenean church of Sant Quirze de Pedret, c.1000.

4. Mozarabic architecture: the church of San Miguel de Escalada near León.

5. Mozarabic painting: an illustration of St John from a tenth-century manuscript which was probably executed at San Miguel de Escalada.

6. *Above:* National mythology: Santiago Matamoros (St James the Moorslayer), from an engraving of *c.*1475.

7. *Right:* Visigothic royal munificence: one of the votive crowns of Guarrazar, now in the Museo Arqueológico Nacional, Madrid.

8. *Left:* Roman Spain: the aqueduct of Segovia.

9. *Above:* Partial reconstruction of the caliphal palace of Madinat az-Zahra near Córdoba.

10. *Below:* A marble trough made for Almanzor in 987.

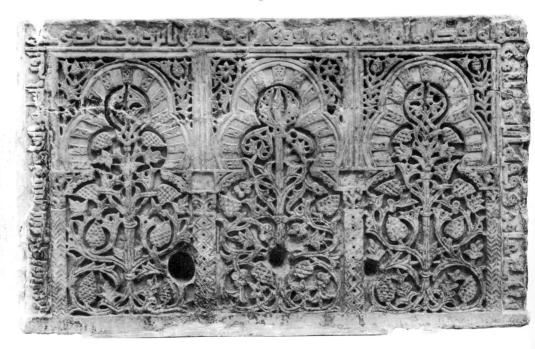

11. Hydraulic
technology: a noria or
waterwheel near
Murcia.

12. Precision
instruments: an
astrolabe made at Toledo
in 1068.

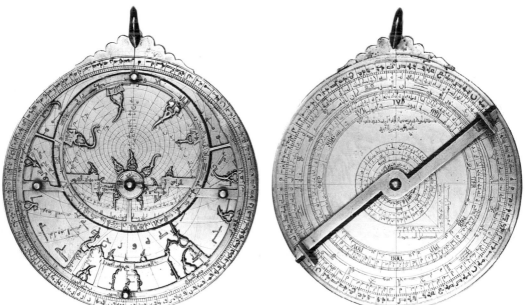

13. A casket of wood and ivory carved at Cuenca for a member of the princely dynasty of Toledo in 1049–50.

14. A silk textile of the eleventh century.

15. *Above:* The Almohad banner captured by Alfonso VIII of Castile at the battle of Las Navas in 1212.

16. *Right:* The Torre del Oro at Seville.

17. James I of Aragon conquers Valencia: fresco of *c.*1300.

18, 19. Mudejar church architecture, in the Aragonese town of Teruel.

20. Mudejar military architecture at Coca.

21. An example of Mudejar ceramics.

22. Averroes (on the left) as represented in a western manuscript of the thirteenth century.

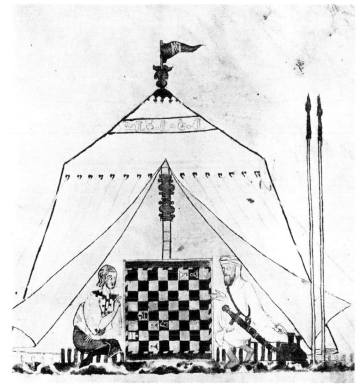

23. *Convivencia?* Christian and Muslim playing chess together, from an illustrated manuscript of Alfonso X's treatise on the game.

24, 25. A monument to
the Jewish community
of later medieval
Spain: the Synagoga
del Tránsito in Toledo.

26. Granada, the Alhambra: the Court of the Lions.

27. Granada, the Alhambra: the Court of the Myrtles.

28. The enforced baptism of the Moors of Granada in 1499: a detail from the Capilla Real, Granada, High Altar by Philippe Biguerny.

affairs – in order to keep their loyalty. For example, the general Zawi ibn Ziri, leader of the Sinhaja tribe, was given the *kura* or province of Elvira: we shall hear more of him shortly. In 1016 one of the generals rose against Sulayman, deposed and executed him.

This was not quite the end of the caliphate of Córdoba. For a further fifteen years a number of short-lived puppet caliphs came and went. The political narrative is extremely confusing and there is no need to go into it here. These were indeed *rois fainéants*, powerless creatures manipulated by generals, civil servants and the urban mob. One of them is said to have 'reigned' for as little as forty-seven days. Most met violent ends. The last of them, Hisham III, was expelled from Córdoba in 1031 and disappeared into obscurity. He was not replaced. The caliphate of Córdoba had come to an end.

The Andalusian *fitnah* of 1008–31 presents us with some portentous moments. The agony of Córdoba and the destruction of the two great palace-complexes which flanked the city marked in the crudest and most violent fashion the end of an era. The intervention of Christian powers from northern Spain in the political affairs of al-Andalus was a reversal of the roles that had obtained forty years earlier and prefigures what was to become more common as the eleventh century wore on.

Politically, the great question in 1031 was this: who was going to succeed to authority in al-Andalus? In one sense it had already been answered: not Córdoba. The *fitnah* had shattered the hold of the centre, and things fell apart. The latent fissile tendencies glanced at in an earlier chapter were allowed free rein. The always fragile political unity imposed by the government of Córdoba shrivelled away. In its place there emerged a number of regional successor states, usually based on the existing administrative units of cities with their associated rural hinterlands. These little statelets, as they have appropriately been called, were ruled by amirs known to historians as 'the taifa kings'. The term derives from the Arabic *muluk al-tawa'if*, meaning 'rulers of the parties', or 'factions', whence these rulers are sometimes called 'the party kings'. The ambiguity latent in the English word is useful, for the suggestions of cheerfulness and jollity and relaxation conveyed by the word 'party' are not inappropriate, as we shall see in due course. The regime of the party kings endured until the last decade of the eleventh century, when unity was once more imposed by a new group of invaders from the Maghrib.

The birth-pangs of the taifa statelets were very far from being cheerful or jolly. Let us look at a few examples, starting with Granada. As we saw, the Berber general Zawi ibn Ziri was granted authority over the province of Elvira by the caliph Sulayman in about 1014. Elvira, the Roman city of Illiberris, is situated in the fertile *vega*, the plain of cultivated land, at the foot of the Sierra Nevada. This was an area which had suffered greatly at the hands of the rampaging Berber armies during the *fitnah* of the years 1009–13. Zawi's descendants would claim that the Elvirans wrote a letter to Zawi imploring him to defend them:

When the people of Elvira saw the dissension among the princes of al-Andalus and the outbreak of civil war . . . they wrote to Zawi, explaining their position. 'If,' they said, 'you have ever before fought the Holy War, you have an even more urgent case for doing so now. There are lives to save, a country for you to defend, and glory to redound to you! We will share with you our lives and possessions; we will give you property and dwellings, and in return we shall have a claim to your protection and defence.' The Berbers agreed to this.

It strains credulity. Elviran experience at the hands of the Berbers had not been such as to make them likely under any circumstances to ask for their return. The most plausible supposition is that Zawi simply seized power by what a later generation of Spaniards would call a *pronunciamiento*, and got the caliph to grant recognition of a fait accompli. The tale of the Elvirans' appeal has the look of a myth spun later on in an attempt to legitimise the rule of Zawi's dynasty (which is usually known as the Zirid dynasty, after Zawi's father Ziri). Among Zawi's first actions upon attaining power was to move its seat from Elvira, the vulnerable city of the plain, to a new site of greater natural defensive potential in the foothills of the Sierra Nevada. This was the origin of the city of Granada. The withdrawal to the hills was the characteristic response of an upstart to the insecurity of his circumstances. It fittingly symbolises the mood of the times.

The seizure of power by Berber generals occurred at several other places in the extreme south of al-Andalus: at Algeciras, Arcos de la Frontera, Carmona, Málaga, Mértola, Morón and Ronda. It also happened across the Straits at Ceuta. The general pattern of events was probably similar to what took place at Granada. The fact is that we are exceptionally well-informed about eleventh-century Granada because of the survival of a volume of memoirs composed by its last ruler 'Abd Allah, the great-great-grandson of Zawi's younger brother, after his deposition in 1090. This work, alluded to by several writers during the Middle Ages, seemed to have been lost until a manuscript was discovered by a French scholar in the library of a mosque in Fez in 1932. An English translation with copious explanatory annotation has recently been published by the Libyan scholar Professor A. T. Tibi. It is an extraordinary and richly rewarding work. 'Abd Allah emerges from his autobiography as a sympathetic if somewhat feeble figure. He was observant and a lively writer. If his autobiography, like many such works, was not altogether innocent of literary guile, the author was not clever enough consistently to present the image of himself and his family that he had chosen. He has a way of dropping, so to say, his literary guard and letting spontaneity break through. His writing has therefore a freshness that is not only engaging in itself but is also of positive help to the historian. His memoirs are wonderfully evocative of the period of the party kings. They furnish much otherwise unknown detail about men and events. In addition – and so much more important for the historian – they enable us to grasp something of the tone and texture of life in that remarkable age. As we shall see, it was different from any previous age in the history of al-Andalus.

This is to anticipate. Zawi's coup at Granada was one characteristic way in which the taifa statelets emerged. There were others. In some places, dynasties of local notables who were already exercising power as the nominal deputies of the government in Córdoba simply continued to do so. It will come as no surprise that this happened most frequently in those provinces furthest from Córdoba, where the government's writ ran most feebly and families of local bosses had been better able to dig themselves in. These also tended to be the least populated and least urbanised provinces. Examples are the party kingdoms that emerged at Albarracín, Alpuente, Calatrava, Toledo and Zaragoza. Albarracín, indeed, owes its name to the Banu Razín, the dynasty which ruled there from 1012 to 1104.

At other places, again, statelets emerged which were run by civil administrators who had achieved prominence under the regime of Almanzor and his son. These men were often technically slaves, or freedmen, and sometimes not of peninsular origin but drawn from the vast hordes of slaves imported into al-Andalus in the tenth century. Take for instance the case of Badajoz, where a certain Sabur al-Saqlabi, 'Sabur the slave', emerged as amir. Sabur is an Arabic form of the Persian Sapor, so he may have been a native of Persia. As a slave and subsequently freedman he was in the service of al-Hakem II. Later, under Almanzor or 'Abd al-Malik, he became the civil governor of Badajoz, Santarem, Lisbon and much of the Algarve. During the *fitnah* he continued to administer this region until his death on 8 November 1022 – we know the exact date because his tombstone has survived – upon which his sons succeeded him. There were several other party kingdoms where the same sort of thing happened, a drift into independent rule under the guidance or the improvisation of locally prominent civil servants of slave or freedman origin.

These 'slave' rulers were not always bureaucrats. Consider for example the taifa state of Denia, on the Mediterranean coast south of Valencia. Here power was taken by a man of slave origin, Mujahid al-'Amiri, who had had a career as a soldier and had risen to high command under Almanzor. The principality of Denia was a corsair state which preyed upon the shipping of the western Mediterranean. Mujahid brought the Balearic Islands under his control, and from these bases set out in 1015 with a fleet of 125 ships transporting 1000 horses to attempt the conquest of Sardinia. (It has been suggested that his family was of Sardinian stock.) His armies were initially successful and overran much of the island. The conquest aroused panic among the mercantile cities of western Italy who saw their commerce threatened. In the following year the combined forces of Genoa and Pisa managed to dislodge Mujahid's troops from Sardinia, though he maintained his hold over the Balearics. Surprisingly, this sea-roving pirate was also a patron of religious scholarship. He assembled a team of learned men at Denia who devoted themselves to the study of *qira'at*, literally 'readings', the elucidation of textual variants in the Koran. Mujahid ruled at Denia until his death in 1044, when he was succeeded there by his son 'Ali.

These rough classifications – military, civil, slave, Berber, local notables – are not exhaustive, nor should they be regarded as permanent; that is, they do not in all cases characterise more than the origins and early history of the statelet in question. It will be obvious enough that each party kingdom was a fragile creation where the ruler's authority could be, and frequently was, challenged. At Badajoz the two sons of Sabur al-Saqlabi were displaced by their chief minister Ibn al-Aftas whose dynasty, the Aftasids, ruled there until 1094. At Valencia the bureaucrats who had emerged as rulers in 1010 were shouldered aside by another bureaucrat in 1018 and he in his turn by a grandson of Almanzor in 1022. At Zaragoza the Tujibid family had been running the show as local bosses from the early tenth century and continued to do so during and after the *fitnah* of the early eleventh: in 1039 they were displaced by a rival local family, the Hudids, who were to rule there until 1110.

The internal political history of each of the party kingdoms was intensely complicated. There is no need here to dwell further on these complications, which would only be confusing, but it is important to bear them in mind for a right understanding of eleventh-century Andalusi history. Their 'external' history, that is their relations with one another, was equally complex. Here were extemporised political units which had emerged as a result of local initiatives during a period of disruption. They had no experience of autonomy, no settled frontiers, no means of mediating disputes more sophisticated than the threat or the use of force perhaps lightly restrained by Koranic precept. The matrimonial customs of Islamic society ensured that every ruler was surrounded by large numbers of relatives, claimants upon his generosity, potential rivals for his power. In the latter capacity they could easily turn to neighbouring princelings who would be only too willing to seek their own advantage in lending a destabilising hand. In so far as the party kings had any models or precedents from the immediate past to guide them, these were furnished by the tenth-century caliphs and by Almanzor: rulers who owed their fame and much of their revenue to incessant predatory campaigning against their neighbours.

'The sheer imperative of survival,' it has been said, 'provided the yardstick of political activity' for the party kings. This entailed unceasing diplomatic manoeuvring and military strife. Here once more the details of names and dates, alliances made and broken, pretenders supported and abandoned, fortresses taken, battles fought, regions devastated, are confusing in the extreme and need not be entered into here. 'Abd Allah's memoirs, with the translator's notes, are as good an introduction as any for the reader who might wish to pursue these matters.

However, the consequences of this undercurrent of instability and strife are of the utmost importance for us. In the first place, there were winners and losers. During the period of maximum disruption between about 1010 and 1040 there were some three dozen of these statelets. They varied greatly in their extent and resources. What was already starting to happen in that early period gained momentum during the 1040s and 1050s: little principalities were gobbled up by bigger ones. By the middle years of the century half a dozen of the larger states stood out as preeminent: Seville and Granada in the south; Badajoz, Toledo and Valencia in a band across the centre of the peninsula; Zaragoza in the northeast. Others existed, but these were the big six. They continued to grow. Zaragoza, for example, swallowed up Tortosa in 1060, Denia in 1076. It is possible that, had the process not been interrupted by intervention from outside, a single principality might have emerged from the confusion. Seville had the strongest chances of filling this role.

In Seville in the 1020s, as in Córdoba after 976, we find a triumvirate in power. As had occurred in the capital, one of its members managed to rid himself of the others. This man, Muhammad ibn Isma'il ibn Abbad – whence the family was known as the Abbadids – was the descendant, at any rate allegedly, of an ancient Arab family. He was by far the biggest landowner in the region, rumoured to own a third of the city's surrounding agricultural hinterland and thus effectively to control its food supply and its commodity trade. He was also the *qadi*, or principal judge of the city. He was, in short, a ripe example of a local boss.

The ambitions of the Abbadid family could be fuelled by the wealth of the city and territory of Seville. In a pre-industrial economy the lower valley of the river Guadalquivir is naturally the richest part of Spain. The olive groves of the Abbadids produced oil that was famous throughout the Mediterranean. The ilexes which clothed the slopes were the home of the kermes beetle, *Coccus ilicis*, whose crushed body yielded a celebrated dye known to the Arabs as *qermazí*, to us as crimson. Plantations of sugar-cane alternated with ranches and stud farms. Seville's commercial prosperity did not begin with the American trade in the sixteenth century. The Guadalquivir had been the artery down which had flowed agricultural surpluses and mineral wealth from before the time when Jonah in the eighth century BC had taken ship for its famous trading port Tarshish (or Tartessos). These cargoes continued to flow, to the enrichment of the Abbadids, eighteen hundred years later. They were joined by more specialised goods. Seville was famed for its manufacture of musical instruments, we are told. Another writer, in classifying the different varieties of tile made there, tantalisingly informs us that a certain sort was 'for the eaves of mechanical clocks'. One wonders what these clocks were like.

It was under Ibn Abbad's son al-Mu'tadid (1042–69) and grandson al-Mu'tamid (1069–91), able and ambitious rulers the two of them, that the taifa state of Seville reached the height of its power. Al-Mu'tadid pursued a vigorously expansionary policy. In 1044 Mertola was conquered, in 1051 Huelva and in 1053 its neighbour Niebla. Algeciras followed in 1055. The absorption of the Algarve was completed with the acquisition of Santa María de Algarve in 1057 and Silves in 1063. Morón, Arcos and Ronda followed shortly afterwards: their rulers were suffocated in the bath-house of al-Mu'tadid's palace while on an ostensibly peaceful diplomatic mission to Seville. In 1067 Carmona was swallowed. The great prize of Córdoba fell to al-Mu'tadid in 1069, and the distant one of Murcia to his son in 1078.

Al-Mu'tadid was an accomplished poet. He celebrated his triumphs in vainglorious verse:

What is called happiness has now been established:
I sat down to receive it in the parlour of honour.
If Thou, O God, wishest to grant a favour to mankind,
Make ME the guiding lord of Arabs and non-Arabs!

His pretensions and those of other taifa rulers were mocked by some. Another poet wrote, 'Among the things which distress me in the land of al-Andalus are names like *Mu'tadid* and *Mu'tamid*: names of royalty out of place, like a cat which speaks in a puffed-up way like a lion.' ('Names of royalty' because these were the honorific titles or 'throne names' of two ninth-century caliphs of Baghdad.) Grotesque the Abbadids may have appeared to some, but the fact was that by the 1070s Seville was incomparably the most powerful of the party kingdoms.

In the eleventh century the city of Seville probably outstripped Córdoba in size and wealth. Córdoba had of course suffered very severely in the disorders of the years after 1008. So had other parts of al-Andalus, especially the south and east which were ravaged by the Berber armies between 1010 and 1013. Relative peace returned to large areas of the country with the taifa regime, despite the dynastic strife of the ruling families. There are signs that economic recovery was rapid. The peace of the taifa kings may not have been the peace of 'Abd al-Rahman III or al-Hakem II, but it was sufficient for the restoration of confidence, the tending and marketing of produce and livestock, the re-establishment of local and long-distance trading networks. In consequence the statelets of eleventh-century Spain were rich. Their rulers used this wealth for, among other things, the patronage of the arts.

The exercise of such patronage, as we have already seen, was a traditional duty of princes. The changed circumstances of the eleventh century gave it a special edge. In the tenth century cultural patronage, like government, had been centralised. It had been at Córdoba that the principal manifestations of it had occurred – the enlargement of the great mosque, the palace-complexes of Madinat az-Zahra and al-Madina al-Zahira. It had therefore been to Córdoba that artists and craftsmen – and scholars like Maslama – had been encouraged or compelled to come, draining the provinces of talent. The switching-off of this centripetal current in the eleventh century reactivated the creative energies of provincial centres, energies which were further stimulated by princely encouragement. As in the Italian Renaissance, cultural rivalry ran in tandem with political. The rulers of the party states vied with one another in public works, in building mosques or palaces, attracting poets and scholars, commissioning artists in stucco or ivory or glass or bronze. A second major consequence of the taifa regime was therefore a flowering of the arts throughout the provinces of al-Andalus.

At Cuenca, about a hundred miles east of Toledo, there flourished in the middle years of the eleventh century a school of accomplished ivory carvers. (This is, incidentally, another sidelight on the far-flung trade of the period: ivory has to come from either India or East Africa.) Why should so rarefied a skill have blossomed in so remote and inhospitable a place? As it happens, we know that the ruling dynasty of Toledo owned large landed estates in the Cuenca region. Some of the surviving ivory caskets which were made there bear inscriptions identifying the patron for whom they were made, and these turn out invariably to be members of the ruling family. For example, the superb casket illustrated in Plate 13 was made in 1049–50 to the commission of Isma'il, the son of al-Ma'mun who ruled at Toledo from 1044 to 1075. The same patron commissioned the exquisite circular casket which is now in the treasury of the cathedral of Narbonne in southern France. Isma'il seems to have been governor of Cuenca at this time. The conclusion is inescapable, that the 'Cuenca school' of ivory carving was sustained by princely patronage. One could not ask for a better example of the surge of provincial creativity.

The products of the Cuenca school that have come down to us have survived because they were rare, precious and highly prized. (The casket made for Isma'il in 1049–50 is now in the Museo Arqueológico Nacional in Madrid. Formerly it belonged to the Castilian bishopric of Palencia. It is a fair guess that the casket came into the hands of king Alfonso VI as part of the spoils from his conquest of Toledo in 1085 and was presented by him to bishop Raymond of Palencia, who was one of his closest counsellors.) The same could be said of artworks in other media, such as the fine silk textile illustrated in Plate 14 which is now in the Musée de Cluny in Paris. Inevitably, a great deal that was less prized or made of more perishable materials – wood, leather, glass, ceramics – has not come down to us. Much of the building of the period we can only read about. We know from an inscription that al-Mu'tamid restored a mosque in Seville in 1079 after it had been damaged in an earthquake, but no trace of the building remains. Almanzor's grandson surrounded Valencia with walls – 'no finer walls in al-Andalus,' said a contemporary – but they were torn down centuries ago in the hectic expansion of the city. He also built a stone bridge – 'the most handsome bridge in al-Andalus' – across the river Turia. The Hudids built themselves a palace at Zaragoza of which a few bits and pieces survive, such as the magnificent stucco archway now to be seen in the Museo Arqueológico Nacional in Madrid. Here and there on the slopes below the Alhambra in Granada one can still see a few stretches of the walls erected by the Zirid rulers.

Several of the taifa princes were patrons of religious or scientific learning. We have already mentioned the Koranic scholars whom Mujahid gathered round him at Denia. Al-Ma'mun employed the botanist and agronomist Ibn Wafid in the royal gardens of Toledo, and commissioned the astronomer al-Zarqal to construct the clypsedra or waterclock which became famous throughout al-Andalus. Some of the rulers were themselves highly cultivated men. Al-Muqtadir of Zaragoza (1046–82) was said to have been 'a real prodigy of nature in astrology, geometry and natural philosophy', and his son al-Mu'tamin (1082–85) composed a treatise on mathematics. Al-Muzaffar of Badajoz (1045–68) is said to have compiled a fifty-volume encyclopaedia which was 'a repository of art, science, history, poetry, literature in general, proverbs, biographical information and so forth'. Perhaps he had some help from his court scholars: royal authorship is often a somewhat opaque business. Of one dynasty's literary talent, however, we can be quite certain: the Abbadids of Seville.

Both al-Mu'tadid and al-Mu'tamid were extremely gifted poets, and as the most imposing of the taifa rulers they were in a position to act as patrons of poets on an ample scale. We have already met a composition by al-Mu'tadid in praise of himself. Here is part of a love poem from his hand:

> A gazelle's are her eyes, sun-like is her splendour,
> Like a sandhill her hips, like a bough her stature:
> With tears I told her plaintively of my love for her,
> And told her how much my pain made me suffer.
> My heart met hers, knowing that love is contagious,
> And that one deeply in love can transmit his desire:
> She graciously then offered me her cheek –
> Oft a clear spring will gush forth from a rock –
> I told her, 'Let me now kiss your white teeth,
> For I prefer white blossoms to red roses:
> Lean your body on mine' – and then she bent
> Toward me, granted my wish, again, again,
> Embracing, kissing, in mutual fire of desire,
> Singly and doubly, like sparks flying from a flint.
> Oh hour, how short thou wast in passing,
> But your sweet memory will linger on forever!

And here is a poem which encapsulated his philosophy of life:

By my life! Wine does make me talk much,
And I like to do what my companions like:
I divide my time between hard work and leisure,
Mornings for affairs of state, evenings for pleasure!
At night I indulge in amusements and frolics,
At noon I rule with a proud mien in my court;
Amidst my trysts I do not neglect my striving
For glory and fame: these I always plan to attain.

His son al-Mu'tamid was even more accomplished. Here he remembers
his youth in Silves:

Salute, oh Abu Bakr, my dwellings in Silves,
And ask them: do they still keep our tender pact of love?
Give the Castle of the Verandahs the greetings
Of a youth who constantly longs for that castle,
The dwellings of fierce lions and of beauteous maidens:
What lion caves they were, what charming boudoirs!
Many a night I spent, enjoying their shadows,
With maidens round-hipped, yet slim of waist:
Their white and brown beauty pierced my heart
Like white blood-spilling swords and points of brown lances!
And those nights playfully spent on the river dam
With a girl whose armband was like the curve of the crescent!
She would pour out wine for me in her bewitching glances,
And in the cup at times, at times in her kisses:
The tunes of her lute thrilled me, as if
I heard in those chords the clash of swordblades.
Then she let her robe fall, her splendid form seeming
To be a bud unfolding from a cluster of blossoms.

This is enough to show the predominantly hedonistic tone of the
Abbadid court at Seville. It was a society of extravagance, refinement,
spectacle, indulgence, gesture. Many anecdotes confirm this. A
favourite wife of al-Mu'tamid was a Christian girl from the north. He
found her weeping one day for the winter snows which she would
never see again in Seville. To comfort her he assembled an army of
gardeners who planted by night a forest of almond trees in blossom
outside her apartments in the palace. In the morning he led her to the
window: 'See my love, there is your snow!' Sheer literary convention,
of course: similar stories are told of other princesses in other times and
places. But it is significant that in eleventh-century al-Andalus it was to
the Abbadid court that the story became attached.

The poets who were attracted to Seville by the patronage of the
Abbadid dynasty caught the prevailing tone. Ibn Hamdis is a good

example. A native of Sicily born in 1055, he fled from his native Syracuse when it was conquered by the Normans and made his way via Tunis to Seville. Al-Mu'tamid put him to the test of improvising second lines, to follow his own firsts, in the description of a glass-worker's furnace which they could see winking at them in the night from the window where they stood.

Al-Mu'tamid:	'Look at the fire glowing in the darkness,'
Ibn Hamdis:	'Like the lion's glances in the darkness of night!'
Al-Mu'tamid:	'See him open both his eyes, then close them,'
Ibn Hamdis:	'Like a man whose eyelids suffer from trachoma.'
Al-Mu'tamid:	'Fate deprived him of the light of one of them;'
Ibn Hamdis:	'Has a mortal being ever escaped his fate?'

This performance was so pleasing to the ruler that he took Ibn Hamdis into his service on an annual salary. Here is one of his characteristic poems, celebrating a party at which the drinks were floated along a stream to the drinkers who sat on its banks:

> I remember a certain brook that offered the impiety of drunkenness to the topers sitting along its course, with its cups of golden wine,
> Each silver cup in it filled as though it contained the soul of the sun in the body of the full moon.
> Whenever a glass reached anyone in our company of topers, he would grasp it gingerly with his ten fingers.
> Then he drinks out of it a grape-induced intoxication which lulls his very senses without his realising it.
> He sends the glass back in the water, thus returning it to the hands of a cupbearer at whose will it had floated to him.
> Because of the wine-bibbing we imagined our song to be melodies which the birds sang without verse,
> While our cupbearer was the water which brought us wine without a hand, and our drink was a fire that shone without embers,
> And which offered us delights of all kinds, while the only reward [of the cupbearer] was that we offered him to the ocean to drink.
> It is as if we were cities along the riverbank while the wine-laden ships sailed the water between us,
> For life is excusable only when we walk along the shores of pleasure and abandon all restraint!

Of all the poets and scholars of this period the one who has achieved the most posthumous fame is Ibn Hazm of Córdoba (994–1064), whom we have already briefly glimpsed surviving the Berber sack of the city in 1013. Ibn Hazm was unusual in that he was an independent author, not one attached to a court. He was brought up close to the centres of power in and near Córdoba, both his father and grandfather having been prominent servants of the state. A career in politics or administration seemed to be opening out in front of him, and indeed for the first part of his adult life he did pursue precisely such a career. But it was Ibn Hazm's ill-judgement or misfortune to have backed the wrong horse. He became an unwavering supporter of the restored Umayyad caliphal family, and that cause sank for ever after the removal of Hisham III from the scene in 1031. Ibn Hazm had already abandoned active involvement in politics in the late 1020s, to devote the rest of his life to study. His known and proclaimed allegiance to Umayyad legitimacy necessarily excluded him from the patronage of the taifa kings, among whom he made many enemies. The seclusion of his life on the family estates near Niebla was from time to time interrupted by bouts of persecution, especially in his later years after Niebla had been absorbed by Seville, for the pretensions of the Abbadid dynasty of Seville aroused his special scorn. Despite these ups and downs, however, Ibn Hazm produced several very distinguished works.

His major works of theology, philosophy and jurisprudence – bound together by the unifying theme of the quest of the soul for God – have remained almost unknown outside the Islamic world save to a handful of specialists. Ibn Hazm is remembered today outside that community for two other works. The first of these is his *Tawq al-hamama*, 'The Ring of the Dove', a treatise on love, partly in prose and partly in poetry, composed when the author was in his early thirties. It is a work of extraordinary psychological subtlety and penetration, tirelessly illuminating the almost limitless human capacity for self-deceit to which love is so often the trigger. It has been translated into most western languages. The second work for which he is remembered today in non-Islamic circles is that known by its abbreviated title *Kitab al-Fisal*, 'The Book of Sects'. This has often been described as a work dealing with 'comparative religion', but the description is a little misleading. The author's intention in the *Fisal* was to assert and demonstrate the rightness of Islam against all other faiths and deviant forms of Islam – an orthodox (of course) and rather commonplace purpose. What has interested historians is the knowledge of other faiths which Ibn Hazm displayed. He had evidently read widely in the Bible and the Talmud. This did not make him sympathetic to either Christianity or Judaism. Ibn Hazm's mind was made up from the start. There is no 'inter-faith dialogue' in the *Fisal*. It is a monument to learning, not to tolerance.

How did Ibn Hazm manage to find out so much about Christianity? Presumably, by reading Christian texts. By his day several such had been translated into Arabic for the use of the Mozarabs, the 'arabised'

Christian communities of al-Andalus who had come to adopt the language of their conquerors for the purposes of daily life. There survives, for example, the manuscript of an Arabic translation of the Gospels made at Córdoba in 946 by a man named Isaac Velázquez, and another containing a textbook of ecclesiastical law in Arabic translated by a priest named Vincent in 1049–50 and dedicated to his bishop who was named 'Abd al-Malik. It appears that such books could be bought on the open market. Ibn 'Abdun, the author of a tract on the municipal government of Seville in about the year 1100, recommended that scholarly books should not be sold to Christians 'except those that deal with their own law'; the phrase probably meant specifically Christian texts such as the Bible, works of church history, canon law, and so forth. If such texts were being produced for sale we can see readily enough how an enquirer like Ibn Hazm could have satisfied his curiosity.

It must be stressed how rare he was. The Muslim writers of eleventh-century al-Andalus had, by and large, singularly little to say about Christianity. They seem to have regarded the Christian communities in their midst with a grudging tolerance. It is significant that preconceptions and oversimplifications often mark their references to them. One writer alludes to a Christian village in terms of its church bells, its wine shop and its grazing swine: three things detestable to a Muslim, but stereotypes the lot of them. It is so much less effort to fall back on caricature than it is to investigate the real thing.

The Christian communities were equally uninterested in Islam. Politically, they followed a course of quietism. The contemporary *Life* of John of Gorze is revealing here. It will be recalled that John could not present his letters of credence to the caliph because of the hostile animadversions on Islam contained within them. When he was visited by a bishop, presumably of the Christian community of Córdoba, John insisted heatedly that he should be allowed to present the letters of his master Otto I. But the Spanish bishop counselled moderation in the following words:

Consider under what conditions we live. We have been driven to this by our sins, to be subjected to the rule of the pagans. We are forbidden by the Apostle's words to resist the civil power. Only one cause of solace is left to us, that in the depths of such a great calamity they do not forbid us to practise our own faith . . . For the time being, then, we keep the following counsel: that provided no harm is done to our religion, we obey them in all else, and do their commands in all that does not affect our faith.

In other words, keep your head down and you'll be all right. Christian intellectuals among the Mozarabs showed no interest in studying the sacred texts of Islam or even in finding out informally what Muslims believed. Back in the mid-ninth century a Christian traveller from Córdoba to the principality of Pamplona discovered a Latin biography of the Prophet Muhammad in the library of the monastery of Leyre. Its information was grotesquely biassed and misleading but it was accepted at the time as reliable because it fortified an already existing prejudice. It has been pointed out that more accurate information could have been obtained 'by asking any Muslim in the street' back home in Córdoba. But on the Christian as on the Muslim side an image or stereotype was found preferable to the laborious, and perhaps disturbing, investigation of reality.

It is difficult to know what the day-to-day relations of Christians and Muslims may have been like in the cities of al-Andalus. They lived side by side. In some cities the Mozarabs inhabited distinct Christian quarters of the town, in others they seem to have lived intermingled with their Muslim neighbours. They were brought together in the mundane affairs of daily life. Ibn 'Abdun urged that Muslims should not empty the cesspits of Christians, nor take employment as their grooms and muleteers. The fact that he had to make these prohibitions is a sure sign that such things went on. Christians and Muslims traded together, doubtless in many other commodities besides books. Ibn 'Abdun also urged Muslim women to keep out of Christian churches lest they should 'eat, drink and fornicate with the clergy'. (It is interesting to find the accusation of sexual licence being flung by a Muslim at Christians; it was a standard part of Christian polemic against Muslims.) Another source casts a fascinating ray of light on the matter of intercommunal relations when it reveals that certain among the better-off Muslims were accustomed to use Christian monasteries as wine-bars where they could drop in for a tincture of the liquid forbidden to them under Islamic law.

If the 'conversion curves' of Professor Bulliet, briefly discussed in Chapter 3, are even approximately correct, then by the age of the party kings the Christians will have been in a small minority in the cities of al-Andalus. Matters may have been different in the countryside. This is a difficult question to investigate because the great bulk of our surviving evidence relates to the towns and not to the country. However, it seems likely that there were fairly large tracts of the countryside, especially perhaps its more mountainous and less accessible parts, into which Islam had hardly penetrated at all. It may be that archaeology will one day be able to reveal something of these rural Christian communities to us. For the present we have to rely on stray allusions in the written sources. In his autobiography 'Abd Allah of Granada twice alludes to areas of his kingdom, one in the Málaga region and the other round Aledo, that harboured Christian populations: and he does so quite casually, as though there were nothing surprising in the fact. Did religious and cultural factors assist to dig ever deeper and wider the gulf that separated townsman from country-dweller? We cannot tell. But in these rural Christian communities we would seem to be confronted by societies which had not been assimilated to the dominant culture of al-Andalus, and perhaps felt resentfully alienated from it. There were 'internal frontiers' between Muslim and Christian inside al-Andalus as well as the 'external frontier' zone which separated the taifa kingdoms from the Christian princes of northern Spain.

No such frontier separated Muslims and Jews. Although there did exist some country-dwellers among the Jews of al-Andalus, the vast majority of them lived in the cities. These urban Jewish communities could be sizeable: there were at least twelve synagogues in Toledo. Surviving records – patchy, it need hardly be said – suggest a prosperous bourgeois community. Jewish businessmen in Spain traded with their co-religionists and others in Morocco, Tunisia, Egypt, Sicily and Provence. As with the records of Islamic commerce during this period, so with Jewish one is struck by the extent of its ramification. Consider for example the network revealed in this letter from an unnamed merchant (A) to a colleague (B), both of them natives of Alexandria, which dates from shortly after the year 1100. A reports to B that a common business associate (X) in Fez had sold civet, a musk-like substance used in perfumery which would have been imported from Tibet or Indonesia, on B's behalf for 7½ Andalusi dinars. X had urged A to invest the proceeds for B in silk at Almería, but A decided to give the money back to B: A has just returned from Spain to Alexandria and is sending the gold to B. He will also send ambergris from the Atlantic: this was entrusted to him by Y, a friend of X, for B to sell in Egypt; would B please employ the proceeds on buying Tibetan musk? Spanish Jewry was part of a trading network which spread throughout the Old World. Against this background Hasday ibn Shaprut's links with the Khazars and the Jewish academies of Mesopotamia seem rather less surprising than perhaps they did in the preceding chapter.

Jews rose to positions of prominence in several of the taifa states in the course of the eleventh century. The most remarkable among them was Samuel ibn Naghrila. Born in Córdoba, he left his native city in 1013 to escape the Berbers and made his way by stages to Granada. There he entered the service of the Zirid rulers and rapidly rose to positions of authority. Skilful handling of a succession crisis in 1038 brought 'his' candidate Badis to the throne: from that moment until his death in 1056 Samuel was in effect the first minister of the principality of Granada. 'Abd Allah the memoirist, the grandson of Badis, always refers respectfully to Samuel in his autobiography by the *kunya* or honorific name 'Abu Ibrahim', 'father of Abraham', in tribute to his wisdom and dignity. Samuel was a most versatile man. In addition to commanding troops in the field and running the state of Granada he was also a scholar, a rabbi venerated for his piety, and a talented poet. The following two short pieces, 'War' and 'Wounded Lions', in David Goldstein's translation, display his gifts.

> War at first is like a young girl
> With whom every man desires to flirt.
> And at the last it is an old woman:
> All who meet her feel grieved and hurt.

> At times of distress, strengthen your heart,
> Even if you stand at death's door.
> The lamp has light before it is extinguished.
> Wounded lions still know how to roar.

Samuel's son Joseph succeeded to his father's position as Badis' first minister in 1056. (It is a minor but telling illustration of the far-flung network of Spanish Jewry that Joseph married the daughter of the celebrated rabbi Nissim, of Kairouan in Tunisia.) Joseph came to an untimely end. In 1066 the Granadan *faqih* Abu Ishaq mobilised Muslim opinion against the Jewish community there, and against Joseph in particular, on the grounds that the Jews were ruling over Muslims contrary to Islamic teaching. He disseminated his views by means of an able but nasty anti-Semitic poem, addressed to Badis, inciting the inhabitants of Granada to turn on the Jews.

> I myself arrived in Granada and saw that these Jews were meddling in its affairs.
> They had already divided up the city and its provinces among themselves, and one of these cursed ones is in every place.
> They collect its taxes, they eat in the enjoyment of a plentiful life, and they crunch with their teeth.
> They don the highest-ranking robes while you, O Muslims, are dressed in their cast-off clothes.
> They are entrusted with your secrets of state, yet how can traitors be trusted?
> Were I to say, regarding their wealth, O Badis, that it is like your wealth, I would say the truth.

So hasten to slaughter them as a good work whereby you will earn God's
favour, and offer them up in sacrifice, a well-fattened ram . . .

Abu Ishaq was all too successful in his aim. A pogrom occurred in the
course of which Joseph and large numbers of the Granadan Jews were
put to the sword.

This was an isolated outbreak. By and large the eleventh century was
a time of peace and prosperity for Spanish Jewry. It was also a time of
cultural vitality. Cultural appetites, like economic or matrimonial ones,
ranged far afield. We hear of a Spanish-Jewish community (town
unnamed) who recruited a teacher from eastern France, possibly a
pupil of the great scholar R. Rashi of Troyes (1040–1105). Jewish
students from Spain would go to Mainz to sit at the feet of the famous
R. Gershom. Inside Spain Jewish learning, like Islamic, followed
wherever patronage was to be had. One of the greatest writers of this
period was Solomon ibn Gabirol. In the course of his short life – he died
in his early thirties in about 1055 – he composed a philosophical work,
'The Fountain of Life', which was later to be influential in western
Europe via a translation into Latin. He also left a body of very
distinguished secular and religious poetry. Ibn Gabirol's first patron
was Yekutiel ibn Hassan, a Jew who held high office at the court of
Zaragoza until his execution as the result of a court intrigue in 1039.
After this he found a patron in none other than Samuel ibn Naghrila of
Granada, to whom he dedicated a fine panegyric:

> . . . But go the Samuel who has come to our land
> As [the prophet] Samuel went to Ramah and to Mizpah.
> He has searched out understanding, learnt her mysteries,
> Gathered her in from her wandering exile,
> Despoiled her riches, made of them his treasure,
> Entrusted himself to her silver and her gold.

Solomon ibn Gabirol's literary output shows that Jewish as well as
Islamic culture benefited from the replacement of the caliphate of
Córdoba by the mosaic of taifa states. A third significant consequence of
their endemic rivalries lay in their vulnerability to exploitation. We saw
in the last chapter how the caliph al-Hakem II had intervened in the
internal political affairs of the Christian states of Spain in the middle
years of the tenth century. In the eleventh the tables were turned:
the taifa statelets were the suppliants and the Christian rulers the
interveners.

The 'year of the Catalans' in 1010, when armies led by the counts of
Barcelona and Urgel campaigned on behalf of the caliph Muhammad
II, was only the most prominent of several occasions when Catalan

troops operated as mercenaries during the Andalusi *fitnah*. Al-Andalus already enjoyed a reputation, among western Christians, for fabulous wealth. Now the Catalans could see it at close quarters, and even take a lot of it home with them – or try to. After a battle with the Berbers at the river Guadiaro, near Ronda, in June 1010, many of the Catalan troops were drowned because they were so laden down with gold and silver. The count of Barcelona, Ramón Borrell, had been handsomely paid for his services: at his death in 1018 he left 'a great quantity' of gold to the cathedral church of Barcelona. The Catalans were not alone in grasping these opportunities. Count Sancho of Castile was another ruler who did nicely out of the *fitnah*.

The exaction of gold was turned into a systematic policy as the eleventh century progressed. The mechanics of the operation were simplicity itself. An agreement would be made between a taifa ruler and a Christian king by the terms of which the latter undertook to provide military aid in return for a substantial annual tribute in gold coin. It was no more and no less than a protection racket. Fernando I, king of León and Castile (1037–65), was the first really skilful operator, a racketeer on the grand scale. By the end of his reign he was taking annual tributes from the taifa princes of Zaragoza, Toledo and Badajoz, and occasional ones as opportunity arose from Seville and Valencia. He felt so secure about the continuance of the payments that he divided up the profits from them among his sons at his death in 1065.

These annual tributes, which were known as *parias*, were of the utmost significance. They were a major item of revenue for kings, and therefore opened up all sorts of new avenues of opportunity for royal action. Passed on through the agency of kings, they enriched noblemen, soldiers, bureaucrats, churchmen and merchants. They gave the Christian kingdoms of Spain a bubble reputation for limitless wealth which was to act as a magnet drawing adventurers across the Pyrenees to share in it. These latter were to bring with them assumptions and ideas which would have far-reaching effects upon the relations between Christians and Muslims within the Iberian peninsula.

The system was inherently unstable. Shifting relationships of power among both Christian and Muslim states could affect the rate and the direction of the flow of gold. Christian rulers could vie with one another for the tribute from any individual taifa state. The ruler of that state could exploit this rivalry to his own advantage. Take the case of Zaragoza. Here was a taifa principality far from the southern heartlands of al-Andalus, based on the valley of the river Ebro. Its western and northern flanks marched with Castile, Navarre, Aragon and Barcelona. Competition for its tribute was keen. Between 1058 and 1062 the gold was flowing towards Barcelona. Fernando I managed to divert it towards Castile. Despite bids from the Aragonese in the early 1060s the Castilians contrived to hold onto it until their grip slackened during a period of strife between the sons of Fernando I which broke out in 1068. At this point the king of Navarre stepped in as Zaragoza's tribute-taker.

The dealings between Sancho IV of Navarre and al-Muqtadir of Zaragoza are illuminated for us by the survival of the texts of two treaties agreed in 1069 and 1073. Here are some extracts from the earlier of them.

If any people from France or elsewhere who are hostile to al Muqtadir Billah, may God exalt him, should attempt to cross from the aforesaid regions through the passes of the said king Sancho, whom God preserve, or by other routes, let him not join with them . . . in any ill-will or hostility against his friend the said al-Muqtadir Billah, may God exalt him; and let him not make common cause with any authority, whether Muslim or Christian, in hostility against him, neither secretly nor openly, neither in word nor in deed. Furthermore, similarly al-Muqtadir Billah undertakes for himself towards his friend the aforesaid lord king Sancho, whom God preserve, that he will not make common cause nor unite with any authority, whether Christian or Muslim, in any way to his disadvantage or in any hostile manner. But let both be bound together in one brotherhood and in one affection with sincerity of intent, just as in the alliance which was confirmed and strengthened between them before this one [a reference presumably to the original alliance of the year before, 1068].

The cost of the deal to Zaragoza is revealed later on:

In token of which al-Muqtadir Billah undertakes for himself towards his friend the lord king Sancho, whom God preserve, to render to him willingly of his riches, to wit, 1000 pieces of good gold every month, just as confirmed in the former treaty. And he shall give to him therefrom 5000 pieces of good gold in advance payment for the five coming months, the first month being the month of April Era 1107 [= AD 1069]: and of the aforesaid 5000 let Sancho have 2500 pieces of good gold at the hour of this treaty; and for the remaining 2500 pieces he will send a vassal chosen from among his good men to Zaragoza that he may collect them at the end of this coming month of May.

Through the stilted legal jargon we can sense the hard-nosed bargaining, the veiled threats, the histrionic gestures of despair, which must have taken place before the drafters set it all down on parchment. But we do not have to guess at these things: 'Abd Allah of Granada is at hand to tell us about them in his memoirs. His dealings were for the most part with Alfonso VI, the son of Fernando I who came out on top in the struggle with his brothers and ruled as sole king of León-Castile from 1072 to 1109. He resumed his father's assertive policies towards

the taifa kings and added Granada to his list of tributaries. Here is 'Abd
Allah describing his negotiations with Alfonso VI in about 1075.

I prepared to meet the king and I gathered round me those of my men whom I
could trust and equipped myself as the occasion demanded. I met him near
Granada and of necessity showed him every respect. He received me with
cheerful countenance and kindly manner and promised to protect me as he
would his own territory.

Then negotiations began, and envoys plied back and forth. Through them he
. . . was reported as issuing the following ultimatum: 'I have pondered the
matter, but have not wanted to take a hasty decision before hearing your
views. If you receive me with courtesy and are prepared to meet my demands, I
shall leave you in peace; if not, I shall stand by him who has concluded a treaty
with me [a reference to an enemy of 'Abd Allah named Ibn 'Ammar, of whom
more presently].' He then demanded 50,000 gold pieces. I pointed out to him,
however, that the country's resources were meagre, that I could not possibly
afford to pay that amount, and that it would so weaken me as to make me easy
prey for Ibn 'Abbad [i.e. the ruler of Seville]; for, should he seize Granada, he
would grow strong and refuse to obey him [i.e. king Alfonso]. So my reply was:
'Take from me what I can afford to pay and leave me a little on which to subsist.
Whatever you leave you will find with me at your disposal whenever you ask
for it.' Alfonso accepted my plea after much effort on my part and I finally
agreed to pay him 25,000 pieces, half the amount he had demanded. Then, as
presents for him, I got together a large number of carpets, garments and vessels
and placed all these things in a large tent. I then invited him to the tent. But
when he saw the presents he said they were not enough. So it was agreed that I
should increase the amount by 5000 pieces, bringing it to a total of 30,000.

Kings were not alone in profiting from the taifa regime. The eleventh
century was a time of opportunity for freelance operators. From a
certain angle, Samuel ibn Naghrila was one such: a refugee from
Córdoba, he made a career for himself in Granada. There were others
who travelled more widely in search of reward, and who crossed
religious and cultural frontiers as well as political ones. 'Abd Allah's
enemy Ibn 'Ammar was one of the most remarkable of these. A native
of the tiny taifa statelet of Silves born in 1031, he sought out the court of
the Abbadids of neighbouring Seville as a young man. There his
brilliance as a poet brought him to the notice of the ruling dynasty and
he was provided with an annual pension (like Ibn Hamdis a generation
later). He and the heir Muhammad (later to be the ruler al-Mu'tamid)
became close friends – too close, some whispered – and after the
Abbadid acquisition of the Algarve Ibn 'Ammar was the natural choice
to accompany the crown prince when he was sent there to cut his teeth
as a ruler. In 1058 he was suddenly exiled by the prince's father al-
Mu'tadid, for what offence we do not know. He spent ten years in exile

at the court of Zaragoza. After the accession of his old friend in 1069 Ibn 'Ammar was recalled to Seville to resume his career as poet, courtier and minister. All went well until 1078. In that year Ibn 'Ammar managed to acquire the taifa state of Murcia, ostensibly on behalf of his sovereign, in effect for himself. He governed there, to all intents and purposes an independent ruler, for a couple of years. Al-Mu'tamid was powerless to eject him, and had to content himself with composing a poem which poured scorn on Ibn 'Ammar's claims to distinguished ancestry. Ibn 'Ammar riposted in verses which mocked al-Mu'tamid and his immediate family. A copy of this poem in Ibn 'Ammar's own hand was sent by one of his enemies to the court of Seville. At about the same time Ibn 'Ammar was betrayed in Murcia and forced to flee. He made his way to the court of Alfonso VI for a short time, then went back to Zaragoza where he spent the years 1081–84. Captured in war in the latter year, he was sold by his captors to al-Mu'tamid, sent back to Seville and there killed by his old friend and patron in person. The weapon which al-Mu'tamid used for the job was an axe which he had been given by king Alfonso VI.

Ibn 'Ammar's career is paralleled in some respects by that of the most famous of all adventurers on the Christian side, the Castilian warrior Rodrigo Díaz, known to posterity (as perhaps in his lifetime) as El Cid, 'the Boss'. The growth of legend about his exploits after his death has served to shroud the historical figure beneath a cloak of Catholic and patriotic piety. However, enough reliable and near-contemporary evidence about his doings has survived to enable us to penetrate the mythic cover. Rodrigo Díaz was a Castilian nobleman who rose high in service to the sons of Fernando I by means of his skills as soldier, diplomat and courtier in transactions with the taifa kings. He was exiled by Alfonso VI in 1081, seemingly on account of somewhat over-zealous dealings with the taifa state of Toledo at a time when the king's interests counselled a milder approach: Rodrigo was evidently a man not easily amenable to control. Like Ibn 'Ammar at the same date, he spent his exile in the service of the ruler of Zaragoza. Rodrigo's military talents made him invaluable as a mercenary commander against Zaragoza's enemies, whether Christian or Muslim. Among his most celebrated exploits in these years were his defeat and capture of the count of Barcelona in 1082, and, two years later in 1084, his defeat of the king of Aragon and capture of a whole string of distinguished Aragonese prisoners. Successful soldiering of this sort and all that went with it – especially the highly lucrative ransoming of important captives – made Rodrigo rich as well as famous.

In 1086 Rodrigo was reconciled to Alfonso VI and returned to Castile.

However, relations between the two men deteriorated again and in 1089 Rodrigo took himself off into exile once more. This time he struck out as a freelance, in the literal and original meaning of the term. Renowned as a commander and wealthy from the spoils of successful warfare, he could attract enough troops to form his own private army. During the remaining ten years of his life he campaigned up and down the region of eastern Spain known as the Levante. Sometimes he fought Christians like the count of Barcelona (again), sometimes the Muslim rulers of the taifa states. He was his own man and went his own way. He pillaged the countryside, he exacted tributes and he ended up by besieging and taking the city of Valencia – somewhat as Ibn 'Ammar had taken the nearby city of Murcia in 1078. Rodrigo ruled there for the last five years of his life, prince of a little taifa statelet all his own. He died there, peacefully, in 1099.

This chapter has been concerned with the Andalusi *fitnah* of the years between 1008 and 1031, the collapse of the system constructed by the great caliphs of the preceding century, and its consequences. Some of these were heartening and liberating: the diffusion of cultural energies and the marvellous works of art and literature which have come down to us from eleventh-century Spain. Others were matter for regret and anguish of spirit: the political fragmentation of al-Andalus, the constant strife among the taifa statelets, their vulnerability to humiliating financial exploitation by their Christian neighbours.

One final consequence of the political volatility of the taifa period was the end of Andalusi dominance in the affairs of the Maghrib. We saw in the last chapter how the tenth-century caliphs of Córdoba had taken trouble to keep themselves well-informed about developments in the Maghrib, to 'defuse' if possible any restiveness among the Berber tribes who lived there and to prevent piracy on the waters of the western Mediterranean. The fragmentation of authority in the succeeding age meant that Spanish Islam could present no single, coherent policy in its relations with northwest Africa. The taifa rulers of Seville might have played a commanding role across the Straits, given their position of near-dominance in al-Andalus from the 1050s onwards, and given Seville's commercial contacts with Morocco. They might have done, but they did not.

A story told of the shrewd al-Mu'tadid of Seville is timely here. Towards the end of his reign, in the mid-1060s, a minister submitted to him a routine report which happened to mention that word had come in that a Berber tribe in southern Morocco had recently founded a new city at Marrakesh. The minister made light of it as a matter of fugitive interest. Al-Mu'tadid demurred. 'If God grants you a long life you will see the coming of those people here!' Then he gave orders for the governor of Algeciras to fortify Gibraltar against invasion.

The people from Marrakesh did indeed come to al-Andalus, with disastrous consequences for al-Mu'tadid's own family, among many others. That cultivated prince, his son al-Mu'tamid, was to be dethroned by them and end his days a captive in Morocco. So was 'Abd Allah of Granada. The world of the party kings was suddenly and brutally swept away when the cats came face to face with real lions.

6

THE MOROCCAN
FUNDAMENTALISTS

At the end of the eleventh century the Iberian peninsula was invaded by the devotees of an Islamic fundamentalist sect from the Maghrib known as the Almoravids. Coming initially as the allies of the taifa rulers, the newcomers rapidly turned against them and subdued all of al-Andalus to their control. But their dominion did not last long. Corrupted and enervated by the fleshpots of southern Spain, they 'went soft'. Revolts against them occurred in the middle years of the twelfth century, and the Christian rulers of the north took advantage of their vulnerability to make territorial conquests at their expense. Meanwhile, back in Morocco, another fundamentalist sect (but of a markedly different character) grew up in the second quarter of the twelfth century to challenge the Almoravids. This was the sect of the Almohads. (The names of the two sects are confusingly similar, but there is nothing that can be done about it.) The Almohads had extinguished Almoravid dominion in Morocco by about 1150 and went on to cross the Straits and conquer al-Andalus during the years 1171–73. By this time the three major Christian powers – León-Castile, Aragon-Catalonia and the new kingdom of Portugal – were formidably strong. Despite a generation of Almohad success in Spain, culminating in their great victory at Alarcos in 1195, this strength told. The Almohads were decisively defeated at the battle of Las Navas de Tolosa in 1212. In the course of the next forty-odd years the Christian rulers conquered nearly all of the territory of al-Andalus. Córdoba fell to them in 1236, Valencia in 1238 and Seville in 1248. These conquests were to prove permanent.

That is to sketch in outline the politico-military history of al-Andalus between about 1080 and 1250. This chapter will amplify the story. The following one will explore the social and cultural history of the period.

In the fourteenth century the great Tunisian scholar Ibn Khaldun, pondering the history of the Berber peoples, worked out a theory to account for what he perceived as recurrent patterns of cyclical change. The key to understanding these patterns, he thought, lay in what we would today call environmental factors. The exceptionally harsh and inhospitable natural environment of southern Morocco, around and beyond the Atlas ranges, had two important social effects. It made the Berber peoples physically tough, and it gave them the impetus to maintain a strong social solidarity. The Berbers, therefore, are formidable fighters. Something further has to happen to make them irresistible. In Ibn Khaldun's own words:

Vast and powerful empires are founded on a religion. This is because dominion can only be secured by victory, and victory goes to the side which shows most solidarity and unity of purpose. Now, men's hearts are united and coordinated, with the help of God, by participation in a common religion . . . Religious fervour can efface the competitiveness and envy felt by the members of the group towards each other, and turn their faces towards the truth. When once their eyes have been fixed on the truth, nothing can stand in their way, for their outlook is the same and the object they desire is common to all and is one for which they are prepared to die . . .

Periodically, when these elements combine, an explosion will occur. The Berbers will break out against their neighbours who inhabit more favoured environments and conquer them. Immediately, however, a rot will start to set in. The influence of a softer climate and culture will dilute religious fervour and dissolve group solidarities. Soon the conquerors will have been subtly made captive by the vanquished. Before long a new cycle of conquest, by a new group of 'outsiders', will take place.

Ibn Khaldun found in the rise and fall of the Almoravid empire a good illustration of his theory. Modern enquirers – social anthropologists, sociologists of religion and such like – though they use a different terminology, have tended to endorse his suggestions. The moment of crystallisation or explosion came in the middle years of the eleventh century. The spark was provided by the coming of an Islamic teacher named Ibn Yasin to the Berber tribal confederation known as the Sanhaja.

The Sanhaja peoples inhabited the southwestern fringes of the Sahara in the regions of (in modern terms) southern Morocco and northern Mauretania. They had adopted Islam in the tenth century but had received little instruction in the faith and its observances. Ibn Yasin's mission, which began in or about 1039, was designed to deepen knowledge and purify practice. He made the shakiest of starts. The Sanhaja would not listen to his teaching and Ibn Yasin was forced to flee to the Atlantic coast accompanied by the very few disciples whom he had been able to attract. There he founded a *ribat*, that is to say a religious community (bearing some resemblance to a Christian monastery) whose members devoted themselves to living a pure and ascetic life and to spreading the faith to the peoples who lived thereabouts by example, preaching and charitable works. A *ribat*, conventionally situated on the frontiers of Islamic territory beyond the reach or the protection of civil power, had to be capable of defending itself. There was therefore necessarily an element of military discipline and readiness about the life of the community. Ibn Yasin and his followers came to be known as 'the people of the *ribat*', *al-Murabitun*: the term was later corrupted by the Romance-speakers of Spain to *almoravid*, which gives us the name by which they are generally known to historians. The term *ribat* has left its mark upon the place-names of the Islamic world: for example, Rabat in Morocco or La Rábita in southern Spain.

Devout, disciplined and armed, Ibn Yasin's community flourished. Converts to Islam were made. This 'new force of revivalist Islam' began to spread like wildfire in a fragmented society to which it held out the hope of a supra-tribal, supra-feuding means of achieving harmony and coherence, a healing (if fragile) unity. Like Muhammad (to whom his followers implicitly likened him) after the *hijra* or flight from Mecca to Medina in 622, Ibn Yasin bided his time. Then he launched himself upon the Sanhaja tribes who had scorned his teaching. Between 1042 and his death in 1059 all the Sanhaja peoples submitted to Almoravid authority. A new power had been born in western Islam. Ibn Yasin was succeeded as commander of the movement by one of his original disciples, Abu Bakr, who delegated leadership of the northern sector to his kinsman Yusuf ibn Tashufin. It was Yusuf who led his men over the Atlas to the plain of Morocco. There he established a new base for further operations, at Marrakesh, in the early 1060s. It was the news of this foundation which al-Mu'tadid of Seville heard with such a grave sense of foreboding. The northward expansion of the Almoravids continued unchecked. With the conquests of Tangier in 1079 and Ceuta in 1083, all Morocco lay at Yusuf's feet.

The arrival of the Almoravids on the shores of the Mediterranean brought them into contact with the taifa rulers of al-Andalus. It is important to take the measure of the cultural gap which yawned between them – wider and deeper by far than the Straits of Gibraltar. The taifa statelets, as we have seen, shared in the culture of Middle Eastern Islam which in turn had inherited much from the civilisations of antiquity. The Almoravids were outsiders, peoples of the *bled*, unsophisticated tribesmen, materially and culturally impoverished. Yusuf dressed in skins, reeked of camels and spoke Arabic only with difficulty. It is impossible to imagine him at the elegant soirées of the Abbadid court of Seville. Indeed – and this is crucial – he would never have dreamed of going to such a godless assembly. The Almoravid leadership were puritans, ascetics, zealots. They saw their role as one of purifying religious observance by the reimposition where necessary of the strictest canons of Islamic orthodoxy.

From what today might be called a fundamentalist viewpoint there was much that could be criticised about the rulers of the taifa principalities. The rulers of al-Andalus had long ceased to pay even lip service to the nominal authority of the caliph in distant Baghdad. But Yusuf regarded himself as the caliph's deputy, as the inscriptions on Almoravid coinage make plain. In other words, the taifa rulers were in a state of rebellion against legitimate Islamic authority. Secondly, there was the matter of the *parias*. The payment of tribute by Islamic rulers to non-Islamic ones is forbidden by the *Shari'ah*, the Revealed Law of Islam: a Muslim cannot be subject to a non-Muslim. Yet this was precisely what was expressed in the tributary regime of eleventh-century Spain. Furthermore, in their pressing need to raise money to meet the demands of rulers like Alfonso VI, the taifa princes were compelled to levy taxes which were not authorised by canonical tradition. A comparable breach of *Shari'ah*, thirdly, could be seen in the exercise of authority by Jews over Muslims, as most notably in the state of Granada – all too easily visible from Africa – between 1038 and 1066 by Samuel ibn Naghrila and his son Joseph. The poem of protest against this state of affairs by the Granadan *faqih*, or doctor of the law, Abu Ishaq, quoted in the last chapter, was an indication of the seriousness with which conservative religious opinion could regard the matter. It was imprudent of the taifa princes to disregard the counsel of their learned men.

These were major breaches of the law of Islam. There were plenty of lesser ones too. For instance, the science (as it was then considered) of astrology was much cultivated in princely circles in al-Andalus. The taifa rulers, like any others, had the keenest interest in peering into the future and employed the appropriate experts to help them do so, much as governments of today use economic forecasters. Al-Mu'tamid of Seville employed a Jewish rabbi from Córdoba as his official astrologer.

Al-Mu'tamin of Zaragoza – the son of al-Muqtadir who was party to the treaties with the king of Navarre discussed in the preceding chapter – was said to have been skilled in astrology to the point of predicting the date of his own death in 1085. The autobiography of 'Abd Allah of Granada reveals his fascination with astrology and includes a spirited defence of it. But orthodox opinion frowned. The *Hadith*, that is the 'Traditions' of Islam which enjoy a status as doctrine second only to the Koran, discourage it. 'Even when the soothsayers tell the truth, they lie.' A leading Andalusi *faqih* of this period strongly condemned astrological study.

Or again, there was the matter of the generally hedonistic tone of court life under the taifa rulers, amply illustrated in the poetry quoted in the previous chapter. 'Their minds were occupied with wine and song,' wrote one contemporary: it was not meant as a compliment. 'Abd Allah was frank in his memoirs about the drinking habits of his father and grandfather, and if he was reticent about his own we should remember that he was writing as a captive in Almoravid hands.

The taifa rulers, then, laid themselves open to criticism from orthodox Islamic opinion on a range of issues. Apart from the views already quoted, there were influential voices publicly raised in opposition. Here is Ibn Hazm, shortly before his death in 1064:

By God, I swear that if the tyrants were to learn that they could attain their ends more easily by adopting the religion of the Cross, they would certainly hasten to profess it! Indeed, we see that they ask the Christians for help and allow them to take away Muslim men, women and children as captives to their lands. Frequently they protect them in their attacks against the most inviolable lands, and ally themselves with them in order to gain security.

It will be recalled that Ibn Hazm detested the taifa rulers: we cannot expect an unbiassed opinion from him. Here then is another voice, that of the poet al-Sumaysir:

Call the kings and say to them,
   'What have you brought about?'
You have handed over Islam into enemy captivity
   and [yourselves] remained seated [and inactive].
We should rise up against you
   since you have given your support to the Christians.
You take no account of the breaking of the bonds of community
   so that you have even broken the bonds of the community of the Prophet!'

The specific focus of the criticisms of Ibn Hazm and al-Sumaysir was the habit of dealing with and submitting to the Christian powers which was embodied in the *paria* relationship. The trouble was that the relationship could not indefinitely remain one that was characterised by cash payments only. Behind the tribute-taking kings of the eleventh century loomed the warrior aristocracies on whom their power rested. These were potentially menacing figures whose loyal cooperation had to be secured with lavish handouts not just in gold but also in slaves, horses, booty and land. Kings could find themselves pushed into policies that were more territorially acquisitive by the expectations and perhaps the demands of their vassals. This was one way in which tribute-taking could merge insensibly into conquest. In 1055, for example, Fernando I of León-Castile conquered the cities of Lamego and Viseu, in what is today central Portugal: the surviving Moorish inhabitants were disposed of as slaves. In 1064 he conquered Coimbra: its Moorish inhabitants were forcibly expelled and the government and resettlement of the city were entrusted to one of the king's leading vassals who acquired ample lands in the countryside nearby. In 1065 king Fernando had designs on Valencia which were frustrated only by his death and a struggle between his three sons over the succession.

Of these three, the one who came out on top was Alfonso VI, whom we have already met towards the end of the last chapter negotiating with 'Abd Allah of Granada in about 1075. Alfonso's most famous military achievement was the conquest of Toledo in 1085. This operation demonstrates another way in which tribute-taking could turn into conquest. The last taifa ruler of Toledo, al-Qadir, was feckless and inadequate. Alfonso VI, as the military 'protector' of the Toledan ruler, found himself compelled to intervene to shore up al-Qadir's crumbling authority. The resultant set of ad hoc arrangements was messy and fragile, obviously unsatisfactory as a long-term solution to the problem of what to do about Toledo – no ordinary city, we should bear in mind, but the ancient capital of the Visigothic kings with all the numinous resonance that that carried with it. So king Alfonso took steps to substitute his own directly-exercised authority for the uncertain power which he had indirectly exerted through the shaky medium of al-Qadir. Protection merged into intervention and that into a takeover. It is a common progression in incipient imperial relationships.

The fall of Toledo to Alfonso VI caused panic in al-Andalus and forced the remaining taifa rulers into the arms of the Almoravids. Led by al-Mu'tamid of Seville, they invited Yusuf to bring an army across the Straits to assist them against the king of León-Castile. In 1086 Yusuf came. The armies met at Sagrajas, near Badajoz, on 23 October 1086. The Almoravids inflicted a decisive defeat upon the army of Alfonso VI.

It is plain from the memoirs of 'Abd Allah that there was little love lost between the taifa rulers and the Almoravids. 'Abd Allah and his colleagues feared the Almoravids but needed them. Yusuf despised the supplicants but was prepared to help them because they were fellow Muslims, albeit disreputable ones. For the Andalusians the alternative to calling in the Moroccan fundamentalists was to go under to an increasingly hawkish Christian leadership. It is said that al-Mu'tamid of Seville swayed the final decision with the remark that he 'would rather be a camel-driver in Morocco than a swineherd in Castile'.

Al-Mu'tamid did indeed end his days in Morocco, though not in quite so lowly a situation as a driver of camels. Shortly after the initial intervention in the affairs of al-Andalus in 1086 Yusuf moved against the taifa rulers, as was to have been expected. He was angered by their failure to give him adequate support in further campaigns against the Christians. He was being urged to turn against them by the doctors of the law, and encouraged by the number of defections to him to believe that he could do so successfully. In 1090 he dethroned 'Abd Allah of Granada and his brother Tamim of Málaga, and exiled them to Morocco – where 'Abd Allah composed his autobiography a few years later. In 1091 it was the turn of al-Mu'tamid of Seville. Before his death in captivity at Aghmat, near Marrakesh, in 1095 he composed several moving elegies lamenting his fate.

> I was the ally of bounty and the lord of generosity,
> A friend of people's souls and of their spirits;
> My right hand was always ready to bestow boons,
> And to snatch lives of foes in fierce affray;
> My left hand would grasp the rein of fiery steeds,
> And hold them firm among the clashing spears!
> Today I am a captive in the throes of poverty,
> Exposed to ills and fevers, with my wings broken.

Or again:

> You enfold my legs like a streaked serpent,
> Grasping them like a lion's sharp fangs:
> Desist! – even if those fetters kindle a fire
> Which sets my arms and every joint aflame –
> For fear of him who once could send men by his boons
> Or by his sword, either to Paradise or to Hell!

In 1094 the taifa state of Badajoz went under to the Almoravids. In 1102 they absorbed the Cid's principality of Valencia when his widow Jimena was forced to evacuate it. Finally, in 1110, they conquered Zaragoza.

True, they never did succeed in repossessing Toledo, though they came within an ace of doing so several times. They inflicted another resounding defeat on the Castilians at Uclés in 1108. They sent raiding parties into Castile. For the first quarter of the twelfth century they kept up a steady pressure upon the Tagus valley which, roughly speaking, formed the southern frontier of the kingdom of León-Castile. For much of this time the city of Toledo was an isolated outpost. Just outside Toledo itself, on the south bank of the Tagus and within sight of the city, a monastery had been established soon after 1085: in 1113 it was abandoned in the face of Almoravid attack and not re-established until about 1127. The only area where any Christian gains of territory were made in this period was in the Ebro valley – the furthest removed from Almoravid reach – where the king of Aragon, Alfonso *el Batallador*, 'the Battler', conquered Zaragoza in 1118 and Tudela in 1119.

The most significant effect of the coming of the Almoravids was the reunification of al-Andalus, as in the great days of the caliphate of Córdoba in the tenth century. This time, however, al-Andalus was not an independent state but a colony administered by governors sent from Marrakesh by the Almoravid amir (who was at least in theory the deputy of the Abbasid caliph in Baghdad). This reunification was the fruit of a much more aggressive Islamic fervour than the stately pieties of the age of 'Abd al-Rahman III. Relations between Muslims and Christians in the Iberian peninsula became more hostile during the Almoravid period. Yusuf's attitude to his own co-religionists was intolerant: it was not to be supposed that he would look more tolerantly upon the Christians – or indeed the Jews – among his new European subjects. We hear of the destruction of a church at Granada by the Almoravids in 1099. A stray surviving papal letter of 1117 addressed to the Christian community of Málaga reveals that its bishop, Julian, had been imprisoned by the Almoravid authorities for the previous seven years. In the winter of 1125–26 Alfonso *el Batallador* of Aragon led a raid down the Levante coastline to the region of Granada and persuaded large numbers of the Christian inhabitants to return with him to Aragon to escape Almoravid persecution – and to colonise the lands conquered by the Aragonese in the Ebro valley. By way of reprisal the Almoravid amir Ali, the son of Yusuf, in 1126 forcibly removed many Andalusi Christians to Morocco. A poignant glimpse of these exiles is granted to us in a note at the end of a surviving manuscript of the Gospels in Arabic translation:

This book was written by bishop Michael, son of 'Abd al-Aziz, servant of the servants of the Messiah, the Word of God the Father Eternal, for Ali, the son of 'Abd al-Aziz the son of 'Abd al-Rahman: it was completed on Friday 23 July of the Spanish Era 1175 [= 1137 AD] in the city of Fez across the sea, in the eleventh year after the removal of the Andalusi Christians to this place (may God restore them to their homeland!). He copied it in the fifty-seventh year of his age.

Almoravid persecution of these Christian communities helped to fuel anti-Islamic feeling in the Christian kingdoms. Their rulers had already been hit hard, in their pockets, by Almoravid expansion. We have seen that the income from tributes paid by the taifa rulers was one of the major sources of royal revenue, perhaps *the* major source, for kings such as Alfonso VI. The Almoravid reunification of al-Andalus turned the supply of gold off just as twisting a tap stems a flow of water. This had the effect of plunging the Christian kingdoms into a state of fiscal crisis for the first third of the twelfth century. This parlous state of government finance probably goes far to account for the difficulties faced by Alfonso VI's daughter Urraca in trying to govern León-Castile during the seventeen unhappy years of her reign (1109–26).

Financial difficulties brought about by the suspension of tributes were not confined to the Iberian peninsula. The most important beneficiary of Alfonso VI's new-found wealth had been not among his own subjects but a French monastic house, Cluny, situated in the Maconnais region of southern Burgundy. The monastery of Cluny was the most renowned religious house in eleventh-century western Christendom. Its body of what were called 'customs' – comprising such things as the Cluniac interpretation of the Benedictine Rule, special forms of liturgy and ceremonial, distinctive routines of prayer and worship, a developing musical tradition and so forth – were widely admired and frequently adopted by other monastic communities. In this fashion a loosely-affiliated network of Cluniac houses came into existence which stretched across the Pyrenees into northern Spain by the second quarter of the eleventh century. The Cluniacs believed in 'the beauty of holiness': the tone of their monasticism was dignified, grand and opulent. They may be said – and it is not meant unkindly – to have 'targeted' rich and influential patrons such as the feudal aristocracy of France and those very wealthy kings in Spain who were suddenly doing so nicely for themselves out of the tributes paid by the taifa statelets of al-Andalus. But to say that the Cluniac monks were drawn to Spain as wasps to a jar of honey, and to leave it at that, would be much too cynical. The traffic went two ways. The Cluniacs were specialists in intercessory prayer for the souls of the sinful. There were plenty of uneasy consciences among the kings and noblemen of eleventh-century Europe, apprehensive of what would befall them when they faced that dread tribunal – frequently depicted in stone or paint within their churches – to answer to God for their sins. Alfonso VI of León-Castile probably compassed the death of one of his brothers and certainly kept the other in lifelong captivity. There, surely, was an uneasy crowned head.

His father Fernando I had entered into an agreement with Cluny by which he paid the monks an annual render of one thousand gold pieces (the *dinars* of al-Andalus). Alfonso VI confirmed this arrangement and in 1077 doubled the annual render. By the standards of the eleventh century two thousand gold pieces was a colossal sum. (Precise monetary equivalents in the values of today cannot be established, but it is safe to say that we should be thinking in terms of annual payments of several million pounds.) It was largely on the strength of the Alfonsine subsidy that abbot Hugh of Cluny embarked on the rebuilding of the abbey church of Cluny, the biggest and most ambitious edifice built in western Europe since the days of the Roman empire. The Cluniac economy was dependent upon the continued flow of gold from al-Andalus via the king of León-Castile to Burgundy. When the Almoravids cut off the supply it was more than abbot Hugh's building operations that were threatened. Cluniac finances were dealt a blow from which it took the abbey half a century to recover.

Alfonso VI's dealings with Cluny extended further than the contract by which prayers were bought for gold. The Cluniac imprint upon the Spanish church at large was a lasting one. The churchman who most vigorously stamped this impression was Bernard, native of Périgord, monk of Cluny, abbot of the Leonese monastery of Sahagún, and from 1086 until his death at a great age in 1124 the first archbishop of the reconstituted primatial see of Toledo. We shall return to him in a moment. Of Alfonso's many successive wives, one was a Burgundian lady, Constance, who just happened to be the niece of abbot Hugh of Cluny. After the disaster of Sagrajas in 1086 Alfonso sent an appeal to France for military assistance, and naturally turned to Cluniac-Burgundian aristocratic circles. One of those who responded was duke Odo of Burgundy, nephew of queen Constance, and he came accompanied by his cousin Raymond. Odo returned to France after an inconclusive campaign in 1087 but Raymond stayed on in Spain. He married the king's daughter Urraca, was made count of Galicia, and would have reigned as king-consort had it not been for his early death in 1107. Raymond was only the most prominent among the French noblemen who were starting to flock to Spain, enticed by the lure of treasure and adventure, or invited by king Alfonso with all the prospects that such an invitation might imply. A further example is provided by Henry, yet another kinsman of queen Constance, who came to León-Castile in about 1092. He too was rewarded with a royal daughter (though an illegitimate one) and a county, this time of Portugal. His son was to be the first king of an independent Portugal.

The warrior-aristocrats from France who went to fight in Spain were men whose culture had been formed by epic tales such as those which dealt with Charlemagne's invasion of Spain in 778. Indeed, the *Chanson de Roland*, the Old French epic which is focussed upon the tragic events in the pass of Roncesvalles, seems to have been composed in the form in which it has come down to us in the latter part of the eleventh century. To go to fight the infidel in Spain was to follow in the footsteps of Charles the Great, the emperor to whom all looked admiringly, even reverently back: for the knight of that age, this was the path of glory. We can hardly doubt that the tales of Charlemagne and all his peerage were known to such as Rotrou, count of Perche in Normandy, who can be traced fighting in the service of king Alfonso *el Batallador* of Aragon on several occasions in the early twelfth century and who was appointed by the king to govern Tudela after its conquest in 1119; or to the brothers Gaston count of Béarn and Centulo count of Bigorre who also served the king of Aragon in the field and as governors of, respectively, Zaragoza and Tarazona.

The religious culture of the feudal aristocracy largely consisted of going on pilgrimages and of fighting in causes that ecclesiastical leaders – themselves, in this small world, usually drawn from noble families – identified as sacred. One of the most popular destinations for the pilgrims of this period was the tomb of St James at Santiago de Compostela in northwestern Spain. The shrine was a potent magnet in drawing men and women to Spain and acquainting them with the opportunities which awaited them there. As for warfare, although the idea of holy war was many centuries old in Christian tradition, in the eleventh century it was being developed into a notion with greater potential for the justification of aggression in relations between Christendom and Islam: the idea that war against the infidel might be work of positive spiritual merit for the Christian knight. Herein lay the seeds of the idea of crusade. Urban II, the pope who launched the First Crusade in 1095 with a speech at Clermont to an audience largely consisting of French warrior-aristocrats, was himself a French noble-man and a former monk of Cluny. Among the thousands who took part in the expedition which captured Jerusalem in 1099 were Rotrou count of Perche, Gaston count of Béarn and Centulo count of Bigorre. Another French nobleman and former monk of Cluny, a friend and contemporary of the pope, who was among the audience at Clermont in 1095, who wanted to join the crusade but in the event was prevented from doing so, was the new archbishop of Toledo.

Bernard of Toledo was a man of prodigious energies and unswerving self-confidence. Given his background it is not surprising to find that he was something of a hardliner in his dealings with Muslims. After the conquest of Toledo Alfonso VI had permitted to its surviving Muslim inhabitants the continued possession of their principal mosque and freedom of worship within it. In 1086 Bernard overrode this. He took over the mosque and converted it into his cathedral. He seems to have done the same with the mosques of all the villages in his diocese from the Tagus north to the Sierra de Guadarrama.

This was the age of that movement of reform in the church which is often known as the 'Hildebrandine' reform after its leading figure Hildebrand, pope Gregory VII (1073–85). The reformers wanted to purify what they saw as a corrupt church by cutting it loose from its connections with the lay world. Thus their insistence on clerical celibacy, and their opposition to lay control over such matters as the appointment of bishops and abbots. A clergy so purified, they further argued, should be the directing force in the shaping and instructing of a more fully Christian society in which the laity should be assigned godly tasks and supervised in their fulfilment of them by the clergy. The clergy would themselves be directed by a chain of command which led through bishops and archbishops back to the pope. The channelling of secular violence into clerically sponsored enterprises – in a word, crusades – was a significant element in the reformers' programme.

Bernard of Toledo was the leading reformer of his generation in the Spanish church. He brought it into a new and much closer relationship with Rome. To give but one example of this: Spanish ecclesiastics were encouraged to attend church councils held by the pope at which reforming legislation was promulgated – such as Clermont in 1095 – and to enforce it upon their return home. Bernard imported like-minded clergy from France and steered them into influential positions in the Spanish church. Nearly every diocese in Castile was occupied by one of Bernard's protégés during the first half of the twelfth century. One of them, Raymond, bishop of Osma from 1109 to 1124, was his successor at Toledo from 1124 to 1152. Bernard was associated with Alfonso *el Batallador* of Aragon in the foundation of a military confraternity in 1122: the knights who joined it promised 'never to live at peace with the pagans [i.e. the Muslims] but to devote all their days to fighting them'.

It may be wondered what all this has to do with the history of Islamic Spain. The answer is, a great deal. During the first half of the twelfth century the character of relations between Christians and Muslims underwent a change. Both sides became more aggressive. On the

Muslim side this was brought about by the coming of the Almoravids. Changing attitudes on the Christian side were in part a reaction to this, but perhaps owed rather more to the imported notions brought to Spain by Cluniac monks, French military adventurers, reforming churchmen, pilgrims to Compostela and the emissaries of the Hildebrandine papacy. The net result, on the Christian side, was the replacement of a policy of exploitation of their Muslim neighbours (as under the *paria* regime) by a programme of crusading conquest.

It must be stressed at once that such a shift of attitude did not happen overnight. We must beware of simplifying the allegiances of the twelfth century, of presenting a wholly unreal image of the Iberian peninsula as a kind of pitch whereon a Christian team slogged it out against a Muslim one. Here are two cautionary examples.

At Zaragoza the last ruler of the Hudid dynasty, 'Abd al-Malik, was dethroned by the Almoravids in 1110. For the next twenty years he held out in the rump of the kingdom, a tiny principality based at Rueda, to the west of Zaragoza. After his death in 1130 his son Sayf al-Dawla became a vassal of king Alfonso VII of León-Castile, surrendering Rueda and being compensated with military commands on the Tagus frontier near Toledo. Like a good vassal he accompanied the king on campaigns against al-Andalus, and attended great state occasions like Alfonso's imperial coronation in 1135. In the early 1140s he seems to have been active in stirring up anti-Almoravid feeling in southern Spain; whether as the king's agent or on his own initiative we cannot tell. He played a prominent part in the uprising against Almoravid rule in Córdoba in 1144 and briefly held power there in the early months of 1145. In the general collapse of Almoravid power in the second Andalusi *fitnah* – of which more presently – Sayf al-Dawla made off for Granada and then Murcia, apparently in search of a new principality for himself. It was a dangerous game. He called on king Alfonso for military aid. Some double-crossing seems to have occurred, and Sayf al-Dawla was killed by the king's emissaries in 1146. Alfonso denied complicity but did not punish the guilty men.

Sayf al-Dawla was a renegade, though not an apostate, Muslim. (It is of some interest that the Latin word *renegatus* seems to have been coined during the crusading era.) The second example is of movement in the opposite direction. Reverter was the name of a prominent Catalan baron who was viscount of Barcelona in the 1130s. Captured by the Almoravids, he agreed to take service with them as a mercenary soldier. (It is a little surprising that a sect so hostile to Christianity should regularly have employed Christians not just as soldiers but also as tax-collectors in Morocco; but the practice is well-documented.)

Reverter took a leading part in the resistance to the expansion of the Almohads in the Maghrib and seems to have died there in about 1145. His widow returned to Catalonia, where her tomb may still be seen in Gerona cathedral: it bears an inscription in Latin and Arabic. Of their two known sons, one became a Muslim, joined the Almohads and followed a soldier's career in their service. The other, by name Berenguer, returned to Spain and entered the service of his father's former master, Ramón Berenguer IV of Aragon-Catalonia. The two documents attesting this, of 1156 and 1157, both bear his signature – in Arabic. (Was it perhaps he who composed his mother's epitaph?) He must have done well for himself, because a document of 1168 shows that he was lending money to the government. He is said to have ended his days in the military order of Knights Templar.

The careers of Sayf al-Dawla and Reverter were both in their different ways made possible by the progressive enfeebling of the Almoravid hold on al-Andalus and the Maghrib. The Almoravids had never been liked in al-Andalus outside the limited circles of the rigorist critics of the taifa rulers. They had come as deliverers but they behaved like conquerors. The leadership may have been sincerely devout but the rank and file were not. Almoravid rule has been described by a modern authority as 'an extended looting expedition'. The same historian has written that 'the position of the Almoravids in Spain was that of an illiterate military caste controlling, but apart from, the native society.' To the end of the Almoravid regime there was not a single traceable Berber among its civil servants: instead, Andalusi clerks were shipped over to Morocco. The Almoravids indulged in all the luxuries and delights of al-Andalus but failed to do the job they had been called in to do: the lost territories in the Tagus and Ebro valleys remained in Christian hands. Persecution of and financial extortion from the Christian and Jewish communities alienated the non-Islamic population. Tribal rivalries reasserted themselves, religious fervour cooled. The cyclical process delineated by Ibn Khaldun was under way by the second decade of the twelfth century. The first rebellion against Almoravid rule in Spain occurred at Córdoba in 1119. From about 1125 their hold on Spain was beginning to fray at the edges, after barely a generation.

Simultaneously, the Almoravids were facing a serious challenge to their authority back in Morocco; so serious, indeed, as ultimately to prove fatal. This challenge came from the sect of the Almohads. The founder of the sect was Muhammad ibn Tumart, the son of a chieftain from the slopes of the Anti-Atlas range which overlooks the Sous valley in southern Morocco. As a young man he studied abroad, first in al-

Andalus and then for about ten years in the east, where he was particularly impressed by the religious teachings of the great Persian philosopher and mystic al-Ghazali. Ibn Tumart returned to the Maghrib in 1118 convinced that he had a mission to reform the corruptions of the Almoravids and bring the Berber peoples back to strict Islamic orthodoxy. He set about his task with gusto, in as openly confrontational a manner as possible. He publicly insulted the Almoravid amir 'Ali ibn Yusuf, and on one occasion in Fez pulled 'Ali's sister off her horse because she was riding without a veil. He went about smashing wine-jars and musical instruments. These methods not producing the desired effect, Ibn Tumart took himself off to his tribal homeland where he founded a *ribat* at Tinmal in the foothills of the High Atlas just below the Tizi-n-Test pass which is on the principal route from the Sous valley to the plain of Marrakesh. With the aid of a few followers he started to evangelise the mountain people thereabouts.

Thus far, Ibn Tumart's movement sounds rather like a repeat performance of the early days of the Almoravid sect. There were indeed similarities, but there were important differences too. Ibn Tumart's religious ideas, known to us through his writings edited by disciples after his death, derived from the intellectual heartlands of Islam in the Middle East. Their guiding principle was the unity of God. It was this notion that gave the Almohads their name: *al-Muwahhidun* means 'the Unitarians' or 'the Upholders of the Divine Unity'. This unity was all-pervasive: the world and everything within it was 'plunged in God'. Other sectarians like the Almoravids presented the Islamic faith as a set of rules. Ibn Tumart insisted, of course, on the rules but rejected a stultifying legalism that went no further. The spiritual interiority he preached was a liberating force in the culture of western Islam. It was to find its most formidable philosophical expression in the writings of Ibn Rushd of Córdoba (1126–98), better known in Europe as Averroes.

Ibn Tumart's teaching was not original, but his writings vibrate with a passionate earnestness for the purification of Islam. They confirm the stories told by chroniclers of the charismatic quality of his personality. In 1121 he was proclaimed *Mahdi* by his followers, 'the rightly-guided one' sent by God in the last days to restore righteousness before the Day of Judgement.

One day he stood up to preach and said, 'Praise to God Who does according to His will and accomplishes what He pleases. Nobody opposes His orders nor modifies His commands. May God bless our lord Muhammad, God's messenger, who announced the coming of the imam, the Mahdi who will fill the earth with justice and equity as it has been filled with tyranny and oppression. God will send him to obliterate lies by truth and to replace tyranny with justice. The Extreme West is his place, and his time will be the last of times . . .'

'When the imam finished his speech,' said the caliph 'Abd al-Mu'min, 'ten of his followers rushed up to him. I was one of them. We told him: "O lord, these qualities may be found only in you: you are the Mahdi." And we recognised him as such immediately afterwards even as the Prophet had been recognised by his companions. We swore to be a single corps for attack and defence.' His ten companions recognised him as the Mahdi under a carob tree, and were followed by the Berbers who recognised him in their turn and swore that they would fight for him and dedicate their lives to his service . . .

A further way in which the Almohad movement differed from the Almoravid was in its organisation. Ibn Tumart seems to have set up some hierarchy of command – the precise details remain obscure – which was superimposed upon, and at least to some degree replaced, the tribal organisation of the Atlas peoples. This made the Almohads a more coherent, less fissile force than their Almoravid opponents when they began to campaign against them from the mid-1120s onwards.

Soon the Almohads formed a state within a state in southern Morocco. Ibn Tumart died in 1130 and was buried at Tinmal. His tomb there became and long remained a place of pilgrimage for the devout. The exquisite and now largely ruined mosque that remains there was built by his successor as 'amir of the believers', 'Abd al-Mu'min (he who reported the account of the recognition of the Mahdi, above). During the reign of 'Abd al-Mu'min (1130–63) the Almohads would eradicate the Almoravids and extend their own power throughout the Maghrib from the Atlantic to Tunisia, and also across the Straits – where they would found the town of Gibraltar in 1159 – to Spain.

We too must cross the Straits and return to Spain, bearing in mind that the unpopular rule of the Almoravids was in the process of being further destabilised in the second quarter of the twelfth century by the need to divert resources to the vain attempt to contain the Almohads in the Atlas.

The death of the second Almoravid amir, Ali ibn Yusuf, in 1143 precipitated widespread outbreaks of rebellion in al-Andalus. It was a second Andalusi *fitnah* and it had more or less the same results as the first one back in the early eleventh century. Central power collapsed. Local statelets emerged – sometimes, indeed, referred to by historians as the 'second taifas'. Intervention from outside al-Andalus took place. As in the preceding century, the scene was one of intense confusion. But if we edge a little closer to look at some of these developments we can catch the tone of those muddled mid-twelfth-century years.

Consider first the southwest. Here a religious teacher and mystic, or *sufi*, named Ibn Qasi had founded a sect known as *al-Muridin*, 'the Adept', which had as its centre a *ribat* at Silves. The Almoravids had tried in vain to suppress the sectaries. In 1144 revolts against the Almoravids broke out all over the Algarve. In the ensuing confusion Ibn Qasi appealed to the Almohads for help. An Almohad army crossed to Spain in 1146 and helped Ibn Qasi to take Seville which had held out for the Almoravids. But the allies soon fell out. In the fighting between the Almohads and the Adept the latter had much the worse of it. Ibn Qasi was driven back to Silves where he was assassinated in 1151. The Almohads remained in possession of the Algarve.

In eastern Spain matters took a different turn. After the death of Sayf al-Dawla in 1146 an adventurer named Muhammad ibn Mardanish seized power at Murcia and Valencia. *El Rey Lobo*, 'King Wolf', as he was known to the Christians, was prepared to do deals with the rulers of Castile and Aragon to keep himself in power and the Almohads out. A 'tame' Muslim, he proved more reliable than Sayf al-Dawla. A skilled propagandist, he spoke Romance rather than Arabic, and dressed, rode, ate and fought like a westerner. King Lobo was a survivor. By diplomacy, Christian subsidies and war he maintained his independent principality until his death in 1172. At its greatest extent it embraced roughly the entire southeastern quarter of the Iberian peninsula and held up the Almohad advance for a quarter of a century.

The Christian powers did not fail to profit from this turbulent period in the affairs of al-Andalus. Alfonso VII (1126–57) was the grandson of Alfonso VI, the conqueror of Toledo, whose expansionary policies he sought to emulate. Throughout the 1130s and 1140s he was pushing raids far down into the south from his bases in the Tagus valley. In the confusion caused by the risings against the Almoravids he even managed to take Córdoba in 1146. In the following year he mounted his most ambitious campaign and in alliance with the Genoese, who provided the ships, he took the port of Almería. For the first time in her history Castile had an opening onto the Mediterranean. Both conquests proved ephemeral. The Almohads took possession of Córdoba in 1148, of Almería in 1157.

Further to the west a conquest that was to prove permanent had taken place in the same year as the Castilian-Genoese success at Almería. Count Henry of Portugal and his wife Teresa, the illegitimate daughter of Alfonso VI, had had a son, yet another Alfonso. Confusion may be lessened if we call him by the Portuguese version of his name, Afonso. This prince managed to emancipate himself from the lordship of his cousin Alfonso VII of León-Castile. In 1139 he won a great victory over an Almoravid army, shortly afterwards he assumed the title of king and in 1143 he contrived to get his independent monarchy recognised by the papacy. In 1147 Afonso engaged ships from England and the Low Countries to besiege Lisbon from the sea while he blockaded the city from the landward side. The successful campaign was written up shortly afterwards by an English participant in one of the most vivid pieces of military reportage that survives from the central Middle Ages. The first bishop of reconquered Lisbon was an Englishman, Gilbert of Hastings. It was the beginning of an association that has remained close and cordial ever since. When the campaign was over some of the English ships went on into the Mediterranean and assisted at another Christian triumph there, the conquest of Tortosa, at the mouth of the Ebro, by Ramon Berenguer IV in 1148. Some of the English stayed on in Catalonia as settlers; we shall hear more of them in the next chapter.

There were some heady moments for the Christian powers of the peninsula around the mid-century, but the general trend as we move into the second half of the twelfth century was for the advance and consolidation of Almohad power. The bridgehead established in the Algarve was gradually extended. Granada fell to them in 1154, Almería as we have seen in 1157. The foundation of Gibraltar facilitated a full-scale invasion in 1160. Operations slackened at the death of 'Abd al-Mu'min in 1163 but were then resumed by his successor Yusuf I (1163–84). In Extremadura a Portuguese adventurer named Geraldo sem Pavor, Gerald the Fearless, sometimes called the Cid of Portugal, had established himself at Badajoz. He was chased out by the Almohads in 1169. Pressure on king Lobo in the east was kept up through the 1160s, and at his death in 1172 his kingdom died with him. By 1173 all that remained of al-Andalus was in Almohad hands (with the exception of the Balearic Islands where an Almoravid principality survived until 1203).

The high point of Almohad power was reached in the last quarter of the twelfth century. In 1191 they recaptured Alcácer do Sal which guarded the southern approaches to Lisbon. In 1195 they inflicted a severe defeat on Alfonso VIII of Castile at Alarcos, the most serious Christian reverse since the battle of Sagrajas in 1086. In 1196 and 1197 they breached the Tagus frontier and ravaged on the plain of Madrid, to which they briefly laid siege in 1197. In 1203 they brought the Balearic Islands under their sway. These reverses were felt the more keenly because they were contemporaneous with equally distressing setbacks to the Christian cause in the east. In 1187 Saladin had defeated at the battle of Hattin the largest army ever mustered in the crusading states and had gone on to take Jerusalem. The Third Crusade, though led by the most renowned commander of the day, Richard I of England, had failed to recapture the holy city. At the time of Saladin's death in 1194 Middle Eastern Islam was politically more imposing than at any other time over the previous century. A hundred years of western crusading had produced negligible results.

The initiatives of the Almohads in Spain were facilitated by the divisions between the Christian powers and within individual states. In 1137 Aragon and Catalonia had been united in a federation which, though it had its shaky moments, was to endure. But the western peninsular kingdoms were in a state of disarray. Alfonso VII had divided his dominions into their former components, separate kingdoms of León and of Castile, for his two sons. The division lasted from 1157 until 1230. During the latter half of the twelfth century there was almost endemic quarrelling between Navarre, Castile, León and Portugal. In these circumstances it was impossible to concert a common defence against Almohad expansion. The diplomatic history of the period is exceedingly complex and need not be dwelt on here. Just one example of the sort of manoeuvring that characterised the age will suffice. A leading Castilian nobleman, Pedro Fernández de Castro, quarrelled with king Alfonso VIII, deserted him for the Almohads and fought on the Muslim side at the battle of Alarcos. In the following year he was entrusted by the amir Ya'qub with the command of Muslim troops who were to fight under the command of the king of León, the cousin of the Castilian king, in a co-ordinated Almohad-Leonese attack on Castile. In accordance with this plan Ya'qub laid waste the Tagus valley while Pedro Fernández did the same on the Tierra de Campos north of Palencia. Almohad diplomacy had also succeeded in fanning Navarrese border disputes with Castile into flame: Sancho VII of Navarre (brother-in-law of the crusader Richard I) invaded Castile from the north. So, a year after a defeat that had sent waves of shock throughout western Christendom – registered by monastic chroniclers as far away as Yorkshire – the unhappy victim found himself simultaneously attacked from three different quarters by a Christian enemy, a Muslim enemy, and a close relative whose general was a renegade vassal leading Muslim troops into an area where they had not been seen since the days of Almanzor two centuries before.

Such goings-on were scandalous to the conscience of Christendom. Papal pressure for the mending of fences now became intense. The very elderly Celestine III (born about 1105, pope 1191–98) had conducted two important legatine missions to Spain in 1154–55 and 1172–73 and knew the problems well. He excommunicated the guilty parties, formally reiterated Spain's special status as a crusading zone and despatched an envoy whose brief was to bring about peace between the Christian powers. The pressure was kept up by his successor Innocent III (1198–1216). After much wrangling a general peace was finally attained in 1207. Meanwhile the Almohad authorities, preoccupied with the annexation of the Balearics, had granted a series of short-term truces which gave Castile a breathing space.

Alfonso VIII delivered his counter-blow in 1212. The campaign was planned with care. Pope Innocent sent letters to every bishop in France requesting them to urge their flocks to go to the aid of the Castilian king. He held special rogations in Rome – fasting, processions, prayers – to enlist divine favour for the operations. The new archbishop of Toledo, Rodrigo Jiménez de Rada, went on a recruiting tour in France where he managed to attract considerable numbers of knights from the Midi. Troubadours supplemented his preaching. One poet expressed the hope that his lord would go to join king Alfonso so that he could prosecute a love-affair with his lord's wife.

Native Castilian and French forces mustered at Toledo in late May, soon to be rejoined by an Aragonese army and later by one from Navarre. The armies headed south. Most of the French contingents soon abandoned the campaign, overcome it was said by the mid-summer heat of Andalucía. The Almohad amir Muhammad had had ample time to make his preparations. His troops were encamped on the level plain of Las Navas de Tolosa, just to the south of the Despeñaperros pass through the Sierra Morena: the site is not far away from today's road and rail link between Madrid and Córdoba. The Almohads had blocked a narrow canyon through which the Christian army would have to pass, but a local shepherd led the way through an alternative defile unknown to the Almohad scouts. The allied forces were able to set up camp without molestation. On Monday 16 July battle was joined. It was hard fought, but in the end an overwhelming Christian victory. Muhammad fled, abandoning his standard on the field of battle. King Alfonso presented it to the religious house he had founded at Las Huelgas near Burgos, where it still hangs today. In the aftermath of victory the king reported on it to pope Innocent. His letter vividly conveys the magnitude of the Christian success:

In order to show how immense were the numbers of the enemy, when our army rested after the battle for two days in the enemy camp, for all the fires which were needed to cook food and make bread and other things, no other wood was needed than that of the enemy arrows and spears which were lying about, and even then we burned scarcely half of them . . .

In the forty years that elapsed between the battle of Las Navas and the death of Fernando III of Castile in 1252 nearly all of al-Andalus came permanently under the rule of the kings of Aragon, Castile and Portugal. It is sometimes assumed that the Christian rulers simply walked into possession of a new empire, that the ripe fruit fell from the tree into their outstretched hands. This was not so. There was plenty of uncertainty and risk. But Christian morale was strong, and it steadily grew stronger: especially in contemplation of developments in the Almohad empire.

Almohad military power had been dealt a devastating blow in 1212. There were other ailments which afflicted the regime. The original ideals of Ibn Tumart were abandoned by his successors. A story was told of 'Abd al-Mu'min that in 1155 he was approached by some of his lieutenants with the request that he should declare one of his sons the heir-apparent to the Almohad empire. He refused: godliness, not kinship, should be the mark of the successor to the Commander of the Faithful. Later he was approached again. Once more he refused, but then after reflection he changed his mind. It was a turning-point. A community of believers devoted to the ideals of the Mahdi had become an empire hereditary in the Muminid dynasty. As one modern historian has put it, 'Abd al-Mu'min had 'confiscated the empire on behalf of his descendants'. The wedge that this drove between the leadership and its subjects received further impetus from social forces of the sort identified by Ibn Khaldun. Although the hierarchy of command established by Ibn Tumart had done something to lessen the tribal divisions of Berber society, it had by no means done away with them. These divisions began to reassert themselves in the second half of the twelfth century. The Almohad leadership sought to protect itself by recruiting among the Algerian Bedouin and introducing these mercenary troops into Morocco (rather as Almanzor had introduced Berbers into the armed forces of al-Andalus at the end of the tenth century). These troops had to be paid, which meant higher taxes; and in times of turmoil, as after 1212, they became a disruptive, destabilising force.

New enemies appeared in the Almohad homeland. The tribe known as the Banu Merin were pastoralists who had been dwelling on the fringes of the Sahara in the area round Figuig in eastern Morocco. They had never submitted to Almohad control and had been left to their own devices. Occasionally they would choose to cooperate: there was a small Merinid contingent at the battle of Alarcos in 1195. In the year after Las Navas, suddenly, unaccountably and menacingly the Banu Merin abandoned their desert homelands and migrated northwards in the direction of the Mediterranean coast. From there they would wage war on the Almohads and, ultimately, succeed to their authority in Morocco.

One of the first actions of the amir Muhammad after his flight from the battlefield of Las Navas was to order the refortification of Fez. His son and successor Yusuf II was responsible for the construction of the Torre del Oro at Seville to defend the city against seaborne attack. Both these building operations betray the jumpiness of the Almohad leaders. Time would show how right they were to be apprehensive. Yusuf II died in 1224, gored to death in Marrakesh by a cow. The succession was disputed between rival claimants. Unitary authority in both the Maghrib and al-Andalus collapsed. Here was the opportunity that the Christian rulers had been awaiting.

Two energetic and gifted kings took advantage of the weakness of the Almohad regime: they were James I of Aragon (1213–76) and Fernando III of Castile (1217–52). Alongside them we should perhaps bracket Sancho II of Portugal (1223–48), a ruler less talented but no less energetic, under whom Portugal took on the territorial contours it has retained ever since. Alcácer do Sal was reconquered before his accession, in 1217, by means of a combined operation reminiscent of that which had led to the conquest of Lisbon seventy years earlier. A force of Dutch and German crusaders on their way to Egypt stopped off to put their ships at the service of the Portuguese to blockade the city from the sea. King Sancho II remains a rather shadowy figure. Most of our information about his reign concerns the strife between him and his leading churchmen which eventually led to the king's deposition. His conquest of the Algarve is ill-documented in detail. However, we do know that in the short space of nineteen years, from the capture of Elvas in 1230 to that of Faro by Sancho's successor Afonso III in 1249, all the lands south of Lisbon and west of the river Guadiana were brought under the authority of the Portuguese crown. This was no mean achievement.

We know a great deal more about the conquests of James I of Aragon. This is partly owing to the survival of abundant administrative records, but above all it is through the king's own autobiography, the *Llibre dels Feyts* (literally 'Book of Deeds'). The work is vivid, exuberant, proud, and candid about the royal author's appetites and ideals. In 1228, after a long minority and a series of disruptive baronial rebellions, James decided to take the military initiative. The commercial interests of the great merchant families of Barcelona helped to ensure that the campaign would be a naval one directed against the Balearic Islands rather than an overland strike down the coast towards

Valencia. The fleet set out for Majorca in September 1229: 'so large a fleet that the sea seemed white with sails', as the king later remembered. On the last day of the year Palma was stormed and the Muslim governor of the island captured. In the course of the year 1230 further resistance was overcome. In 1231 Minorca submitted to Aragonese lordship, paying tribute but maintaining a nominal independence. (It was conquered in 1287.) The government of Majorca was entrusted to an exiled member of the Portuguese royal family, Dom Pedro – a colourful character who had spent some years in Morocco as commander of a Christian mercenary force in Almohad service – who directed the conquest of Ibiza and Formentera in 1235. These were the first steps towards the formation of an Aragonese-Catalan maritime empire in the Mediterranean which at its peak in the early fourteenth century embraced Sicily, Malta, Gozo, Jerba, Kerkenna, parts of Sardinia and a tenuous foothold in Greece.

James I advanced down the Mediterranean coastline in the 1230s, using a mixture of diplomacy and force to take the towns which lay to the north of Valencia, little by little tightening his grip on the hinterland of that great prize. Valencia was in a state of turmoil characteristic of this post-Almohad period. In the 1230s it was under the control of Zayyan ibn Mardanish, of the same family as the twelfth-century king Lobo. James laid siege to the city in 1236. Command of the sea, ensured by his recent Balearic conquests, enabled him to mount a naval blockade and prevent relief gettting through from Tunisia. In September 1238 Valencia surrendered and the royal banner of Aragon was raised above it. 'When I saw my standard upon the tower I dismounted, turned myself towards the east, and wept with my eyes, kissing the ground for the great mercy that had been done me,' wrote the king in his autobiography. In the following years the thrust towards the south continued. Alcira surrendered in 1242, Játiva in 1243. Murcia, a vassal of Castile from 1243, fell to the Aragonese in 1266 but was then ceded to Castile. By the time of king James's death in 1276 he had roughly doubled the size of the Aragonese domains that he had inherited.

Territorial expansion on an even larger scale had occurred in Castile under Fernando III. An important condition of its success was the final reunion of León with Castile in 1230. Shortly before his death the last king of an independent León, Alfonso IX, had made extensive conquests in Extremadura which gave him Cáceres in 1229 and Mérida and Badajoz in 1230. Thus the kingdom of León which Fernando of Castile acquired stretched as far south as the river Guadiana. We have no such personal document as James I's autobiography from the hand of Fernando III, and the surviving administrative records of Castile are sparser than those of Aragon. But we do have three contemporary chronicles which furnish detailed information on the first half of the reign. The author of the most important of the three was no less a person than the archbishop of Toledo, Rodrigo Jiménez de Rada, whom we have already met recruiting in France for the Las Navas campaign of 1212. After his great predecessor Bernard, Rodrigo was the most commanding Toledan prelate of the Middle Ages. Short of stature – his tiny shoes and gloves may be seen at the monastery of Santa María de Huerta where he was buried – he was a forceful personality, a gifted orator and an effective administrator. He was also a scholar who employed his considerable intellectual gifts in the service of his see and his country (usually in that order) to present a version of Spain's medieval history which has proved both enduring and, some would claim, misleading. Archbishop Rodrigo was the most important single agent in organising the material and moral support of the Castilian church for the Andalusian campaigns of Fernando III.

All three chroniclers end their histories with the conquest of Córdoba in 1236. They regarded it as the high point of Fernando's triumphs. So in a sense it was: yet it was a campaign forced upon the king by chance rather than design. Córdoba, like Valencia, was in a state of disarray. A body of freelance Christian soldiers of fortune contrived one dark night in the winter to infiltrate and take possession of one of the city's suburbs. From this precarious foothold they appealed for help to Fernando III. It was January, and a wet one to boot. The king was three hundred miles away at Benavente, on the borders of León and Galicia. Bravely – as some thought, rashly – Fernando decided to seize this opportunity. With what troops he could muster he dashed to the south, reinforced the Christian band there and laid siege to the city. Further troops gradually came down from Castile to join him. A Muslim relief force from Seville approached but did not dare to attack. Córdoba capitulated on 29 June. That very evening bishop Juan of Osma, the royal chancellor and probable author of one of the three chronicles, ritually cleansed the mosque and consecrated it as Córdoba's cathedral. On the following day the king formally entered the city, heard mass in the mosque-cathedral and then held court surrounded by his barons and bishops in the palace nearby. The seat of Islamic authority in Spain for over five centuries, the jewel in the crown of al-Andalus, was once again in Christian hands. The bells which Almanzor had looted from the shrine of St James in 997 were sent back to the cathedral of Santiago de Compostela.

The following years were spent subduing the territory round about and extending Castilian conquests in Andalucía. The most glittering prize of all, at any rate in terms of size, beckoned Fernando on: Seville. In the autumn of 1246 the king laid siege to it. As at Valencia ten years earlier, command of the sea was of critical importance. The river Guadalquivir was Seville's water-link with the outside world, and the pontoon bridge which crossed it from the metropolis to the suburb of Triana provided communication with surviving Islamic strongpoints in southern Spain and Portugal. Fernando engaged a Burgos capitalist, Ramón Bonifaz, to assemble a fleet from the burgeoning ports of the Biscayan coastline. The ships arrived in the summer of 1247 and gradually established command of the river. The crucial breakthrough (in the most literal sense) came in the spring of 1248 when Bonifaz's sailors rammed the pontoon bridge and cut the only surviving artery between Seville and the world of Islam. After that, it could be only a matter of time. The summer of 1248 was a very hot one. Both besieged and besiegers suffered from drought, shortages of food and disease. Conditions inside the city slowly became intolerable. Muslim morale broke. In the negotiations which preceded capitulation Fernando showed himself inexorable. In order to make absolutely sure that Seville would remain in Christian hands he had decided that every Muslim must leave it, taking with them what possessions they could carry, so that the city could then be resettled by an exclusively Christian population. These harsh terms were finally accepted on 23 November, and the inhabitants of Seville were given a month to evacuate the city. When the king of Castile made his formal entry on 22 December 1248, behind the thin lines of his cheering soldiers there stretched a ghost-city of deserted tenements and streets, where those cats and dogs which had escaped being eaten during the siege scavenged among the bundles which had proved too much for the malnourished refugees to carry.

Let the last word of this chapter be with the poet ar-Rundi, whose elegy on the fall of Seville was composed some time later.

> Ask Valencia what became of Murcia,
> And where is Játiva, or where is Jaén?
> Where is Córdoba, the seat of great learning,
> And how many scholars of high repute remain there?
> And where is Seville, the home of mirthful gatherings
> On its great river, cooling and brimful with water?
> These cities were the pillars of the country:
> Can a building remain when the pillars are missing?
> The white wells of ablution are weeping with sorrow,
> As a lover does when torn from his beloved:
> They weep over the remains of dwellings devoid of Muslims,

Moorish Spain

Despoiled of Islam, now peopled by infidels!
Those mosques have now been changed into churches,
Where the bells are ringing and crosses are standing.
Even the mihrabs weep, though made of cold stone,
Even the minbars sing dirges, though made of wood!
Oh heedless one, this is Fate's warning to you:
If you slumber, Fate always stays awake.

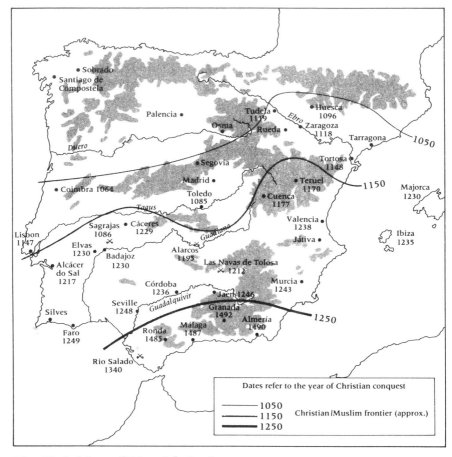

The Shrinking of Moorish Spain

7

CONVIVENCIA

Seville was the most favoured residence of the Almohad rulers of al-Andalus when they were at the apex of their power towards the end of the twelfth century. In a splendid act of piety they rebuilt the city's principal mosque on a colossal scale. All that now remains of the building is its tower, the famous Giralda, constructed in about 1185. The practice of adding towers to mosques was a fairly recent architectural development in the Islamic world which seems to have received a significant impetus from the Almohad leadership. The mosque-shrine of Tinmal had a tower, and 'Abd al-Mu'min added a gigantic tower to the Kutubiyya mosque in Marrakesh. These structures were conceived as architectural manifestoes of Almohad orthodoxy and power. What was intended to be the most imposing of them all, the tower of the mosque of Hassan at Rabat, was begun in the wake of the Almohad victory over Alfonso VIII at Alarcos in 1195. Construction was abandoned on the death of the amir Ya'qub in 1199, never to be resumed. The unfinished tower stands today as a memorial at once to the climax of Almohad power and to its ensuing decline.

These monuments are the most enduring examples of the artistic patronage of the Almohad elite. Generally speaking, the cultural levels in al-Andalus during the caliphal and taifa periods were not matched, let alone surpassed, during the age of the Almoravids and Almohads. There were, it is true, signs of vitality and some notable achievements. The poetry of ar-Rundi, quoted at the end of the last chapter, testifies to an enduring literary energy. The medical treatises of 'Abd al-Malik ibn Zuhr, referred to in Chapter 4, indicate the continuing vitality of scientific studies.

Philosophy was very much alive in the Almohad age. One manifestation of it was the curious philosophical novel by Ibn Tufayl (c. 1110–85), who was physician to Yusuf I. The book was called *Hayy ibn Yaqzan*, 'The Living, son of the Awake' (or 'Alive, son of Awake'). It tells the story of Hayy, who was brought up in isolation from humankind on a desert island, suckled by a gazelle. By means of contemplation and reflection he works out for himself a complete religious and philosophical system. Then he receives a visitor, Asal, from an inhabited island. Asal has been brought up in an Islamic religious tradition which sounds suspiciously like that of the Almohads: wishing to escape from the world the better to engage in religious exercises – somewhat as a man might enter a *ribat* for a spell – he has come to the uninhabited island. When Hayy and Asal compare notes they find that their philosophical positions are identical. Fired with enthusiasm they set out together to convert the people of Asal's island to their own brand of religion and philosophy. But the ruler of the island and his subjects are not interested in what the two enthusiasts have to offer, and reject their teaching.

How right they were, one might be inclined to reflect. The book, thus baldly summarised, sounds insufferably tedious. In actual fact, the tale is told with subtlety and charm. It proved enduringly popular not only in the Islamic world but through the medium of translation in Christendom too. A translation by the seventeenth-century English orientalist Edward Pococke is said to have been among the influences which led Defoe to compose *Robinson Crusoe*.

Ibn Tufayl's novel evidently mirrored current debates about the relations between religion and philosophy which preoccupied the intellectuals of al-Andalus in the twelfth century. Another philosopher and physician who shared these concerns was brought to the notice of the Almohad court by Ibn Tufayl. This was his younger contemporary Ibn Rushd, better known in the west as Averroes, one of the most commanding thinkers of the medieval Islamic world.

Averroes was a member of an old Córdoban family, possibly of *muwallad* or convert origin. His father and grandfather had gained distinction as jurists. He grew up in the troubled years of the second quarter of the twelfth century when Almoravid dominion in al-Andalus was crumbling. The Almohads took over Córdoba in 1148, when Averroes was about twenty-two: he was an early supporter of their regime. Ibn Tufayl's patronage introduced the promising young man to Almohad court circles about the middle of the 1150s. He served in the very important position of *qadi*, or religious judge, successively of Seville, Córdoba and Seville again between 1169 and 1184. He was the personal physician and trusted adviser of the Almohad rulers Yusuf I and Ya'qub. His closeness to the seat of power was most probably the occasion of the most puzzling episode in his life: he fell out of favour, perhaps as the result of some court intrigue of which the details are lost, and was exiled in 1195. He was restored to favour a few months before his death in 1198.

In the course of this exceptionally busy and, save at its end, successful career in public life, Averroes found time and energy to write voluminously. Like Ibn Hazm, at whose work we glanced briefly in Chapter 5, Averroes was one of those rare individuals who are multi-talented. At the age of twenty-seven he made astronomical observations near Marrakesh in the course of which he discovered a previously unobserved star. A lifetime's experience as a physician was concentrated in his *Kulliyat*, or 'Generalities', a compendium of medical knowledge completed in its final version in 1194. Yet it is as a philosopher that Averroes is primarily remembered today – at any rate in the western world, where he is more honoured than in the Islamic – and in particular as a follower and interpreter of Aristotle.

Averroes once wrote that because al-Andalus enjoyed a similar climate to Greece, so the intellectual propensities and talents of the inhabitants of the two regions were akin. Perhaps one could propose a different way of expressing it. By the time of Averroes the reception of ancient Greek science and philosophy in Islamic Spain – and we looked at the beginnings of this in Chapter 4 – had been completed; but the process of grappling with its implications had barely begun. In the field of what we should today call the natural sciences this was a laborious but essentially straightforward job. Take the study of medicine. There was the learning of antiquity – Aristotle, Dioscorides, Galen, and so forth – now available in Arabic: textbooks which had to be edited, introduced, explained, commented upon for a new readership of students. To this corpus of respected but ancient knowledge could be added the considerable, the very considerable, advances in the science of medicine made by the physicians of the Islamic world since antiquity. Averroes wrote commentaries on Galen and Aristotle and his *Kulliyat* summarised existing knowledge. Ibn Zuhr – to whose treatises Averroes modestly regarded his own compendium as merely an introduction – was engaged in the same enterprise.

Averroes was fascinated by Aristotle: he was 'an example which nature has devised to demonstrate supreme human perfection . . . given to us by divine providence that we might know whatever can be known'. He commented upon nearly all the master's works – astronomical, biological, meteorological, medical, logical, ethical. He also commented upon some of Plato's works, notably the *Republic*. Aristotle's philosophical system posed a challenge which Averroes faced up to courageously. Islam is a religion founded on revelation, divine revelation granted to the Prophet and recorded in the Koran. All knowledge is in the Koran and all knowledge is from God. The *qadi* of Seville was nothing if not devout. But Aristotle offered a disquieting alternative: the world and its workings may be understood without recourse to the divine, by human observation and inference. These were dangerous and uncharted waters. Averroes did not sail them alone – his friend Ibn Tufayl and others in twelfth-century al-Andalus were similarly preoccupied – but he explored more searchingly than any of his contemporaries. One of his treatises was entitled 'On the Harmony of Religion and Philosophy'. It could stand as the theme of his life's work as a philosopher. Averroes wrestled with the relations between reason and revelation, philosophy and faith, enquiry and authority. If he did not find solutions – and who ever has? – he opened up perspectives and proposed modes of enquiry. His work was to have great influence in the philosophical circles of western Christendom in the thirteenth and fourteenth centuries. There too a religious tradition founded on revelation had to square up to the implications of a newly-rediscovered Hellenistic alternative. The schoolmen or scholastic philosophers of Paris, Oxford or Naples found that they could lean on Averroes in trying to cope with Aristotle. In Christian Europe he became 'The Commentator'; Dante, who glimpsed him in Aristotle's company, wrote of him as: 'Averrois che il gran commento feo' (*Inferno*, iv, 144) – 'Averroes who composed the great commentary'. St Thomas Aquinas (d. 1274), whose achievement it was to show that reason and revelation could coexist in a Christian philosophy, explicitly cited Averroes no less than 503 times in the course of his work. But we shall return to these matters later.

*

These then are some of the artistic and intellectual achievements of the Almohad age. However, to an ever-increasing extent the history of Moorish Spain in the twelfth and thirteenth centuries is the history not simply of an Islamic state or collection of states in al-Andalus, but of Muslim communities under Christian rule in the expanding monarchies of Aragon, Castile and Portugal. Spanish historians of today speak of experiments in *convivencia* as characteristic of this period: the word means literally 'living together'. They sometimes contrive to suggest that this was something new in medieval European history. It wasn't, of course. The multi-cultural society of, let us say, the Aragon of James I, in which peoples of different faith, ethnicity, language and customs co-existed, had been foreshadowed in the al-Andalus of 'Abd al-Rahman III or the taifa princes. Nor is it true to assert, as is sometimes done, that the Iberian peninsula was unique in this respect in the Europe of its day. Christian, Muslim and Jew co-existed in the Norman kingdom of Sicily and in the principalities set up by the crusaders in Syria and Palestine. True, these other areas of co-existence were fairly short-lived: after Saladin's conquests the Crusader states were but a shadow of what they had once been, and the last of them, Acre, fell to the reconquering Muslims in 1291; in Sicily the Muslim presence was enfeebled by the deportations ordered by Frederick II in the 1230s. Thus the peninsular experiments in *convivencia* lasted longer than they did elsewhere; and this during a period when the climate of European society was gradually moving towards a more explicit unwillingness to tolerate deviations – by Jews, for example, or by those labelled heretics – from the cultural norms laid down by authority.

One must not jump to the conclusion that *convivencia*, because long-lasting, was harmonious. The extent to which it was or was not remains a matter for enquiry. It must be said at once that attitudes expressed on both sides of the cultural divide between Christian and Muslim were hostile. Here is James I of Aragon in his autobiography: 'The Moors are all traitors, and have often made us understand that whereas we treat them well, they are ever seeking to do us harm.' And here is king Sancho IV of Castile, in the book of advice which he compiled or commissioned for the son who was to succeed him as Fernando IV (1295–1312): 'The Moor is nothing but a dog . . . Those things which Christians consider evil and sinful, he considers goodly and beneficial for salvation; and what we think beneficial for salvation, he considers sinful.' From the other side, here is Isa Yabir, a prominent Muslim intellectual of Segovia, who compiled a compendium of the law of Islam for his co-religionists in the middle years of the fifteenth century. His attitude was stark: 'Do not employ the practices, uses or customs of Christians.'

In the light of such attitudes – and leaving aside the difficult question of how representative they are – we cannot expect to find that co-existence was a straightforward business. What actually happened to the indigenous Muslim inhabitants when a town or district came under Christian rule in the twelfth or thirteenth centuries? In the worst case, massacres might occur. These were very rarely, if ever, deliberate. Usually they took place when troops got out of control, whether owing to the indiscipline which characterised all medieval armies or to those explosions of violence which intermittently release the psychological tensions of combat. When the Portuguese captured Santarém in 1147, for example, many of the inhabitants were slaughtered. The killing could be indiscriminate rather than sectarian: in the sack of Lisbon later in the same year the Mozarabic Christian bishop had his throat cut. Some deaths may have been unintended. When Alfonso VIII's troops entered the town of Baeza shortly after the battle of Las Navas in 1212 they found it deserted and set fire to the mosque. Did they know that some of the town's inhabitants had concealed themselves inside? We do not know.

People were too precious to be slaughtered. Slavery was the lot of many Muslims who came into Christian hands, just as it was of many Christians who fell into Muslim hands. Muslim prisoners-of-war were employed as slave labour on the cathedral of Santiago de Compostela in the twelfth century, Christian ones on the Kutubiyya mosque in Marrakesh. When the Aragonese finally took possession of the island of Minorca in 1287 the entire population was sold into slavery, apart from the very rich who were able to emigrate to north Africa on payment of a ransom. Medieval Spain remained a slave-owning society at a time when slavery was gradually disappearing in western Christendom. And this was not just in the frontier areas. We possess, for instance, an undated (probably thirteenth-century) document from the Cistercian monastery of Sobrado, in the far northwest of Spain, which under the heading *Genealogia Sarracenorum* records the slaves owned by the community:

Brother Martin Velázquez bought Ali Gurdu in Toro, and this Ali had a wife named Fatima Regannada: both died pagans. They had a daughter named Obona, who was called Maria after her baptism, and a son who was christened Miguel. Obona married a man named (from?) Valencia who was called Martin after baptism, and they had two sons and a daughter, Domingo who was a weaver, and Maria and Juanino . . .

The list goes on in the published version for two closely-printed pages. The slaves seem to have been employed in lowly but not unskilled crafts – weavers, cobblers, blacksmiths – for the monastic community. Sobrado was not untypical. Many religious communities, and indeed many households, would have possessed a few slaves in twelfth- and thirteenth-century Spain and Portugal.

'The obligation to emigrate from the lands of unbelief will continue right up to the Day of Judgement.' This was a legal ruling attributed to Averroes. Some emigrated under compulsion, like the inhabitants of

Seville in 1248. Some chose to depart, like many of the Muslim population of Toledo after 1085. But there were always some who chose to stay put, whatever the law might say and whatever the risks involved. A person who elected to stay was known in the Romance vernacular as a *mudéjar*, a word derived from the Arabic *al-mudajjar*, rendered in the thirteenth-century glossary of Ramón Martí as 'persons allowed to remain'. Among historians of today the word *Mudejar* is widely used (both as noun and as adjective) to label the culture of the Muslims who lived under Christian rule in medieval Spain – just as the term *Mozarab* is used of the Christians who lived under Muslim rule.

Regulations for the administration of a newly-conquered city were often committed to writing by the Christian authorities in a document known as a *fuero* (with regional variants, e.g. *foral* in Portuguese). These documents can furnish much information about the life of the Mudejar communities – provided one remembers that their content is normative rather than descriptive, that is to say they describe society as it was intended to be rather than as it actually was. An early example is the *fuero* granted to the Mudejars of Tudela by Alfonso I of Aragon in 1119 after negotiations with the community leaders in the wake of conquest. The Mudejars were to be governed by an official of their own choosing according to the conventions of Islamic law 'as in the time of the Moors'. They were permitted freedom of worship. They were guaranteed possession of their property, freedom of movement, freedom to buy and sell. Like their Christian and Jewish co-citizens they were subject to certain annual dues and taxes paid to the crown. Broadly generalising, terms such as these became fairly standard in the course of the twelfth and thirteenth centuries. Much the same guidelines, for example, were laid down by Afonso Henriques of Portugal in a *foral* for the Mudejar community of Lisbon in 1170, perhaps committing to writing a verbal agreement made at the time of the conquest in 1147. A set of regulations which had proved themselves appropriate in one town or region could be extended to others. In this way 'families' of *fueros* could spread their branches from the parent trunk over ample swathes of territory. In this manner the Lisbon *foral* of 1170 was widely extended to the towns of the Algarve during the first half of the thirteenth century. In Castile the *fuero* of Sepúlveda (1076) spawned a numerous progeny in the twelfth century, and the *fuero* of Cuenca (1177: itself descended from Sepúlveda) an even larger one in the thirteenth. Over in Aragon the *fuero* of Jaca (1077, amplified 1134) was similarly widespread.

Thus far the provisions of the law. The new Christian authorities sought to guarantee protection for the Mudejar communities under their charge. Closer examination suggests that *convivencia* may have been a good deal less harmonious than those who framed the laws had hoped. The Tudela *fuero* of 1119 contains a clause which seems to say – its bearing is not completely clear in the text as transmitted – that if Almoravid persecution of Mozarabic Christians should occur in al-Andalus the Christian population of Tudela must not take reprisals on the Mudejars of their town. We have a hint here of the potentially explosive intercommunal tensions which existed in the urban societies of the frontier zone.

There is plentiful evidence in the *fueros* to suggest that in the ordinary course of daily life the Mudejars suffered discrimination. They chose their officers for the management of their own communal affairs; but they had no say in the general municipal administration of the cities where they lived. In some cities, though by no means all, they lived by choice or compulsion in separate ghettoes of their own. Murcia, in the southeast of Castile, forms a good example: Alfonso X concentrated the Mudejars in a new suburb and built a wall between the suburb and the city to keep Muslim and Christian communities apart. In the event of litigation between Mudejars and Christians the former tended to find themselves at a disadvantage. By a clause of the *fuero* of Toledo (1118) – a body of municipal custom widely diffused among Andalusian towns in the thirteenth century – lawsuits between Christians and Muslims were to be heard by a tribunal made up of Christians. In lawsuits where the contending parties were required to find supporters for their oaths it tended to be easier for the Christian party to assemble the requisite support. For instance, in the *fuero* of Sepúlveda it was laid down that a Christian litigant's oath needed the support of three persons – either two Christians and a Muslim, or two Muslims and a Christian, or three Muslims; but a Mudejar's oath needed the support of either three Christians or two Christians and one Muslim (but not two Muslims and one Christian). Again monetary penalties for crimes against Mudejars tended – not invariably but generally – to be lower than those for crimes against Christians.

At the most intimate levels of social life Muslim and Christian had long been aware of their separateness: one has only to consider marital, hygienic or dietary customs. The urban legislation of the conquest period on the whole reinforced these tendencies to apartheid. Segregation was often the rule at the municipal bath-houses: different days for Christians, Muslims and Jews. Christian families were not allowed to employ Muslim (or Jewish) girls as nannies for their children. Certain items or styles or colours of clothing were forbidden to Mudejars.

Sexual relations across the religious or cultural divide were punished savagely. Death by stoning was the normal penalty for a Muslim man who had sexual intercourse with a Christian woman – unless she were a prostitute, in which case he would be publicly whipped for a first offence, and executed only for a second.

Although freedom of worship was granted to the Mudejar communities, any Islamic proselytising was strictly forbidden, as had been Christian preaching designed to make converts in al-Andalus. In both Aragon and Castile the death penalty awaited Christian converts to Islam. Mudejars were required to share in certain Christian observances and obligations. They had to abstain from work on the Christian sabbath. In 1252 Alfonso X laid down that Mudejars and Jews must kneel when they met a Christian priest carrying the Host in a public procession along a street. A Mudejar who took the name of Christ or the Virgin in vain would be whipped for the first two offences and have his tongue cut out for a third. Mudejars were required to pay tithes to the church on any lands that they acquired from Christians. It was regular practice for the Christian conquerors to convert mosques into churches. That is why, of course, the great mosque of Córdoba still stands. Although smaller mosques survived in many cities, the practice of taking over the principal mosque for Christian use effectively prevented the Mudejars from maintaining their social cohesion by means of regular meetings, as an undivided community, for worship.

Were people, as well as buildings, forcibly converted to Christianity? On the whole it would seem not. Lip-service might be paid by some to the duty of encouraging conversions. For example, Alfonso X, echoing in this the earlier words of pope Gregory I, urged Christians:

to labour by good words and suitable preaching to convert the Moors and cause them to believe in our faith and to lead them to it not by force nor by pressure . . . for the Lord is not pleased by service that men give Him through fear, but with that they do willingly and without any pressure.

But the great legal compilation known as the *Siete Partidas*, in which these sentiments occur, was never promulgated as the formal public law of the Castilian kingdom.

Of course, conversions did take place. Sometimes they were brought about, it was believed, by supernatural agency. One spring day in the year 1150 a deaf-mute received the gifts of hearing and speech, miraculously, in the cathedral of Toledo in the presence of king Alfonso VII and archbishop Raimundo of Toledo: as a result, says our source for the incident, several Jews and Moors were converted to Christianity. Just over a century later Alfonso X recorded some similar conversion stories in his collection of poems in honour of the Virgin, the *Cantigas de Santa Maria*. In one of these, for example, a Mudejar woman was converted to Christianity after the Virgin Mary had resuscitated her dead child.

Earthier inducements to conversion existed. Several *fueros* offered manumission from slavery as a reward for conversion. But this was not at all a straightforward matter, for conversion of slaves was not in the interests of the slave-owners. In 1206 pope Innocent III had to write a strong letter to the canons of Barcelona cathedral:

> You should know that it has come to our notice that when a public baptismal ceremony is celebrated in your church, and many Saracens gather for it eagerly seeking baptism, their owners, whether Jews or even Christians, fearing to lose a worldly profit, presume to forbid them . . .

The clergy who had colluded with the slave-owners were given a sharp ticking-off. In the wake of his conquest of Valencia in 1238 king James I of Aragon had held out the promise of manumission upon conversion, but pressure from Christian slave-owners forced a change of policy on the government a few years later: slaves were too precious to be released so lightly. There were some parts of the Iberian peninsula where, it would seem, the issue had never raised its head. In the Sobrado slave-list quoted earlier, for instance, there is not a hint that baptism changed the status of the unfree in any way at all.

The impulse to convert the Mudejars to Christianity tended to come from outside the peninsula. It will be recalled how shocked Otto I's ambassador, the German monk John of Gorze, had been in the tenth century at what he considered too accommodating an attitude on the part of the Mozarabic Christians of al-Andalus towards the Muslims. He had been all for confrontation. There were plenty like him in the twelfth and thirteenth centuries, to whom we shall return later.

The language as well as the faith of the Mudejars came under pressure. We need to remember at this point that Arabic had also been the adopted language of the Mozarabic Christians. For how long did the Mozarabs of a city conquered by a Christian king maintain a culture which differed from that of their 'new Christian' liberators? It is a difficult question. Some of the manifestations of that culture were rather odd. Consider this tombstone which was found in the church of Santa Justa and Santa Rufina at Toledo. The main inscription, which is in Latin, reads as follows: 'In the name of our Lord Jesus Christ. This is the grave of Miguel Semeno. He died on Sunday 4 November in the Era 1194 [= 1156 AD].' Nothing remarkable about this: but what *is* truly remarkable is that the Latin inscription is framed by another one, running round the edge of the stone, which is in Arabic. It reads as follows: 'In the name of Allah, the Compassionate, the Merciful. Mikayil ibn Semeno was he who went forth to Allah, with His mercy, from the abode of this life to the life to come, on Sunday 4 November in the year 1194 [= 1156] by the dating of the Romans. May Allah give light to him.' What a strange intermingling of cultures we have here. Miguel Semeno must have been a Christian, to judge by his name and his burial in a church: but his family were content to commission a gravestone from a mason who would embellish it with the standard funerary pieties of Islam.

The same impression of cultural mixture, even confusion, emerges from evidence of a different nature; documents which record the humdrum transactions of daily life. Let us stay in Toledo. Not long after Miguel Semeno's death, in 1162, a lady named Juliana, the widow of a man referred to as Miguel ibn 'Abd al-Rahman, and her two sons gave a small vineyard to Pedro Abad, the priest of the parish church of St Mary Magdalen. The document recording the grant was drawn up, as was usual, in Latin. However, at the end of it there was appended a note running in the name of the two sons, and in Arabic: 'And I, Pedro ibn Miguel ibn 'Abd al-Rahman will make ready for you Pedro Abad whatever may be necessary for the vineyard which my father – may God have mercy on him! – gave you. And I, Domingo ibn Miguel ibn 'Abd al-Rahman will do likewise . . .' The bearing of this addition is not clear: presumably it referred to some related undertaking or transaction involving the family property. What is of interest, however, is not the content but the form, and the social reality which might have lain behind it. Was Juliana's father-in-law 'Abd al-Rahman a Mudejar? was her husband Miguel the first Christian in the family, baptised with the resoundingly Christian name of the archangel Michael? Christian the family may, indeed must have been by 1162, but the two sons of the next generation thought in Islamic phraseology ('may God have mercy upon him!') and used Arabic for recording legal transactions – and for how much else, one wonders, in the normal course of life? This was something which was long to continue in Toledo. Hundreds of documents in Arabic or with Arabic additions survive from Toledan archives during the century after Juliana's day.

It was largely during this period that the thousands of Arabic loan words made their way into the Romance vernaculars which were fast turning into Castilian, Portuguese and Catalan. The Arabic language as such seems gradually to have died out among the Mudejar communities (except, as we shall see in a moment, near Valencia). When Isa Yabir was meditating his compendium of Islamic law in about 1450 he decided to compose it in Castilian because so few of his fellow Muslims could read Arabic.

The nature and degree of discrimination against the Mudejar communities varied as the Mudejar presence itself varied across the face of the peninsula as a whole. It will be obvious enough that there were more Mudejars in the south than there were in the north. But what we know of the distribution of the Mudejar communities – which is not a great deal – suggests that it would be an oversimplification to think in terms of a straightforward progression from northern scarcity to southern abundance. In the northernmost kingdom, Pyrenean Navarre, there was a surprisingly substantial Mudejar population in Tudela. In neighbouring Aragon the Mudejars might have numbered about a quarter of the population in the thirteenth and fourteenth centuries but they were dispersed for the most part in small rural communities – medieval Aragon as a whole was under-urbanised – and fairly quickly became assimilated to the Christian population. Significantly, it was in this region that the speaking of Arabic seems to have died out most rapidly. In Catalonia the Mudejar population was negligible outside the towns of Lérida and Tortosa. By contrast in the other mainland constituent of the Aragonese federation, Valencia, the Mudejar population was enormous. This was not the case in the city of Valencia itself, from which the Muslim population had been expelled after the conquest, as at Seville. But in the hinterland of Valencia the Mudejars were and long remained comfortably the majority of the population. Here the Islamic faith and the Arabic language kept their vitality down to the sixteenth century.

To the north of the river Duero/Douro, in Old Castile, León and northern Portugal, there were hardly any Mudejars apart from slaves. In the towns between the Duero and the Tagus such as Avila, Segovia, Toledo and Talavera, there was a small but significant Mudejar presence. Further south, between the Tagus and the Guadalquivir (including the Portuguese Alentejo and Algarve) lay a sparsely settled country, much of it held in the form of great estates and ranches by the Military Orders: the towns were few and small. Mudejars survived here and there as a depressed rural peasantry or as gang-slaves on the big estates. Further south still, in Andalusia proper, yet a different scene was to be found. Here were flourishing towns, most of them with Mudejar communities, some modest, others substantial. The archives of several of these cities – Seville, Murcia, Jérez to name only three – have yielded a *Libro de Repartimiento* (literally a 'partition book'), which was an official register of property recording its distribution after the imposition of Christian rule. This is a source of evidence of the utmost importance for the social history of the Andalusian cities in the thirteenth century. Seville's *Libro de Repartimiento* and associated records of property transactions, for example, show that the Mudejars began to drift back to the city with royal encouragement not long after the expulsions of 1248. Settlers, and especially settlers with craft skills, were badly needed. In a grant of 1253, for instance, we hear of a property situated 'between the houses of Muhammad the saddler and Muhammad the toy-maker'.

A saddler and a maker of children's toys: these are characteristic Mudejar callings. In the aftermath of conquest those Mudejars who could afford to seem for the most part to have heeded Averroes' ruling and emigrated either to north Africa or to the remaining Spanish Muslim state of Granada. The Mudejar communities were thus, so to say, mutilated: they lost their elites. Rebellions of the Mudejars took place in Castile in 1264–66 and in Aragon in 1275–77. After them more emigrations and expulsions occurred. The revolts were used as a pretext for the conquerors to go back on undertakings made in earlier surrender agreements. Thus in Valencia the free Mudejar peasant communities were forced to submit to 'seigneurialisation', the imposition of burdensome dues and services which drove down their social status and their standard of living. Add to this the apparatus of social and cultural disadvantage with which the Mudejars were hemmed in, and you are left with what has been called 'a wounded subculture'.

The bleakness of the scene should not be exaggerated. It needs to be repeated that much of the evidence relating to the disabilities suffered by the Mudejars is the normative evidence of legal prescription. It needs to be balanced against what little evidence we have describing everyday life. Church councils in Castile in the early fourteenth century expressed dismay because Christians were taking their Muslim friends to Mass, or hiring Mudejar buskers to play in churches to relieve the tedium of night vigils. If we had only the *fueros* at our disposal we should never have guessed at these cheery goings-on.

However this may be, it does seem to have been the case that the free Mudejars of later medieval Spain and Portugal were typically persons of fairly lowly social standing. In the countryside, small farmers, market gardeners, shepherds; in the towns potters, carpenters, textile- or leather-workers, masons, plasterers, shipbuilders, smiths, book-binders: these are typical callings. They usually followed skilled rather than unskilled callings, and sometimes they were very skilled indeed as technicians or designers – the papermakers of Játiva, for example, or the gunfounders of Tudela, or the anonymous artists whose lovely ceramics may be admired in today's museums. Their most imposing surviving works are architectural. Brick was the most favoured building material of Mudejar artists. The massive castle of Coca, near Medina del Campo, built for the Fonseca family in the fifteenth century, is a characteristic example. They specialised in surfaces decorated with intricate geometrical patterns: externally, in brick, as for instance in the exuberant variety of the church towers of the Aragonese town of Teruel; internally in stucco, as at the Alcázar of Seville, or in wood, as in the cloister ceilings of the church of San Juan de los Reyes in Toledo.

To sum up: the Christian conquerors of al-Andalus in the twelfth and thirteenth centuries treated the indigenous Muslim peoples with a mixture of toleration and persecution. There is sufficient sediment of material here, unfortunately, to muddy the waters of Spanish historical studies with rival 'cases' put for 'tolerance' or 'intolerance', and burdensome celebrations or laments over 'the Spanish character'. Far too much intellectual energy has been dissipated in such trivial pursuits, often by those who should know better. What a historian wants to know is, why the mixture? A large part of the answer lies in the demands of resettlement.

Resettlement (*repoblación*) was the necessary follow-up to conquest. The Christian conquerors' hold on the land could only be secure if the land was settled. The lessons of the twelfth century were plain. The Almoravids had been able to roll back the conquests of Alfonso VI – excepting the almost impregnable city of Toledo – because there had been no time to consolidate them with settlement. The Almohads had been able to treat his grandson Alfonso VII's Andalusian conquests likewise. For so long as the danger of an Islamic comeback from the Maghrib persisted – and it lasted well into the fourteenth century – the encouragement and organisation of settlement was the major peace-time preoccupation of the directing elites of the Christian kingdoms.

The scale of the problem must be appreciated. Under Alfonso *el Batallador* (1104–34) the kingdom of Aragon doubled in size; this enlarged monarchy doubled again during the thirty-odd years of James I's conquests between c.1230 and 1260. Castile stopped at the Tagus in 1100; by 1250 it stopped at the Straits of Gibraltar. Where were the settlers to come from? At a much earlier date, when Leonese and Castilians were beginning to establish themselves on the central *meseta* and Catalans were pushing down to colonise the Llobregat and Penedès, back in the ninth and tenth centuries, the colonists came from the extreme north of the peninsula. Astonishing though this may seem, the mountainous zone stretching along the Pyrenees and westwards through Cantabria into Galicia was probably more densely populated at this period than ever before or since. Land hunger drew settlers down from the mountains to the plain. Their presence there is still attested by place names, such as the scatter of Basque names in Old Castile. These settlers gave the early Christian principalities the sturdiness and stamina they needed to withstand shock. Almanzor might strike, and strike again, for plunder; but not for land.

This source of supply was drying up as the eleventh century wore on. From about 1070, for the next hundred years or so, it was supplemented by an influx of colonists from beyond the Pyrenees. Attention has been mainly focussed upon migration from France, especially southern France, into the Iberian peninsula; and we have already met some of the military and ecclesiastical leaders of the movement in an earlier chapter. While it is true that the French constituted the vast majority of the immigrants who made their way to Spain at this period, the contribution of other nations should not be overlooked. Italians were keenly interested in the commercial opportunities that were unfolding in Spain and beyond. Genoese businessmen followed up their twelfth-century ventures (Almería, 1147) by opening offices in Seville after 1248. Their ships were cruising the eastern Atlantic, discovering the Canaries and probing the west African coast, before the century was out. In 1291 the brothers Vivaldi set out 'for the regions of India by way of the-Ocean': they were never heard of again. The Genoese presence was to be a very important feature of peninsular commercial history for at least the next two centuries.

Settlers came from even further afield. An Anglo-Norman knightly family, the Burdets, established what was for some time in the twelfth century a virtually independent principality based on Tarragona where they had been entrusted with responsibilities for defence and resettlement by the local archbishop. A clutch of documents reveals an unsuspected English colony nearby in the third quarter of the same century. Gilbert *Anglicus* first appears in the surviving records in 1151 when the count of Barcelona granted him some property in recently-conquered (1148) Tortosa: 'the houses of Ovocar Abnaleab and Ali Abenaydo and the house of Ashmet Abenhudna' – the scribe wrestling with unfamiliar Arab names. It is a fair guess that Gilbert had been a member of the naval expedition which had helped the Portuguese to capture Lisbon in 1147 and had then gone on to help the Catalans to take Tortosa in the following year. Gilbert evidently did well for himself; and well by his adopted country. In 1164 he was contributing to public works at Tortosa; by 1168 he was lending money to the Montcadas, the biggest baronial family in Catalonia. A successful entrepreneurial career ended when he entered the monastery of Santas Creus (with all his family papers, fortunately for the historian) in 1172, to spend his declining years there as a monk. The will that he made on that occasion reveals among much else that there were several other Englishmen settled in or near Tortosa. One of the beneficiaries of the will was a certain Robert of Totnes, which may suggest a Devonian origin for our Gilbert: the possibility is plausible, seeing that the fleet had been assembled at Dartmouth in 1147. (The deeds of Devon seadogs long antedate the age of Drake and Raleigh.) Gilbert did not neglect his English relatives: 'I grant to my niece Adeliza the sum of sixty *maravedis* and half of our land in England, with which she may get a husband . . .' Did the gold make its way from sunny Tortosa to the fog-clad skirts of Dartmoor? Did Adeliza's dowry catch her a husband? We do not know.

The career of Gilbert's namesake, the priest of Hastings who became the first bishop of reconquered Lisbon, reminds us that 'ecclesiastical resettlement' went hand in hand with lay. The new religious orders of the period played an important role. The Cistercian monks wanted to settle in remote and inhospitable places. It is not a bit surprising to find them much favoured by twelfth-century rulers harassed by the demands of resettlement. Afonso Henriques of Portugal made his expectations unambiguously clear when he generously endowed the Cistercian house of Alcobaça at its foundation in 1153: 'We have given you [this land] under this condition, that if through your own neglect and without my permission you fail to settle the land you shall forfeit it and never have it back.' In the thirteenth century the new orders of friars, the Franciscans and Dominicans, with their special emphasis on urban mission, were ideally suited to the spiritual colonisation of the Andalusian cities.

The twelfth and thirteenth centuries were an age of demographic growth throughout Europe and of corresponding expansion on every frontier. There was no shortage of colonists, even though there were never enough to satisfy the needs of the peninsular rulers. Then came the demographic disasters of the fourteenth century: poor harvests and widespread famine in its second decade, and then the shattering visitation of the Black Death, initially in the years 1346–50, then in recurrent later outbreaks. The pace of resettlement slackened. Medina Sidonia, conquered in 1249, had only a hundred and fifty households as late as 1367. There were farms not far from Córdoba which lay abandoned from the thirteenth century to the eighteenth. A note of desperation can be heard in some of the *fueros*. Fernando IV's charter for Gibraltar (1310) stated that the town would welcome all manner of persons among its citizens, 'be they bandits or thieves or murderers, or any other man no matter what wrong he may have done . . . or any married woman who has left her husband.' The only criminals exempted from this comprehensive privilege of sanctuary were those guilty of *alevosía*, treason.

Against this background it can be seen why the Christian authorities wanted the Mudejars to stay put and play their part as colonists. In the rural hinterland of Valencia, as we have seen, they did; in the Castilian and Portuguese countryside on the whole they did not. Into the space thus created moved livestock, above all sheep. Grazing needs little manpower. The acquisition of the steppe-lands of the Tagus-Guadalquivir zone, where winter grazing is to be had, made possible the development of large-scale transhumant pastoralism: winter in La Mancha or Extremadura, then the long trek up the *cañadas*, or sheepwalks, to summer pastures round Avila or Soria or Teruel. The military orders acquired vast estates in the south: the holdings of the Order of Santiago amounted to about 750,000 acres. They turned themselves into great ranching corporations with flocks of millions of head of sheep. The merino sheep, introduced into Spain in about 1250, thrives in a dry climate and produces excellent wool. The ranchers set up the famous organisation of the *Mesta* to protect their interests. They exploited the insatiable demand for wool, first from native centres of production such as towns like Cuenca or Segovia, then from the great textile centres of Europe. Genoese shippers were at hand to export the clip to the looms of Florence or Bruges. The wool trade became and long remained Spain's major economic enterprise.

Intellectual and cultural resettlement occurred also in the twelfth and thirteenth centuries: the process by which the learning of the Islamic world was discovered, appropriated, colonised by western scholars, and made widely accessible by means of translation into Latin, the international language of scholarship. This was one of the turning-points in the intellectual evolution of mankind. After the Arabs had broken out of the desert into the civilised lands of the Fertile Crescent they found themselves heirs to the intellectual riches of Hellenistic and Persian antiquity. They were not much interested in its literature, though bits of Homer were translated into Arabic in the ninth century and the *Thousand and One Nights* came to them from Persia. What mainly concerned them were scientific and philosophical treatises and technical descriptions of how things worked. This corpus of learning was translated into Arabic between c. 750 and c. 900. In certain directions, for example astronomical and medicinal, it was also enlarged and refined, becoming more comprehensive and more accurate through the observations of Islamic scientists themselves or through their becoming acquainted with the yet more distant learning of India and China. Ideas as well as commodities travelled with ease throughout the world of classical Islam in the ninth and tenth centuries, united as it was by faith and language and as yet little troubled by disruptive enemies from outside. In the fullness of time the learning of the Middle East reached even the most distant outposts of Islam in the west: the arrival of Dioscorides at the court of 'Abd al-Rahman III in 949 may be said to symbolise the process.

Scientific study, broadly defined, was at a low ebb in early medieval western Christendom; indeed, it barely existed. A time would surely come when western scholars would begin to get an inkling of the riches of Islamic learning, and of its potential for themselves if only it could be made accessible. The scholar who stands at the head of this evolution was Gerbert of Aurillac, who through the patronage of the count of Barcelona was enabled to come to Spain to study in the 960s. In 972 he returned to France and settled at Rheims where he acquired a great reputation as a teacher of mathematics. Some of his surviving letters are concerned with this intellectual interest. In 984, for example, he was writing to a friend asking to borrow 'a little book *On the Multiplication and Division of Numbers* written by Joseph the Spaniard'. Now the term *Hispanus*, 'the Spaniard', was used at that date to signify a recent immigrant from al-Andalus into Christian Spain. Joseph was therefore a Mozarabic Christian – or perhaps, to judge by his name, a Jew – who had brought with him specialised mathematical knowledge to which he gave written form in a textbook (now, sadly, lost or at any rate as yet unidentified). It is as nearly certain as can be, in the absence of categorical proof, that Joseph's book was concerned with the abacus. Gerbert himself wrote a treatise on the abacus which perhaps depended on Joseph's work.

Today we think of the abacus as a toy which helps a child to learn to count. But we must forget the free-standing frame-abacus of today, with its brightly-coloured plastic balls clicking to and fro on taut wires in nursery and play-school. The abacus of a thousand years ago was a horizontal surface of wood or slate, or a tray of sand, marked with vertical lines dividing it into columns; pieces or markings, standing for numbers, could be moved from column to column. The critical innovation here was 'place-value', the numerical value attached to a marker (or digit) by virtue of its position in a series of such markers representing units, tens, hundreds, thousands and so on. It sounds elementary and indeed it *is* elementary, but in the desperately backward mathematical world of tenth-century Europe it was revolutionary and liberating. The abacus made it possible to make rapid and exact calculations of hitherto unmatched complexity.

Gerbert and other early abacists stood at the beginning of a mathematical revolution whose effects may be seen in fields as diverse as music, the design of castles and cathedrals, and the fiscal operations of government. The cathedral of Durham and the abbey church of Saint-Denis, especially the latter, were not built without a confident knowledge of the mathematics of mass and thrust. The English government department which is still known as the Exchequer takes its name, first recorded in the early years of the twelfth century, from the ruled and chequered tablecloth – an abacus – over whose columns and squares counters (note the word) could be moved for purposes of calculation at the audit of government accounts. In about 1115 a certain Thurkill who describes himself as a *compotista*, a computist or accountant, wrote a treatise on the abacus. He illustrated the points he made with material drawn from the fiscal records of the English government. He was one of the civil servants who operated the Exchequer for king Henry I, and an example of the way in which men trained with mathematical skills were valued as bureaucrats.

There were other men in command of exotic learning who were connected with Anglo-Norman courtly and governmental circles. One was Peter Alfonso. This was not his real name, which was Moshe Sefardi, a Spanish Jew who when he was baptised at Huesca in 1106 took these as Christian names, the second of them to honour his godfather who was none other than king Alfonso I of Aragon, *el Batallador*. From one royal entourage he moved, by what means we do not know, to another. Not long afterwards he was in England, where he became physician to Henry I. He was skilled in mathematics and astronomy as well as medicine. Among other works he translated the astronomical tables of al-Khwarizmi (apparently not in Maslama's revision) into Latin. Peter was associated with other English scholars who shared his scientific interests. One such was Walcher, the prior of Malvern, who was one of the earliest men in England to use the astrolabe. Another was Adelard of Bath, who like Peter and Thurkill had connections with governmental circles. Adelard was a wide-ranging scholar in every sense. He had travelled in search of learning to France and southern Italy and Sicily. He translated al-Khwarizmi's tables, this time in Maslama's revision, and Euclid's *Elements* of geometry; composed a textbook on the abacus, a treatise on falconry, a work explaining the astrolabe written for the young prince who was to become Henry II, and a work entitled *Questiones Naturales*, in which in the course of an imaginary dialogue with a nephew the author attempted to sum up what he had learned from the Arabs. There also survives in the British Library a collection of horoscopes, apparently written out in Adelard's own hand, which he cast for prince Henry.

There were two 'contact-points' where western enquirers could gain access to the learning of the Greco-Arabian tradition: the Christian kingdoms of Spain and the Norman principalities of southern Italy and Sicily. (To these might be added the Crusader states set up in Syria and Palestine in the wake of the First Crusade after 1099; but their contribution to intellectual life was pretty negligible.) For a long time it was believed that Adelard of Bath had studied in Spain as well as in Italy, but modern research has cast doubt on the sojourn in Spain. As a rough and ready generalisation we might say that in Italy there was more translation of Greek works directly into Latin than of Arabic works, while in Spain the translation was predominantly of Arabic works, including Arabic renderings of Greek works, into Latin. Take the case of Aristotle's works by way of example: many of them were translated into Latin from the original Greek by the prolific and careful scholar James of Venice who was active in the second quarter of the twelfth century; the contribution of scholars in Spain lay especially in translating commentaries upon Aristotle, especially those of Averroes, several of which were translated by the Scottish scholar Michael Scot who was working in Toledo in the early years of the thirteenth century.

There was nothing organised about the translation movement of the twelfth and thirteenth centuries. Many different scholars were at work, at different times and in different places or at the same time but in different places, usually (though not always) in ignorance of what others were up to. Work was, inevitably, duplicated. Ptolemy's great work on astronomy, the *Mathematike Syntaxis*, known in the Islamic world as *al-Majisti*, hence to the west as the *Almagest*, was translated from the Greek by Henry Aristippus in Sicily in 1160; at about the same time Gerard of Cremona was translating it from the Arabic in Toledo. It is horribly difficult for the modern historian to sort out this anarchic intellectual scene, which is further complicated by the tendency for manuscripts to be ill-copied, unattributed, undated and extravagantly eccentric in their renderings of Arabic names or technical terms. It follows that much modern research on this crucial topic has been devoted to sorting out who was doing what with which texts when and where. The patient scholarship brought to the elucidation of these questions has been fruitful; but at the cost to the layman of tending to reduce discussion of the subject to indigestible lists of names, works and dates interlarded with question-marks. At the risk of oversimplification it will be best to confine ourselves to a few examples.

The most prolific of the translators to work in Spain was the Italian Gerard of Cremona. He came to Toledo as a young man in about 1140 and stayed there until his death in 1187. An obituary notice by his pupils tells us why he came and why he stayed:

He was trained from childhood at centres of philosophical study and had come to a knowledge of all of this that was known to the Latins; but for love of the *Almagest*, which he could not find at all among the Latins, he went to Toledo. There, seeing the abundance of books in Arabic on every subject, and regretting the poverty of the Latins in these things, he learned the Arabic language in order to be able to translate. In this way he passed on the Arabic literature in the manner of the wise man who, wandering through a green field, links up a crown of flowers, made not just from any, but from the prettiest. To the end of his life he continued to transmit to the Latin world (as if to his own beloved heir) whatever books he thought finest, in many subjects, as accurately and as plainly as he could.

One of these pupils, the Englishman Daniel of Morley who was active as a translator in Toledo between about 1180 and 1200, gives us a glimpse of Gerard's methods. He had an assistant, Ghalib the Mozarab (*Galippus mixtarabus*), who translated from the Arabic text into the vernacular by word of mouth to Gerard who then wrote it out in Latin. His pupils listed some seventy works translated by Gerard. The rough categories give an indication of not only Gerard's but also his age's intellectual priorities: twenty-four works on medicine; eighteen on astronomy, astrology, alchemy and divination; seventeen on the mathematical sciences including geometry, dynamics and optics; eleven on philosophy; three on logic.

We do not know how Gerard supported himself during all those years in Toledo. Daniel of Morley remembered going to some public lectures which Gerard gave on astrology, but it is likely that lecturing no more furnished a living stipend in the twelfth than it does in the twentieth century. Perhaps Gerard had resources of his own. They might have been supplemented by a canonry of Toledo cathedral. In the documents of the period a certain *magister Giraldus*, 'master Gerard' (the term 'master' denoting learning), appears among the members of the cathedral chapter at the right dates to fit our Gerard. His first appearance in the surviving documentation was in 1157. This was during the archiepiscopate of Juan (1152–66), who is known to have been a patron of translators. Perhaps his influence secured Gerard this modest item of ecclesiastical preferment.

Another translator to enjoy archiepiscopal patronage was Michael Scot. By 1215 at the latest he was in the entourage of archbishop Rodrigo Jiménez de Rada (whose historical work we touched on briefly in the last chapter). It was during this period in Spain that Michael translated some of Aristotle's works with the commentaries of Averroes upon them. By 1220 Michael was in Italy where he soon entered the service of the emperor Frederick II. He became the official astrologer and alchemist to the imperial court, as well as Frederick's friend and counsellor. His translations of Aristotle's works on natural history may have assisted Frederick in his composition of *De Arte Venandi cum Avibus*, the greatest work on falconry ever written. The rewards of a successful courtier-scholar were great. Michael was offered the archbishopric of Cashel by pope Honorius III – this was at a time when papal–imperial relations were briefly harmonious – but turned it down on the grounds that he could not speak Irish. Like all the best astrologers he foresaw the occasion (though not the date) of his own death. He discovered that he would be killed by a stone of a certain weight so he took to wearing a helmet of his own design which was known as the *cerebrerium*. One day when attending Mass he removed it at the elevation of the Host, whereupon a small stone fell from the vault of the church and wounded his head slightly. When he weighed it he found that it was precisely the weight he had occasion to fear. Having given this scientific proof of his skills he took to his bed and died. This occurred in 1235.

Frederick II has enjoyed a great posthumous reputation as a patron of scholarship, possibly a greater one than he deserves. A thirteenth-century monarch who fully merits this reputation was his first cousin once-removed, Alfonso X of Castile (1252–84). Alfonso has tradition-ally been styled *el Sabio*, usually rendered 'the Wise', though 'the Learned' is more appropriate and accurate. The literary output of Alfonso and his team of collaborators was prodigious. Apart from the poetry and legal works mentioned earlier in this chapter, there were several works which to a greater or lesser degree depended on Arabic models: translations of Arabic fiction, encyclopedias of astronomy and astrology, a guide to precious stones and their medicinal or magical properties, an illustrated account of chess and other games.

Because the Alfonsine corpus was composed in Castilian it achieved little circulation outside the Iberian peninsula, unlike works in Latin. Another reason for the relative neglect of Alfonso the Learned's work beyond the Pyrenees was that by his day western mastery of Greco-Arabic learning had been accomplished. Western Christendom had taken possession of what it needed: what was it going to do with the new learning?

The potentially explosive impact of Aristotelian philosophy, upon Christendom as upon Islam, has already been mentioned. Attempts were made to ban the study of Aristotle's works at the University of Paris in the first half of the thirteenth century. Intemperate academic struggles occurred, until Aquinas showed in his *Summa Theologica* that reason and revelation were compatible, could come together as in the taut harmony of a Gothic archway. Doubtless then as now, academic conflict tended to generate more heat than light, and to be of more pressing concern to the small world of the participants than to others. Some practical applications of the new learning have already been touched on, for bureaucrats and merchants and financiers, for doctors and architects and falconers, and for those to whom was entrusted the perennial and hazardous task of telling rulers what was going to happen next. Most of all perhaps the impact of the new learning can be seen in a slowly dawning change of attitude to the natural world. Instead of being something given, to which the guide lay in the Bible, it became something which invited investigation, for which the tools were experiment, observation and measurement. The dawnings of what we call the scientific attitude may be discerned in the thirteenth century, in for example the work on optics of the great English scholar-bishop Robert Grosseteste (d.1253) and his pupil Roger Bacon (d.1292). Modern science begins in thirteenth-century Europe, based firmly on the plinth furnished by translations from Arabic and Greek. In this perspective the European scientific and industrial revolutions of the seventeenth and eighteenth centuries appear less as new beginnings than as the end of a long haul: perhaps one day they will come to seem last gasps.

In all this welter of translation, this ferment of intellectual excitement in the twelfth and thirteenth centuries, are there any signs that Christian scholars were led to study the religious beliefs of the Muslims with whom they practised *convivencia* and whose secular learning they were so eagerly absorbing? The answer seems to be: few, but interesting. The earliest resulted from an initiative taken by Peter the Venerable, abbot of Cluny, in the course of a visitation of the Cluniac monasteries of Spain in the year 1142. He met two scholars, an Englishman named Robert of Ketton and a German named Hermann of Carinthia, who were together seeking out Arabic works on mathematics, astronomy and astrology – the usual mixture – to translate into Latin. Peter persuaded them to abandon their studies for a while to translate a collection of Islamic religious texts for him. The most important among these was the Koran, translated by Robert of Ketton: the first translation into a western language.

Peter used these texts as his sources for a work of Christian–Muslim polemic, in which there appeared the following oft-quoted sentence: 'I approach you [the Muslims] not with arms but with words; not with force but with reason; not in hatred but in love.' In the light of these sentiments abbot Peter has sometimes been presented as an apostle of toleration and enlightenment in a bigoted age. Not so. At about the same time he was writing to the king of France, Louis VII, who was just about to set out on crusade, expressing the hope that he would smash the Saracens as Moses and Joshua had destroyed the Amorites and Canaanites of old. Peter's polemical work was called *The Abominable Heresy or Sect of the Saracens*. He needed his Islamic texts not because he wanted to understand or to engage in dialogue but because he wanted to trounce the Muslims with a refutation of their creed. His mind was already made up.

Neither Robert's translation nor Peter's polemic circulated at all widely in the twelfth century. (Later on Robert's translation of the Koran was to achieve a much greater currency, after being printed at Zurich in 1543.) This is shown by the next translation of Islamic religious texts, at the hands of a canon of Toledo named Mark. In the years 1209–10 he translated the Koran, dedicating his work to archbishop Rodrigo Jiménez. He followed this up in 1213 with a translation of the *Aqida* or 'Profession of Faith' ascribed to Ibn Tumart, the founder of the Almohad movement, which he dedicated to bishop Maurice of Burgos. Mark's preface to his translation of the Koran makes clear that he thought he was doing something that nobody had ever done before; so completely had the memory of Peter the Venerable's enterprise faded. His translation was more literal and less elegant than Robert's, and thereby a more effective aid to the understanding of Islam. However, like Robert's, it enjoyed only a very restricted circulation.

This interest in sacred Muslim writings shown by the Castilian episcopate about the time of Alfonso VIII's great military offensive is of some significance. Bishop Maurice's neighbour, bishop Diego of Osma (d.1207), had wanted to resign his see in order to go to preach the Gospel to the Moors. The prior (or dean) of Osma, Domingo, wanted to do the same until the pope persuaded him that the Order of Preachers which he founded and which bears his name – the Dominican Friars – should be directed in the first instance at preaching against heresy. During this period of the late twelfth–early thirteenth century there was something of a trend towards the view that the evangelisation of the Muslims should accompany, perhaps even replace, the military confrontation between the west and Islam represented by the crusades. St Francis preached to the sultan of Egypt in 1219, and his first version of the Rule of the Franciscan Order encouraged the brothers to undertake missionary work among the Muslims. In that same year of 1219 a party of Franciscans tried to preach Christianity in Seville before going on to Morocco and martyrdom.

An enhanced concern with mission and associated activities was going to require training, especially linguistic training. In 1192 pope Celestine III wrote to the archbishop of Toledo ordering him to send priests 'instructed in both Latin and Arabic' to Seville and Marrakesh and other Islamic cities to minister to the Christian communities there. Perhaps he had specially in mind the captives held in Almohad hands. In 1198 pope Innocent III wrote to the Almohad amir to give him formal notice of the foundation of a religious order, the Trinitarians, devoted to the ransoming of captives. Another such order, the Mercedarians, was founded in Aragon by St Pedro Nolasco in about 1225. Over the centuries these orders did much good work: both played some part in organising the ransoming of Cervantes and his release from captivity in Algiers in the 1570s and thus, perhaps, in securing *Don Quixote* for the world's literature.

In 1254 Alfonso X established schools of Latin and Arabic in Seville. The royal charter which is our only evidence of this gives no hint as to the king's motives. The school of Arabic was not necessarily for budding missionaries or Mercedarians; it could have been intended primarily to turn out civil servants or diplomats. But there were others who linked the learning of Arabic explicitly with mission. One such was Ramón de Peñafort (1185–1275), one of the most distinguished churchmen of his day, canon lawyer, General of the Dominican Order and confessor to James I of Aragon. In 1240 he resigned his generalship of the Dominicans to devote himself to missions to Islam. He founded schools for the study of Arabic, briefly in north Africa (at Tunis) and more permanently in Spain at Murcia, Valencia and Játiva. The missionaries trained in them are said by Ramón's biographer, doubtless with some exaggeration, to have made ten thousand converts. Another member of this circle was Ramón Martí, also a Dominican, fluent in both Arabic and Hebrew, author of an Arabic–Latin vocabulary for the use of students and of several works of religious polemic. Yet another was Ramón Lull (1232–1315), the unbalanced Majorcan polymath and visionary – knight, poet, novelist, mystic, traveller and tireless lobbyist for the causes in which he believed. After his conversion to the religious life in about 1263 he spent nine years learning Arabic, after which with the help of the king of Aragon he set up at Miramar, near his home in Majorca, a college for the training of missionaries to Islam. At the end of his life he persuaded the churchmen assembled at the ecumenical council of Vienne in 1311–12 to set up schools of oriental studies at the universities of Paris, Oxford, Bologna and Salamanca. It is said, though on doubtful authority, that Lull died a martyr at the age of eighty-four when trying to preach Christianity to the Muslims of Tunisia.

When Lull wanted to learn Arabic he bought a Majorcan slave to teach him. All went well until one day it was reported to Lull that the man had been overheard to blaspheme against the name of Christ. Lull beat him up about the face in punishment. The slave nourished resentment against his master, managed to gain covert possession of a sword and tried to kill him. Lull survived the attack, though he was badly wounded in the stomach. The slave was imprisoned, and Lull debated with himself what to do next. He did not want the man tried and executed, for he was grateful to him for his teaching; on the other hand he did not want him set free to make another murderous attempt. Lull was in such a quandary that he went to a nearby monastery and prayed for guidance for the space of three days: but no guidance came. On his way home he heard that the man had hanged himself in prison. At this Lull 'cheerfully gave thanks to God, for on the one hand he had clean hands in the matter of the Moor's death, while on the other he was free of that grave perplexity about which he had shortly before so earnestly prayed'. Not a pretty tale, but one which may fittingly end a chapter on the peninsular experiment in *convivencia*.

8

NASRID
GRANADA

By about 1250 the greater part of the Iberian peninsula had thus come under the rule of the kings of Aragon, Castile and Portugal. There remained one Moorish principality which was to survive for a further two and a half centuries – the amirate of Granada. When Almohad dominion in Spain was crumbling in the 1220s and 1230s a certain Muhammad ibn Yusuf ibn Nasr – from which latter ancestor his family is often known to historians as the Nasrids – contrived to set up a small independent state which from 1237 was based upon Granada. By the mid-1240s the amirate had taken on the shape which it was to keep, with minor fluctuations, until its demise in 1492: a wedge of territory stretching from the Mediterranean coast north of Almería to the Straits of Gibraltar, rarely extending more than sixty miles inland. Its political status had also been settled. In 1246 Fernando III laid siege to Jaén, an outpost of Muhammad's dominions some forty miles north of Granada. Muhammad surrendered Jaén, became a vassal of the king of Castile and agreed to pay an annual tribute, like the *parias* of the eleventh-century taifa kings, fixed initially at half his yearly revenues. In outline, this relationship of clientage persisted until the surrender of Granada in 1492. Among the earliest expressions of it was the service of five hundred Granadan horsemen at Fernando's siege of Seville in 1247–48.

The amirate of Granada was small and vulnerable. In the first place, it was economically weak. 'The Christians pushed the Muslims back to the seacoast and the rugged territory there, where the soil is poor for the cultivation of grain and little suited to growing vegetables.' We owe this observation to the great scholar Ibn Khaldun (1332–1406) who lived in Granada for a time in the 1360s. Granada was not self-supporting in foodstuffs. Cereals and olive oil had to be imported from the Maghrib, in return for specialised crops such as sugar, raisins, figs and almonds, and industrial products among which the renowned Granada silk was the most important. Much of this carrying-trade was in the hands of Genoese shippers.

The power of the amir was restricted by the continuing strength of tribal feeling in a society which, outside a few big towns such as Almería, Málaga and Granada itself, was rural, poor and conservative. The amirate was never a unitary state but rather a loose federation of tribes or lineages (*linajes*). Every settlement had its tribal elite, more usually competing tribal elites, and its local bosses – what later generations of Spaniards would come to call *caciques*. The amir's role was to conciliate and cajole, to wheel and deal, to bribe and browbeat. It was a difficult and often a dangerous role to play. Generally speaking, the amirs managed it rather successfully down to about 1400. Thereafter the principality was in a state of almost constant strife between the different lineages. The political history of fifteenth-century Granada is bewilderingly complicated and quite unrewarding.

Saddled with the obligation to pay out fluctuating but always considerable annual sums to the rulers of Castile in tribute, the amirs were compelled to extort taxes which went well beyond the levels sanctioned by Islamic tradition. There was already a major inbuilt moral blemish at the very heart of the amirate. Under Islamic law no state may be the vassal of a Christian one, yet this was precisely what Granada was throughout its history. So there was always plenty for Islamic jurists to criticise. Furthermore, Granada was isolated from the mainstream of Islamic culture, her population was swollen with Muslim immigrants from the Christian kingdoms, and she recruited among the Berbers of Morocco who were noted at this as at other times for their intransigence. All these factors helped to breed what has been described as a siege mentality. Late medieval Granada was a tense, volatile, unharmonious society.

In the light of the foregoing one might well wonder why Granada survived for so long. One reason was that it was extremely well fortified. Along its northern and western frontiers a chain of castles, on average about five or six miles apart, was constructed largely on the initiative of Muhammad II (1273–1302). Town defences were kept in good repair. Enormous numbers of modest watchtowers were constructed, not just on the frontiers but throughout Granadan territory, to serve as local strongpoints in the event of attack. The statesman and historian Ibn al-Khatib (d. 1375) reckoned that there were about

14,000 such in the emirate. Dozens of them may still be seen today. The Nasrids commanded good armies, particularly strong in contingents of lightly-armed cavalry recruited in Morocco. The tribal confederation from which they came, the Zanata, has given Spanish the term *jinete*, 'horseman', whence English 'jennet'. Don Juan Manuel, the nephew of Alfonso X of Castile, who knew the frontier well, wrote of them with guarded respect in his *Libro de los Estados* composed in 1328–30: 'Because they are so lightly equipped they can travel great distances . . . they cover the ground at an amazing speed . . . two hundred Moorish cavalry can do more damage than six hundred Christian.'

In addition, Granada could call on the military assistance of the formidable dynasty of the Banu Merin, or Merinids, which had emerged in Morocco as heirs of the Almohads somewhat as the Nasrids had done in Spain. Merinid power was at its height between about 1270 and 1340. There were several occasions when the Merinids intervened in Spanish affairs, whether solicited or not by the amirs of Granada. Nasrids and Merinids supported the Mudejar revolts against Castilian rule that convulsed Andalusia in 1264. When Alfonso X was absent from Spain in 1275, pursuing his madcap dream of becoming Holy Roman Emperor, the Merinids again invaded the south, encouraged by Muhammad II of Granada. They defeated two Castilian armies and took huge booty. Eventually they retreated to Morocco, but retained two bridgeheads on the Spanish side of the Straits, at Algeciras and Tarifa. Sancho IV of Castile took Tarifa in 1292. It was heroically defended against Merinid counter-attack in 1294 by Alfonso Pérez de Guzmán. Legend would later magnify the exploits of 'Guzmán el Bueno', Guzmán the Good, but the story that he refused to surrender Tarifa even to save the life of his son, a prisoner in Moorish hands, is a true one. It has echoed down the centuries as a dread example of the soldier's duty, and one can hardly doubt that it was in the mind of General José Moscardó during his fateful telephone conversation with his son from the alcázar of Toledo in 1936. Fernando IV unsuccessfully besieged Algeciras in 1309. A Catalan fleet secured Gibraltar for him in the same year, but it was recaptured by the Merinids in 1333. The last serious Merinid invasion occurred in 1340, but it was heavily defeated by Alfonso XI of Castile at the battle of the river Salado. The king followed up this victory by the long and ultimately successful siege of Algeciras in the years 1342–44. (Incidentally, this was possibly the earliest occasion in European history when cannon was used in siege-warfare – and, interestingly, by the defence, not by the attackers.) The besieging armies included French and English contingents, the latter led by Henry of Grosmont, earl of Derby. Geoffrey Chaucer, whose patron John of Gaunt was the son-in-law of Henry, would later find a role at the siege for the knight who was among his pilgrims to Canterbury:

> In Gernade at the seege eek hadde he be
> Of Algezir . . .

Merinid power declined rapidly thereafter, but during the first century of the amirate of Granada it had been an important asset. This is to simplify an extremely complicated story. One example of the sort of complications that could arise will suffice. In 1282 the *infante* Sancho, later Sancho IV, rebelled against his father Alfonso X of Castile. Sancho enlisted the help of Muhammad II of Granada. In desperation Alfonso turned for military aid to the Merinids of Morocco. So Merinids and Nasrids found themselves at war in support of two rival Christian factions.

The Nasrid rulers of Granada had to be extremely adroit diplomats. Vulnerable as they were, they had to exploit the potential divisions among their neighbours: Aragonese against Castilians, Catalans against Genoese. They had to be wary of the Merinids as well as beholden to them. They had to try to prevent their enemies exploiting the tribal divisions within their own states. Luck as well as skill was with them in the fourteenth century. While Alfonso XI was besieging Gibraltar in 1349 the Black Death struck the Castilian forces; the king himself succumbed early in 1350 and the siege was abandoned. Gibraltar remained in Muslim hands until 1462. In the second half of the century Castilian attentions were distracted from Granada by three separate but related circumstances: prolonged instability and conflict within the royal dynasty and the higher ranks of the nobility; war with the kingdoms of Aragon and Portugal; and involvement in the long-drawn-out series of hostilities between England and France which historians call for convenience the Hundred Years War. In consequence, between 1350 and 1405 there was peace between Granada and her Christian neighbours. It was not unbroken peace. There were occasional 'incidents' to threaten it. In 1394, for example, the Master of the military order of Alcántara invaded the amirate in irresponsible disregard of the existing truce, only to be defeated and killed. In 1397 a couple of Franciscan friars were executed for publicly preaching Christianity in Granada. But generally speaking these were two generations of peace.

It was during the long reign of the amir Muhammad V (1354–59, 1362–91) that the Alhambra at Granada took on its final form. The Zirid rulers of the taifa state of Granada in the eleventh century had established their citadel, as we saw in an earlier chapter, on the rocky spur of the Sierra Nevada which overlooks the plain of the river Genil and the modern city of Granada. A few stretches of its eleventh-century walls still stand here and there, and some other materials, for the most part fragmentary, from the palace of the Zirid amirs may be seen in the Museum of Hispano-Islamic Art now housed in the nearby palace of Charles V. It was this eleventh-century nucleus which was transformed by the Nasrids.

The Alhambra was more than just a palatial dwelling-place for the amirs. Like 'Abd al-Rahman III's Madinat az-Zahra it contained a fortress and its garrison, mosques, baths, government offices, lodgings for resident or visiting dignitaries, gardens, stables, workshops. However, what the visitor of today goes to the Alhambra to see is precisely what would not have been visible to the fourteenth-century visitor – the amiral family's private apartments and their linking courtyards. These offer a unique architectural ensemble, the only reasonably complete surviving palace-complex of a medieval Islamic ruler, in a natural setting of unparalleled grandeur against the backdrop of the Sierra Nevada.

Muhammad V's architects, craftsmen, engineers and gardeners created for him a series of palaces which allows the visitor to comprehend in a concentrated form all the major elements in the Islamic architectural aesthetic. Spatial entities are combined and recombined. Mass and aperture are so grouped as to maximise the effects of the play of light and shade. Decoration in wood, tile and above all stucco is applied to walls and ceilings. Water is used, as for example in the Patio de los Arrayanes, the Court of the Myrtles, to multiply columns and arches by reflection, to cast light into shade and spread ripple over decoration. The piled 'honeycomb' work in stucco, which would then have been painted, can be literally breathtaking, as witness the gasps of tourists as they contemplate the extraordinary 'exploding firework' effect of the ceiling of the Sala de los Dos Hermanas just off the famous Patio de los Leones. Contemporaries recognised that a wondrous work of art had been created. This is conveyed, for example, in several of the poems of Ibn Zamrak, the chief minister of Muhammad V in the latter part of his reign. Here is one of them: the Sabika to which it refers is the spur on which the Alhambra stands.

Stay awhile here on the terrace of the Sabika and look about you.
This city is a wife, whose husband is the hill:
Girt she is by water and by flowers,
Which glisten at her throat,

Ringed with streams; and behold the groves of trees which are the wedding
   guests, whose thirst is being assuaged by the water-channels.
The Sabika hill sits like a garland on Granada's brow,
In which the stars would be entwined,
And the Alhambra (God preserve it)
Is the ruby set above that garland.
Granada is a bride whose headdress is the Sabika, and whose adornments are
   its flowers.

In the Sala de los Reyes in the Alhambra there survives a ceiling painted
with frescoes which were executed by an artist who worked in a
western-Christian rather than an Islamic tradition. The amirs, therefore, were prepared to patronise artists who came to them from outside
the Nasrid state. Traffic went in the other direction too. Pedro I of
Castile rebuilt the alcázar of Seville in the 1360s and employed
Granadan artists and craftsmen much of whose work may still be seen
there. His Jewish treasurer Samuel ha-Levi used them too, for the
synagogue which he built a few years earlier in Toledo, the Synagoga
del Tránsito.

Masons and bricklayers, carpenters and plasterers were not the only
persons to move to and fro across the frontiers of the Nasrid state of
Granada. Others did so involuntarily, such as the captives taken in
frontier skirmishes or carried off into slavery after a sudden enemy
descent from the sea. Ibn al-Khatib reported that Christian captives
worked on the building of the Alhambra. The celebrated traveller Ibn
Battuta (d. 1378), sometimes called the Islamic Marco Polo, left an
account of a slave raid that he witnessed on the coast between Marbella
and Málaga in about 1352. Attempts were made to defuse potential
trouble. Officials known as *alcaldes entre cristianos y moros*, judges
between Christians and Moors, were appointed to deal with frontier
incidents. Their work was supplemented by locally-appointed officers,
alfaqueques, whose special job it was to arrange for the release of
captives by means of ransom or exchange, and *rastreros*, or scouts,
appointed by town councils as a sort of frontier police force to
investigate incidents and complaints. All these officials found themselves travelling across the frontier in the performance of their duties.

The *romances fronterizos*, or frontier ballads, that were composed in
the later Middle Ages bear witness to the strains and opportunities that
life along the frontier involved. Most of them were concerned with the
deeds of noblemen and knights. One that was not is the famous ballad
'Moraima'. It is a lament spoken by a beautiful Moorish girl who has
been raped by a Christian, an Arabic speaker, who gained entry to her
house at night by posing as a relative seeking sanctuary.

I am Moraima,
a beautiful Moor,
I was hurt by a Christian
who knocked at my door,
speaking good Arabic
to deceive me the more.
'Come open, Moraima,
Allah keep you from harm.'
'But how can I open?
I don't know who you are.'
'I'm a Moor and your uncle,
your uncle Mas'ud,
and I've just killed a Christian,
the law's after my blood –
if you don't let me in
I'll be finished for good.'
To my grief, when I heard him
at once I went down,
threw a shawl on my shoulders
instead of my gown,
I ran straight to the door
and I pulled it right round.

How many Moraimas might there not have been in real life in fourteenth- and fifteenth-century Andalusia?

*

The peace of the second half of the fourteenth century was shattered early in the fifteenth. Castile and Granada were briefly at war between 1405 and 1410. The advantage lay with the Castilians, whose ruler the *infante* Fernando, regent for his nephew king Juan II (1406–54), conquered the strategically important fortress town of Antequera in 1410. (The siege offers another example of *convivencia* and its strains. The Castilian nobleman Juan de Velasco had a Moorish trumpeter in his service who was at the heart of a plot to set fire to the besieging camp. It was scotched just in time.) After this campaign relations between Castile and Granada returned to the state of uneasy peace which had prevailed beforehand. But the terms of the relationship were altering. The long-enfeebled dynasty of the Merinids was finally extinguished, and no strong successor was to emerge in Morocco until the sixteenth century. If the Nasrids of Granada were to seek help from north Africa they would have to look much further to the east. They did, in the event, appeal to the Mamluk rulers of Egypt on at least three occasions during the fifteenth century, but the Mamluks had problems of their own and were powerless to help. Moroccan naval forces were run down after about 1350, allowing the Christians command of the sea, as was observed by Ibn Khaldun in a characteristically incisive discussion of Mediterranean seapower. In 1415 the Portuguese captured Ceuta, thus placing control of the Straits finally and firmly in Christian hands.

Tribal conflicts within the amirate during the fifteenth century weakened its power of resistance to predators. So too did a faltering economy. The Genoese grip tightened: the mighty merchant dynasty of Spinola secured a monopoly of the export of fruit from Granada, driving down the price of a traditional and vital export. Some of Granada's products were successfully produced elsewhere: the Valencians and the Portuguese found that they too could make and market ceramics which consumers found attractive. Yet if the economy stagnated, tribute-paying and defence ensured that taxes did nothing of the kind. It has been calculated that the average inhabitant of the amirate paid over three times the amount of tax paid by the average Castilian in the fifteenth century. It did not help to endear the amirs to their subjects.

Granada would fall to Christian attack when her enemies had resolved their quarrels, when the political will to conquer had affirmed itself, and when the appropriate strategy had been devised and tested. In 1412 the kingdom of Aragon had come under the rule of a cadet of the Castilian royal family – none other than Fernando, the hero of the conquest of Antequera. From then onwards a closer union of the crowns could be anticipated. It finally occurred in 1474, when Fernando (of Aragon) and Isabel (of Castile), husband and wife from 1469, succeeded to their conjoint but separate thrones. For the first time for nearly eight hundred years a single political authority governed the major part of the Iberian peninsula.

It had been Isabel's uncle Enrique IV of Castile (1454–74) – a much maligned monarch, not least by his niece's propagandists – who had been responsible for developing a new strategy against Granada in a small mid-century war (1455–58). This was based upon systematic devastation of the countryside, designed to shatter morale and imperil food supplies, thus to bring Granada to her knees without the risk of pitched battle. The internal troubles of Enrique's reign did not permit prolonged campaigning along these lines, but the experiment had been an encouraging one. This was how Granada was ultimately to be reduced to submission.

In 1453 the Ottoman Turks had conquered Constantinople and brought the Byzantine empire finally to an end. The advance of Islam in the eastern Mediterranean, of which this was the most resonant episode, contributed to a sense that some decisive blow should be struck for Christendom elsewhere. The spread of printing diffused more widely the vernacular chronicles of medieval Spain which presented the ruler's God-given task as the reconquest of territory from the Moors. The newly-fashionable humanist scholars hailed Fernando as another Augustus – the Roman emperor who (among much else) had initiated the conquest of the one region of Spain, Galicia, not yet under Roman control. Messianic expectations and prophecies focussed on the new monarchs. A poem composed before 1474 hailed the imminent union of the Spanish kingdoms and the conquest of Granada. Ballads and prophecies foresaw Fernando's conquests as embracing not merely Granada, but Africa, Jerusalem and the empire of the Turks. Royal propagandists presented the conquest of Granada as a new crusade. A measure of their success is that Fernando and Isabel have been remembered by Spaniards from that day to this as *los Reyes Católicos*, 'the Catholic Monarchs' above all others.

The war for Granada started, like so many earlier ones, with a frontier incident in the winter of 1481–82: Granadan raid and Castilian reprisal. Though it was to continue for ten years, the end was never in doubt. Apart from Granada's debilitating weaknesses, already indicated, Castile was vastly superior in manpower, artillery and generalship. (The Granada war was a training-ground for such great commanders as Gonzalo de Córdoba, known as *el Gran Capitán* (1453–1515), later to become famous in Fernando's Italian wars of 1495–97 and 1501–04. He acquired a lot of land in the amirate as a result of the war, so the Granada campaigns also made him rich.) In 1482 the son, named Boabdil, of the reigning amir rebelled against his father. The Castilians were lucky enough to capture Boabdil in 1483. Fernando decided to set him up as a puppet amir (Muhammad XII) whom he could use as a stalking-horse for his designs over the whole territory of the amirate. This diplomatic ace secured, Fernando prosecuted the war steadily by means of devastation and siege. Ronda fell to him in 1485; Loja in 1486; Málaga in 1487; Baza in 1489; Almería in 1490. Granada itself was besieged for eight months in 1491. Terms of capitulation were arranged in December. Castilian troops took over the Alhambra on 1 January 1492. On the following morning the Catholic Monarchs received the keys of the city from Boabdil: curiously enough, they had chosen to dress themselves in Moorish costume for the ceremony. Among those who witnessed it was Christopher Columbus, who was in attendance upon the court in his quest for royal sponsorship of his projected voyage of discovery into the Atlantic.

In the arrangements made for the treatment of the conquered, Fernando and Isabel showed themselves – as in so much else – traditionalists. The Moors of the amirate of Granada were granted the rights enjoyed by Muslims living under Christian rule in other parts of Castile and Aragon: the unhindered practice of their faith and customs, the administration of their community law by their own officers. There were local variations. Generally speaking there was less disruption in the countryside than in the towns. Málaga, which offered strong resistance, suffered severely: most of its 8000-odd Muslim inhabitants were sold into slavery, only the richer being allowed to escape this fate by payment of a heavy ransom. The city of Granada was lightly treated, and Boabdil himself was granted a sort of sub-kingdom, a little principality of his own in the mountainous lands to the south of Granada known as the Alpujarras. In the event he chose to emigrate to Morocco in 1493: he lived out the remainder of a long life there, and died in Fez in about 1532.

As in the wake of the thirteenth-century conquests of Valencia and Seville, many Muslims chose, like Boabdil, to emigrate. Events were to show how prudent they were. The two key figures in the administration of Granada after 1492 were the governor, the Conde de Tendilla, and the archbishop, Hernando de Talavera. The latter, in particular, was a most remarkable man. By training he was a monk, by temperament a man of charitable disposition and wide sympathies. He was a rigorous upholder of the most exacting standards in a Spanish church whose intellectual, moral and pastoral condition was deplorable. He had played a leading role in the important reforming church council held in Seville in 1478. He was the queen's confessor, and therefore a man who was influential in the highest circles. He became bishop of Avila in 1484 and was promoted to Granada in 1492: evidently, a suitable man for a difficult assignment. Talavera was by instinct a conciliator. Naturally, he was keen that the Muslims of his new diocese should become Christians: but he was determined to use encouragement rather than pressure, to ease his flock over the hurdle of conversion by instruction and understanding, to go as far as he could to meet his potential converts. Thus, for example, his initiatives in having Christian scripture and liturgy translated into Arabic, his encouragement to his clergy – and his own attempts – to learn the language, his insistence that the terms of capitulation agreed in 1492 be observed, and his successful efforts, until 1499, to keep the Inquisition out of Granada.

The times were against him. Only a few weeks after the surrender of Granada the government had decreed the expulsion of the Jews from

Spain. It was one symptom of the end of *convivencia*. In 1499 the Catholic Monarchs paid a visit to Granada. They were accompanied by Francisco Ximénez de Cisneros, archbishop of Toledo and primate of the church in Spain. Cisneros was a prelate of a much more zealous temper than Talavera, whose conciliatory policy he overrode. Enforced mass baptisms became the order of the day. By January 1500 Cisneros was reporting that 'there is now no one in the city who is not a Christian, and all the mosques are churches.' The results of the change of policy were unsurprising. Rebellion against Castilian rule broke out in the Alpujarras late in 1499 and spread to other parts of the former amirate. It was suppressed in the years 1500 and 1501. At first the rebels, and then the Muslim population as a whole, initially in Granada but shortly afterwards (1502) throughout Castile, were offered the choice between emigration or conversion. Since emigration was permitted only on payment of a fairly substantial sum to the government and on other widely unacceptable conditions – for example, emigrants had to leave their children behind – it proved an unrealistic option for most Muslims. So they remained, and became automatically 'Christians'. The hardline policies of Cisneros had the support of queen Isabel. But her husband refused to allow the extension of these policies to his own kingdom of Aragon. His grandson and successor Charles V similarly swore in 1518 not to expel or forcibly convert the Aragonese Muslims. But in 1525 he went back on his word and offered them the choice of expulsion or baptism. After this date Spanish society was, at least officially, exclusively Catholic.

In practice, of course, it was nothing of the kind. The Moriscos, as we must now call them, remained an unassimilated and alienated minority. Part of the trouble is that there was no follow-up to the nominal conversions of 1499–1502 and 1525. The ordinary parish clergy of sixteenth-century Spain were for the most part ignorant and slothful, altogether incapable of undertaking the slow, patient, tactful work of assimilation which alone – as Talavera had realised – could have achieved the integration of the Moriscos into Catholic Spanish society. Islamic law permits the practice of *taqqiya*, the concealment of true belief during a time of persecution. These 'New Christians' of sixteenth-century Spain outwardly conformed to the requirements of the church which they had been compelled to join while secretly maintaining allegiance to the Islamic faith of their ancestors. They might be forced to bring their children to church for baptism, but they would wash the consecrated water off as soon as they got home. Compelled to undergo Christian marriage ceremonies, they would also celebrate marriage secretly according to their own rites. Documents known as *aljamías* survive from this period, expositions of Islamic religious practice written in the Spanish language with Arabic characters. Despite the attentions of the Inquisition, rituals of washing, prayer and fasting continued unchecked. In countless day-to-day details the Moriscos differed from their 'Old Christian' neighbours. They had different names, wore different clothes, abstained from pork and wine, lived in houses of different structure furnished in different ways.

For a generation or so after 1525 the Moriscos were for the most part unmolested. However, in the 1550s and 1560s tension between the Morisco communities and the authorities began to mount. This was partly because the Moriscos were suspected of sympathy with Spain's most dreaded Mediterranean rival, the Turks, who had established a kind of unofficial dependency in the shape of the 'corsair-state' on the coastline of modern Tunisia and Algeria by the middle of the century. It was partly because Spain's emergent role as the sword of the Counter-Reformation made it embarrassing to be accused of nurturing these Islamic vipers in her very bosom. Add to this a decline in the prosperity of the Granada silk industry, in which many of the Moriscos were engaged, in the 1550s and 1560s, and an ill-judged attempt from 1566 onwards to stamp out traditional Moorish customs. The unsurprising result was widespread Morisco revolt in 1568–70, known as the Second Revolt of the Alpujarras (the first one having been that of 1499–1501). The rebellion was put down with great brutality by king Philip II's half-brother the *infante* Don Juan – better known to English-speakers as Don John of Austria, victor of Lepanto in 1571 – and the crisis passed.

One step taken by the king in the wake of the uprising was further to complicate the Morisco problem. In order to break up the concentration of Morisco settlement in the Granada region – defeated and disaffected communities perilously close to the waters sailed by the Barbary corsairs – he ordered the Morisco population to be dispersed throughout Castile. Accordingly a large number of persons, perhaps in the region of 100–150,000, were forcibly resettled elsewhere. But they remained unassimilated in their new homes. Philip might have successfully defused the threat of further insurrection in Granada, but only at the cost of spreading the Morisco problem throughout the kingdom of Castile.

It was left for his son, Philip III, to banish the question definitively – by banishing the Moriscos themselves. On the advice of his leading minister the duke of Lerma the king had all the Moriscos expelled from Spain between 1609 and 1614, exactly nine centuries after the initial invasion by Tariq and Musa. It is reckoned that something like 300,000 people were expelled. This was a big slice out of a total Spanish population of perhaps eight million. But in some areas it was a very big slice indeed. For example, the Moriscos had formed about a third of the population of the old kingdom of Valencia and as a result of the expulsion whole tracts of that countryside lay deserted for the rest of the century. The loss of the Moriscos must be measured in qualitative as well as quantitative terms. Although they were not rich in possessions, the Moriscos were famous for industry and thrift in the callings they followed – artisans and craftsmen, muleteers, small traders, peasant farmers. Their expulsion cost the sagging economy of seventeenth-century Spain very dear. 'This most barbarous act in the annals of mankind', as cardinal Richelieu called it, was a folly as well as a crime. Some of those expelled were able to take their revenge. Al-Maqqari, who composed his great history of Spanish Islam some twenty years after the expulsion, noted in its last paragraph that some of the Moriscos entered the service of the sultan of Morocco who 'allotted them for their residence the port of Salé [on the Atlantic coast], where they have since made themselves famous by their maritime expeditions against the enemies of God'. This was the origin of the infamous 'Sallee Rovers' who were to terrorise the Atlantic coasts of Europe from the Tagus to the Bristol Channel for the next two centuries.

The expulsion of the Moriscos was not quite the end of Moorish Spain. Some of them contrived to slip through the net and stay. Secret Muslims were still being brought before the Inquisition throughout the seventeenth century: a case is even recorded from as late as 1728. But to all intents and purposes the Moorish presence in Spain ended in the reign of Philip III.

9

AN AUGUST
POMEGRANATE

The loss of the last slice of al-Andalus in 1492 induced a mood of grief and regret in the Islamic conscience. Al-Maqqari's history of the Maghrib, completed in about 1630, is peppered with the phrase 'may Allah return it to Islam' (and variants) when he refers to the cities of Spain and their departed glory. He never did, though hopes that He would lasted for a long time. It used to be said that there were houses in Fez and Marrakesh inhabited by the descendants of those who were able to emigrate in and after 1492 where the keys to properties in Almería or Ronda, Málaga or Granada, hung in readiness for a return to al-Andalus.

Nostalgia is the enemy of historical understanding. Back in the eighth century the author of the *Chronicle of 754* had movingly commended the fruitfulness and fairness of his country even in the midst of the tribulations of the Berber conquest. Alluding to the arrival of one of the early Arab governors in Spain in 734 he wrote that,

He found it, even after all that it had been through, to be abundant with every good thing and, even after all its suffering, to be filled with beauty, so that you could say that it was like an August pomegranate.

It's a lovely image, with its suggestions of warmth, ripeness, fecundity, plenty and repose. The nostalgia of writers like al-Maqqari has had the effect of infusing this kind of imagery into our mental picture of Islamic Spain. This won't do. The witness of those who lived through the horrors of the Berber conquest, of the Andalusian *fitnah* in the early eleventh century, of the Almoravid invasion – to mention only a few disruptive episodes – must give it the lie. The simple and verifiable historical truth is that Moorish Spain was more often a land of turmoil than it was a land of tranquillity.

Great is truth: but whether it can pierce the armour-plating of legend, in this context, remains to be seen. Here is Stanley Lane-Poole, author of a work on *The Moors of Spain* published in 1897.

The history of Spain offers us a melancholy contrast. For nearly eight centuries, under her Mohammedan rulers, Spain set to all Europe a shining example of a civilised and enlightened state . . . Whatsoever makes a kingdom great and prosperous, whatsoever tends to refinement and civilisation, was found in Moslem Spain. In 1492 the last bulwark of the Moors gave way before the crusade of Ferdinand and Isabella, and with Granada fell all Spain's greatness . . . There followed the abomination of desolation, the rule of the Inquisition, and the blackness of darkness in which Spain has been plunged ever since . . . So low fell Spain when she had driven away the Moors. Such is the melancholy contrast offered by her history.

There is room here for no more than this brief selection from his preface. The reader must take on trust that Lane-Poole's book (and its illustrations) is the embodiment of the romantic interpretation of Andalusi history propagated, as was mentioned in Chapter 1, by such as Washington Irving and Richard Ford.

Nearly a century after Lane-Poole's time these views are still widely current. Reviewing a book about the events of 1492 in the *Independent* newspaper on 21 June 1991, none other than Mr Anthony Burgess wrote that after the fall of Granada, 'the magnificent Emirate of Córdoba, where beauty, tolerance, learning and good order prevailed, was only a memory.' Indeed it was. But had they ever prevailed? Beauty? Yes, a fair amount of it, here and there. Tolerance? Ask the Jews of Granada who were massacred in 1066, or the Christians who were deported by the Almoravids to Morocco in 1126 (like the Moriscos five centuries later). Learning? Outside the tiny circles of the princely courts, not a great deal of it to be seen. Good order? Among the feuding Berber tribesmen? Or the turbulent *muwallad* rebels like Ibn Hafsun? Or the taifa statelets of the eleventh century? Or the Moroccan fundamentalists who succeeded them? Or the *linajes* of Nasrid Granada?

So the nostalgia of Maghribi writers was reinforced by the romantic vision of the nineteenth century. This could be flavoured with a dash of Protestant prejudice from the Anglo-Saxon world: it can be detected in Lane-Poole's reference to the Inquisition. A powerful mixture! But that is not yet the end of this receipt. In the second half of the twentieth century a new agent of obfuscation makes its appearance: the guilt of the liberal conscience, which sees the evils of colonialism – assumed rather than demonstrated – foreshadowed in the Christian conquest of al-Andalus and the persecution of the Moriscos (but not, oddly, in the Moorish conquest and colonisation). Stir the mix well together and issue it free to credulous academics and media persons throughout the western world. Then pour it generously over the truth.

Those who are too idle to prepare decent food can buy pungent sauces in supermarkets to disguise the absence of flavour in the meat or fish they smother with them. The past, like the present, is for most of the time rather flavourless. 'Nothing, like something, happens anywhere.' Larkin's line should be the historian's motto. But in the cultural conditions that prevail in the west today the past has to be marketed, and to be successfully marketed it has to be attractively packaged. Medieval Spain in a state of nature lacks wide appeal. Self-indulgent fantasies of glamour or guilt do wonders for sharpening up its image.

But Moorish Spain was not a tolerant and enlightened society even in its most cultivated epoch. The Mozarabic Christian communities whom John of Gorze met on his embassy to Córdoba were cowed and demoralised. Ibn Hazm, so often and misleadingly presented as a beacon of enlightenment, was learned but not open-minded. The Christians of al-Andalus were second-class citizens like Christians under Muslim rule elsewhere in the world such as the Copts of Egypt. What else should we expect to find? The treatment of the Mozarabs by their Islamic rulers foreshadows that of the Mudejars by their Christian ones. If the disabilities experienced by the Mudejars can be known in more detail than those of the Mozarabs, that is owing to the changing nature and survival rate of our sources: we know far more about the thirteenth and fourteenth centuries than we do about the tenth and eleventh.

We waver on the brink of a cycle of argument already dismissed in Chapter 7 as trivial. Let us draw back and turn elsewhere. In the vast perspective of human history the critically important function of Moorish Spain was to act as a channel for the transmission of knowledge from east to west at one of the most sensitive periods in Europe's rise to dominance. It is fashionable in some quarters to condemn this view as 'Eurocentric'. This is rather bewildering. Like it or not, European hegemony is the most prominent feature of the history of the world between 1300 and 1900. Anything that may assist in explaining the rise of the west is presumably of interest to the historian; or should be.

The interaction between Islamic and Christian civilisations in the medieval west was an extremely fruitful one. It may have gone well beyond the translation of scientific and philosophical works touched on in Chapter 7. Did the Islamic idea of *jihad* influence the development of the western idea of crusade? Did the Muslim institution of the *ribat* furnish a model for military orders such as the Order of Santiago? Was the poetry of the troubadours influenced by the love-lyrics of al-Andalus? Was the organisation of the *Divina Commedia* affected by Dante's reading of the *Libro della Scala*, an account of Muhammad's journey to heaven in the company of the archangel Gabriel which might have been brought from Spain to Italy by his mentor Brunetto Latini, Florentine ambassador to the court of Alfonso the Learned in 1260? Did the high regard for literacy and penmanship in the Islamic world afford an instructive example to Christendom? These and many others are questions which have provoked much discussion. They remain open. Whatever the agreed solutions which might, however improbably, emerge one day, the contours of a multi-faceted debt to medieval Islam are clear enough in outline.

The traffic was all one way. Moorish Spain was the donor, western Christendom the eager recipient. The Muslims of al-Andalus had nothing to learn from their Christian neighbours and were incurious about them. Geographers' accounts of Christian Spain tended to be cursory in the extreme: it was cold, the inhabitants were barbarians who ate pigs, you could get slaves there – that was about the sum of it. The Muslim discovery of Europe did not begin until several centuries after the fall of Granada. Christian reactions to the Muslims *as Muslims* must be distinguished from western interest in the knowledge that arrived by way of al-Andalus. In this respect the Christians were as incurious as their Muslim neighbours, as ready to accept stereotypes and myths, as unwilling to investigate the truth. Peter the Venerable was better placed, thanks to Robert of Ketton and Hermann of Carinthia, to understand the faith of Islam than any Christian had ever been before: but he didn't want to. An image of Islam had already gained currency in the west and abbot Peter was satisfied with that. His attitude, on the Christian side, was paralleled by Ibn Hazm's on the Muslim.

The religious history of the Iberian peninsula in the Middle Ages may be summarised, from one point of view, as the persistent and wilful failure of two faiths and cultures to make any sustained attempt to understand one another. Human enough; pretty bleak. The trouble with such a judgement is that historians in making it have to rely on the testimony of those who could write. For most of the period discussed in this book that meant a small intellectual elite. Intellectuals are not renowned for their grasp of everyday reality, nor for cheerfulness and optimism. Judgements might have been rosier if one had found oneself spending the Easter vigil at a Mudejar pop concert in the local cathedral; or downing a few bottles of Valdepeñas with like-minded Muslim pals at one of Toledo's monastic wine-bars.

NOTES ON FURTHER READING

A formal bibliography would be out of place in a work of this kind. I confine myself to listing a few books, all of them in English, which will enable the enquiring reader to pursue the subject further. The best introduction to medieval Spain as a whole is provided by two complementary volumes in Macmillan's 'New Studies in Medieval History', now under the general editorship of Maurice Keen: Roger Collins, *Early Medieval Spain: Unity in Diversity 400–1000* (New York, 1983) and Angus MacKay, *Spain in the Middle Ages: from Frontier to Empire 1000–1500* (London and Basingstoke, 1977). W. Montgomery Watt, *A History of Islamic Spain* (Edinburgh, 1965) is a reliable if pedestrian survey. Thomas F. Glick, *Islamic and Christian Spain in the Early Middle Ages. Comparative Perspectives on Social and Cultural Formation* (Princeton, 1979) contains many new insights. The most useful work of reference is the magnificent *Encyclopedia of Islam* (new edition, Leiden and New York, 1960–): the latest volume (1993) has just reached the letter N.

More detailed monographs on different themes or periods are provided by, for example: Roger Collins, *The Arab Conquest of Spain* (Cambridge, Mass., 1989); David Wasserstein, *The Rise and Fall of the Party-Kings. Politics and Society in Islamic Spain 1002–1086* (Princeton, 1985); Bernard F. Reilly and John Lynch, *The Conquest of Christian and Muslim Spain 1031–1157* (Cambridge, Mass, 1992); Benjamin Z. Kedar, *Crusade and Mission. European Approaches toward the Muslims* (Princeton, 1984); James M. Powell (ed.), *Muslims under Latin Rule 1110 1300* (Princeton, 1990); L. P. Harvey, *Islamic Spain 1250–1500* (Chicago, 1990); J. N. Hillgarth, *The Spanish Kingdoms 1250–1516* (2 vols, New York, 1978). The proceedings of the quincentennial conference held at Granada in

1991 have been published under the editorship of Salma Khadra Jayyusi and the title *The Legacy of Muslim Spain* (Leiden, 1992): its fifty-odd essays (all in English) investigate every aspect of the history and culture of al-Andalus.

Colin Smith, *Christians and Moors in Spain* (2 vols, Aris and Phillips, Warminster, 1988, 1989) is an attractive anthology from the Christian sources which has now been joined by volume 3, Arabic sources, edited by Charles Melville and Ahmad Ubaydli (1992). Amin T. Tibi, *The Tibyan. Memoirs of 'Abd Allah ibn Buluggin, last Zirid amir of Granada* (Leiden, 1986) is an enthralling eleventh-century autobiography. Among several fine translations of Hispano–Arab poetry, the most recent is Cola Franzen's *Poems of Arab Andalusia* (San Francisco, 1989).

Two superb exhibitions were held as part of the quincentennial celebrations in 1992. Their handsome and scholarly catalogues now furnish the most convenient introduction to the art of Moorish Spain. They are: Jerrilynn D. Dodds (ed.), *Al-Andalus: the Art of Islamic Spain* (New York, 1992) and Vivian B. Mann, Thomas F. Glick and Jerrilynn D. Dodds (eds.), *Convivencia: Jews, Muslims and Christians in Medieval Spain* (New York, 1992). Geoffrey Goodwin, *Islamic Spain* (San Francisco, 1990) is a volume in the series 'Architectural Guides for Travellers' which helpfully catalogues the principal sites. Oleg Grabar, *The Alhambra* (Cambridge, Mass., 1978) treats Moorish Spain's most famous architectural ensemble.

INDEX